MOSES

EXCELLENCE IN LEADERSHIP

Vol. II

by Theodore H. Epp
Founder
Back to the Bible

Back to the Bible

Lincoln, Nebraska 68501

200,000 printed to date—1987
(5-5352—3M—87)
ISBN 0-8474-1201-6

Printed in the United States of America

Contents

Chapter 1

Israel Becomes a Nation

By the end of the time of plagues which God brought on Egypt, Moses was established beyond any doubt, both before Egypt and before Israel, as God's man for the great task of leading the Israelites.

The Bible says, "Moreover the man Moses was very great in the land of Egypt, in the sight of Pharaoh's servants, and in the sight of the people" (Ex. 11:3). After the Israelites had been delivered from the Egyptians, the Bible records: "Israel saw that great work which the Lord did upon the Egyptians: and the people feared the Lord, and believed the Lord, and his servant Moses" (14:31).

Only as Moses' leadership was fully established with Israel was he able to proceed in leading them out of Egypt, through the desert and to the land of his fathers.

From Exodus 12:40,41 we learn that the Israelites had been in Egypt for 430 years: "Now the sojourning of the children of Israel, who dwelt in Egypt, was four hundred and thirty years. And it came to pass at the end of the four hundred and thirty years, even the selfsame day it came to pass, that all the hosts of the Lord went out from the land of Egypt."

God's Promises to Abraham

God's program for the people of Israel actually began with His call of Abraham, who was then known as Abram. God's call and promise of blessings on Abraham and his descendants are recorded in Genesis 12:1-3: "Now the Lord had said unto Abram, Get thee out of thy country, and from thy kindred, and from thy father's house, unto a land that I will shew thee: and I will make of thee a great nation, and I will bless thee, and make thy name great; and thou shalt be a blessing: and I will bless them that bless thee, and curse him that curseth thee: and in thee shall all families of the earth be blessed." Note especially the words "I will make of thee a great nation."

God's promise to Abraham was confirmed to Abraham's son Isaac. God told Isaac, "Sojourn in this land, and I will be with thee, and will bless thee; for unto thee, and unto thy seed, I will give all these countries, and I will perform the oath which I sware unto Abraham thy father; and I will make thy seed to multiply as the stars of heaven, and will give unto thy seed all these countries; and in thy seed shall all the nations of the earth be blessed; because that Abraham obeyed my voice, and kept my charge, my commandments, my statutes, and my laws" (26:3-5). Note especially the words "I will perform the oath which I sware unto Abraham thy father" (v. 3).

God's promise to Abraham was confirmed again to Jacob in a dream: "And, behold, the Lord stood above it [the ladder], and said, I am the Lord God of Abraham thy father, and the God of Isaac: the land whereon thou liest, to thee will I give it, and to thy seed; and thy seed shall be as the dust of the earth, and thou shalt spread abroad to the west, and to the east, and to the north, and to the south: and in thee and in thy seed shall all the families of the earth be blessed" (28:13,14).

Genesis 35:9-12 also confirmed to Jacob the promises God had made to Abraham: "And God appeared unto Jacob again, when he came out of Padan-aram, and blessed him. And God said unto him, Thy name is Jacob: thy name shall not be called any more Jacob, but Israel shall be thy name: and he called his name Israel. And God said unto him, I am God Almighty: be fruitful and multiply; a nation and a company of nations shall be of thee, and kings shall come out of thy loins; and the land which I gave Abraham and Isaac, to thee I will give it, and to thy seed after thee will I give the land." Verse 11 is especially significant: "God said unto him, I am God Almighty: be fruitful and multiply; a nation and a company of nations shall be of thee, and kings shall come out of thy loins."

Near the end of Jacob's life there was a famine in the land of Canaan, and food was available only in Egypt. The Bible records how Jacob's sons went down to Egypt and acquired food from their brother Joseph, although they were unaware at first of Joseph's identity. Later, Joseph disclosed his identity to his brothers and arranged to bring Jacob and the rest of the family to Egypt.

Although Jacob had looked forward to seeing his beloved son Joseph again, he was reluctant to leave the land of Canaan. However, God assured Jacob that he should go to Egypt and reiterated the Abrahamic covenant to him. God told Jacob, "I am God, the God of thy father: fear not to go down into Egypt; for I will there make of thee a great nation: I will go down with thee into Egypt; and I will also surely bring thee up again" (46:3,4). Notice that God planned to make a great nation of Jacob and his descendants in Egypt.

This fact is also evident from Deuteronomy 26:5, which records the words of Moses concerning his ancestor Jacob: "A Syrian ready to perish was my father, and he went down into Egypt, and sojourned there with a few, and became there a nation, great, mighty, and populous." Notice again the words "became there a nation."

Israel's Independence Day

So the Scriptures indicate that the descendants of Abraham actually became a nation while they were in Egypt. Before this time they were not known as a nation. A common expression concerning God's chosen people before this time was "children of Israel." This expression is derived from the fact that Jacob's name was changed to "Israel," for the angel of the Lord told him, "Thy name shall be called no more Jacob, but Israel: for as a prince hast thou power with God and with men, and hast prevailed" (Gen. 32:28).

Following this time, Jacob is commonly referred to as "Israel" and his descendants are referred to as the "children of Israel." The Book of Exodus uses the expression "children of Israel" several times in the first chapter (vv. 1,7,9,13). The 12 sons of Jacob were designated by the expression "children of Israel," and the 12 sons were destined to become the heads of the 12 tribes of Israel.

Before the Israelites were delivered from Egypt, God also referred to them as "my people," and through Moses he told Pharaoh, "Let my people go" (Ex. 5:1). But even though the descendants of Jacob were known as the "children of Israel" or "my people," they were not known as the "nation" of Israel. They became a nation on the day they left Egypt, so the day of the Exodus was truly an independence day for them.

That the time of the Exodus was also the time of the birth of Israel as a nation is evident from what God told Moses and Aaron in the land of Egypt: "This month shall be unto you the beginning of months: it shall be the first month of the year to you. Speak ye unto all the congregation of Israel, saying, In the tenth day of this month they shall take to them every man a lamb, according to the house of their fathers, a lamb for an house" (12:2,3). This was actually a fulfillment of what God had told Jacob: "Fear not to go down into Egypt; for I will there make of thee a great nation" (Gen. 46:3). The words of Exodus 12:2,3 tell of the time referred to in Deuteronomy 26:5 which says that Jacob "became there [in Egypt] a nation, great, mighty, and populous."

The month referred to in Exodus 12:2,3 is the month of April, known to the nation of Israel as "Abib." From that point on Israel was to keep the Feast of the Passover during this month. Deuteronomy 16:1 refers to this: "Observe the month of Abib, and keep the passover unto the Lord thy God: for in the month of Abib the Lord thy God brought thee forth out of Egypt by night." The Feast of the Passover was a remembrance of the beginning of the nation of Israel. As such, the Passover reminded the Israelites of everything that was foundational to the nation itself.

Just as the Israelites needed to be reminded of their beginning as a nation, those of us who know Jesus Christ as Saviour need to be reminded of the deliverance we have experienced. Colossians 1:12-14 refers to this deliverance: "Giving thanks unto the Father, . . . who hath delivered us from the power of darkness, and hath translated us into the kingdom of his dear Son: in whom we have redemption through his blood, even the forgiveness of sins.''

Israel's redemption from Egypt constituted the first step in the life of the nation. The people stepped into freedom! Before that time they had been merely a group of slaves, but then they became a free nation. God redeemed them by blood and by His power.

Important Time Divisions

There are at least three important divisions in time. The first one occurred when Israel became a nation, which is the subject being considered in Exodus 12. At this time, God interrupted the ordinary course of the peoples' existence, and their previous history was disregarded; from this time forth they were known as a nation. The redemption of Israel constituted a new step in the nation's life.

A second important division in time occurred when the Lord Jesus Christ entered this world through the nation of Israel. The birth of Christ changed the marking of calendars; the chronology of the civilized world is dated from this time.

A third important division in time occurs when an individual trusts Jesus Christ as his personal Saviour. Although the popular expression says that life begins at 40, for the Christian, life begins at Calvary. Every member of the human race is born into this world dead in trespasses and sins (Eph. 2:1-6). Because of the sin nature that each person possesses, all are separated—or alienated—from God (4:18). But when a person receives Jesus Christ as personal Saviour, he becomes a "new creature: old things are passed away; behold, all things are become new" (II Cor. 5:17). The new birth marks the beginning of a new life.

Just as the past of the individual Israelites was disregarded, as far as national history was concerned, after they became a nation, so also the past life of an individual is disregarded by God when that person trusts Christ as Saviour. His spiritual life begins at that moment. This life is available by trusting in Christ as Saviour, for at that time a person experiences a spiritual birth. The Bible says, "Except a man be born again, he cannot see the kingdom of God" (John 3:3). The Bible also says, "He that hath the Son hath life; and he that hath not the Son of God hath not life" (I John 5:12).

Chapter 2

Israel's Journey in Three Stages

Israel's journey from Egypt to Canaan occurred in three distinct stages. All three stages are outlined in Exodus 6:6-8. The first stage is seen in verse 6. God said, "I will bring you out from under the burdens of the Egyptians, and I will rid you out of their bondage, and I will redeem you with a stretched out arm, and with great judgments."

The second stage is seen in verse 7, where God said, "I will take you to me for a people, and I will be to you a God."

The third stage is expressed in verse 8 in which God said, "I will bring you in unto the land, . . . I will give it you for an heritage."

Illustration of the Believer's Life

These three stages in Israel's journey from Egypt to Canaan also illustrate three stages in the individual believer's life today. The New Testament says, "Now these things happened to them as an example, and they were written for our instruction" (I Cor. 10:11, NASB).

Each believer should ask himself, In which one of these stages am I spiritually? Israel in Egypt is symbolic of the believer's being occupied with the things of the world. Israel in the desert is symbolic of the believer's being occupied with the self-life. During this time Israel grumbled and complained against Moses and against God, even though God was performing miracles to take care of them. God had to have much longsuffering and mercy toward Israel at this time. Israel in Canaan symbolizes the believer's being occupied with the things of God or the God-life. So if you know Jesus

11

Christ as Saviour, in what stage is your spiritual life? Are you concerned about the world, about self or about God?

The one who has trusted Jesus Christ as Saviour can be occupied with the things of the world so that he is in bondage just as the children of Israel were in bondage under the Egyptians. Such a believer is a slave to the world.

A believer who is occupied with self is self-centered and expends his energy for selfish delights. Perhaps he would not do the things the world does, but what he does is to satisfy his own selfish desires.

The believer who is occupied with Christ is experiencing the abundant life. Jesus said, "I am come that they might have life, and that they might have it more abundantly" (John 10:10). If the believer is to have an overcoming life, he must recognize the truth of Ephesians 6:12: "For we wrestle not against flesh and blood, but against principalities, against powers, against the rulers of the darkness of this world, against spiritual wickedness in high places." To do spiritual warfare, the believer must be in fellowship with the Lord through the Word and much prayer (Eph. 6:17,18). Only then can he overcome evil.

God's plan for Israel included total deliverance. The Lord promised to deliver Israel from condemnation, from burdens and from bondage. God said, "I will bring you out from under the burdens of the Egyptians, and I will rid you out of their bondage, and I will redeem you with a stretched out arm, and with great judgments" (Ex. 16:6). The Passover and deliverance through the Red Sea accomplished all of these for the Israelites. This was deliverance from the world.

God promised to be with the Israelites in their desert experience and to take them to Himself: "I will take you to me for a people, and I will be to you a God: and ye shall know that I am the Lord your God, which bringeth you out from under the burdens of the Egyptians" (v. 7). At this point, the Israelites were not ready for the warfare they would encounter in the land. God used the desert experience to prepare them for this warfare.

The people of Canaan heard how God delivered the Israelites from the Egyptians, and as a result they feared the Israelites. However, the Israelites themselves were not spiritually strong enough to conquer as God wanted them to conquer. He had to take time to train them out in the desert. They needed to be delivered from the self-life.

Having been delivered from the world and from self, Israel needed to be delivered to God for true warfare and rest in the land. God promised this to them in Exodus 6:8: "And I will bring you in unto the land, concerning the which I did swear to give it to Abraham, to Isaac, and to Jacob; and I will give it you for an heritage: I am the Lord." It was not enough that God had promised the land to the Israelites. First they had to enter the land and then conquer it. Finally, as they believed God, they were to follow through and take possession of the land He had promised to them. This was spiritual warfare and involved being occupied with the things of God and especially with God Himself.

God Works for the Believer

God has a similar plan, or program, for the believer. First, the believer is delivered from the guilt and condemnation of sin by the redemptive work of Jesus Christ. This is altogether God's work through Christ in behalf of the believer. It is something God has done for us; it is not something we do ourselves. It is totally the work of God. Ephesians 1:7 speaks of this work of God for us: "In whom we have redemption through his blood, the forgiveness of sins, according to the riches of his grace." Ephesians 2:5 says, "Even when we were dead in sins, [he] hath quickened us [made us alive] together with Christ, (by grace ye are saved)."

The Book of Romans has much to say about the deliverance of the believer from the guilt and condemnation of sin. "Being justified freely by his grace through the redemption that is in Christ Jesus" (3:24). "But God commendeth his love toward us, in that, while we were yet sinners, Christ died for us. Much more then, being now justified by his blood, we shall be saved from wrath through him. For if, when we were enemies, we were reconciled to God by the death of his Son, much more, being reconciled, we shall be saved by his life" (5:8-10).

So first of all, as believers we have been taken from the world, where we were condemned. But God has also made provisions for us to be released from the slavery and bondage of sin. This is what Romans 6 is all about. Notice especially verses 3-6: "Know ye not, that so many of us as were baptized into Jesus Christ were baptized into his death? Therefore we are buried with him by baptism into death: that like as Christ was raised up from the dead by the glory of the Father, even so we also should walk in newness of life. For if we have been planted together in the likeness of his death, we shall be also in the likeness of his resurrection: knowing this, that our old man is [literally, was] crucified with him, that the body of sin might be destroyed, that henceforth we should not serve sin."

This is all God's doing, and it is all part of the first step that has been accomplished *for* us through the Lord Jesus Christ. All of this is made effective for us by the work of the Holy Spirit, producing life in us. His life-giving ministry is mentioned in John 3:5,6: "Jesus answered, Verily, verily, I say unto thee, Except a man be born of water and of the Spirit, he cannot enter into the kingdom of God. That which is born of the flesh is flesh; and that which is born of the Spirit is spirit."

So the first stage of the believer's life with the Lord is redemption from the guilt, condemnation, power and slavery of sin. If you have trusted Jesus Christ as your personal Saviour, this has been accomplished in your behalf. You need to thank God for this and live accordingly.

God Works in the Believer

The second stage of the believer's life with the Lord is deliverance from the weakness of the self-life and training for usefulness for God. This training is accomplished by Christ's work *in* us. The Scriptures emphasize more what Christ does in us than what He does through us.

In this regard, note the following verses: "Being confident of this very thing, that he which hath begun a good work in you will perform it until the day of Jesus Christ" (Phil. 1:6).

"According as he hath chosen us in him before the foundation of the world, that we should be holy and without blame before him in love: having predestinated us unto the adoption of children by Jesus Christ to himself, according to the good pleasure of his will, to the praise of the glory of his grace, wherein he hath made us accepted in the beloved" (Eph. 1:4-6).

"Hope maketh not ashamed; because the love of God is shed abroad in our hearts by the Holy Ghost which is given unto us. . . . For if, when we were enemies, we were reconciled to God by the death of his Son, much more, being reconciled, we shall be saved by his life" (Rom. 5:5,10).

"In whom ye also trusted, after that ye heard the word of truth, the gospel of your salvation: in whom also after that ye believed, ye were sealed with that holy Spirit of promise, which is the earnest of our inheritance until the redemption of the purchased possession, unto the praise of his glory" (Eph. 1:13,14; see also 3:16-20).

God has provided all that we need in order to live in victory over sin and thus please Him in all that we do. This is emphasized in II Peter 1:3,4: "According as his divine power hath given unto us all things that pertain unto life and godliness, through the knowledge of him that hath called us to glory and virtue: whereby are given unto us exceeding great and precious promises: that by these ye might be partakers of the divine nature, having escaped the corruption that is in the world through lust." In Hebrews 13:21 we learn that God works in us "that which is wellpleasing in his sight."

So we learn that Jesus Christ did something for us—He died on the cross to pay the penalty for our sin. But we also learn that Jesus Christ wants to do something in us, and it is important that we cooperate with Him in order to mature spiritually. God did something for Israel when He delivered them from Egypt, but in the desert He was working in them to accomplish His will in their lives.

When Jesus spoke with the woman at the well, He said, "Whosoever drinketh of the water that I shall give him shall never thirst; but the water that I shall give him shall be in him a well of water springing up into everlasting life" (John 4:14). Notice especially the words "in him." When we trust Jesus Christ as Saviour, He takes up residence in our lives to accomplish His will in us. Eternal life is like a well within us—it sustains our lives, for it is the life of Jesus Christ in us.

God Works Through the Believer

In the third stage of the believer's life with the Lord he is delivered from the disgrace of the self-life and is established as a mature, functioning vessel in the hands of the Holy Spirit. In this case, the Holy Spirit works *through* us. We choose to be the servants of the Lord, and thus we are His bondslaves, allowing Him to work through us. Jesus referred to His work in and through us when He said, "If any man thirst, let him come unto me, and drink. He that believeth on me, as the scripture hath said, out of his belly shall flow rivers of living water" (John 7:37,38). The Holy Spirit makes the things of Christ real to us and then works out the life of Christ through us. We must always remember that the Lord Jesus Christ cannot do His work *through* us until we allow Him to do His work *in* us.

The nation of Israel provides the sad example of how long it takes some to allow God to accomplish His purpose in their lives. The trip from Egypt to Canaan should have lasted no longer than two years at the most to provide all the training Israel needed. But because of disobedience the nation wandered 40 years in the wilderness before God could accomplish His purpose. As individual believers, we need to make sure that it doesn't take a long desert experience for us to learn the lessons God wants to teach us.

If we are to have victory over evil and the Evil One as we wrestle against principalities and powers, we need to obey the instructions of the Word of God. "Wherefore take unto you the whole armour of God, that ye may be able to withstand in the evil day, and having done all, to stand" (Eph. 6:13). The following verses list the armor that the believer is to put on—truth, the breastplate of righteousness, the preparation of the gospel of peace, the shield of faith, the helmet of salvation and the sword of the Spirit (vv. 14-17). All of this armor is necessary and is provided for the purpose of enabling us to be victorious in our spiritual warfare.

Consider also that the Lord Jesus Christ has ascended into heaven and has provided the Holy Spirit to live within each believer. It is important for us to get beyond just seeing what Christ has provided *for* us in delivering us from the guilt and condemnation of sin. This is tremendously significant and is foundational to all else, but we need to go beyond that stage in our lives with the Lord. God wanted far more for Israel than just to deliver them from Egypt; He wanted them to enter the land, to conquer it and to possess it by faith. Jesus Christ has given us the Holy Spirit to make us effective in all that we do for Him.

In Ephesians 1 the Apostle Paul prayed for believers, "That ye may know . . . what is the exceeding greatness of his power to us-ward who believe, according to the working of his mighty power" (vv. 18,19). This power is available to those who have trusted Jesus Christ as personal Saviour. Ephesians 2:5,6 reveals why we have such power—because of our position in Christ: "Even when we were dead in sins, hath quickened us together with Christ, (by grace ye are saved;) and hath raised us up together, and made us sit together in heavenly places in Christ Jesus."

Personal Emancipation

Have you really been emancipated from the guilt and condemnation of sin as the nation Israel was emancipated from Egypt? Have you trusted Jesus Christ as your personal Saviour? It does not matter how religious you are or how much religious activity you may be engaged in. The important question is, Have you personally placed your trust in Jesus Christ as your only hope for salvation? It's possible to be extremely religious and yet to be lost because no decision has been made to receive Christ as Saviour.

Do not make the mistake of thinking that a religious atmosphere or religious activities take the place of a personal relationship with Jesus Christ. In my own case, I was reared by wonderful Christian parents, so I had a religious atmosphere. But it wasn't until I was 20 years old that I really recognized that I was lost and needed to personally trust Jesus Christ as my Saviour. Outwardly, I did the things that are normally expected of Christians, but inwardly I had never made the decision to personally trust Christ. I was a member of a church, but I was not a member of the Body of Christ. In spite of all the religious atmosphere and activities, had I

Chapter 3

Saved by Blood

The process of God's redemption of Israel provides an example of how He redeems every sinner through the Lord Jesus Christ. Israel's redemption is beautifully divided into two aspects, helping us to clearly see all that is included in the great salvation God has provided for mankind.

Two Aspects of Redemption

The first aspect of God's redemption of Israel concerns blood. Exodus 12 records that each household was to kill a lamb and apply its blood to the upper and side posts of the door. Without the shedding and application of the blood every Israelite family would have lost the firstborn of their children and their animals. There was no deliverance without the shedding and application of the blood of a lamb.

This shedding of blood typifies the shedding of Christ's blood for the forgiveness of sin. Hebrews 9:22 says, "And almost all things are by the law purged with blood; and without shedding of blood is no remission [forgiveness]." The shed blood of Christ provides deliverance from condemnation for all who trust Him as Saviour. John 5:24 records the words of Christ regarding this matter: "He that heareth my word, and believeth on him that sent me, hath everlasting life, and shall not come into condemnation; but is passed from death unto life." Deliverance from condemnation is possible only because Christ shed His blood for us—"while we were yet sinners, Christ died for us" (Rom. 5:8).

What a significant parallel the individual believer's life is to the nation of Israel. The only means of deliverance from condemnation for the Israelites was the shedding and application of blood. Romans 8:1 proclaims, "There is therefore now no condemnation to them which are in Christ Jesus." First John 5:12 promises, "He that hath the Son hath life."

The second phase of salvation concerns power. By God's power He delivered the Israelites from the slavery of Egypt and then took them to the desert for training. There they had to depend totally on God's leadership and power for all of their needs.

So, too, the individual believer needs to rely totally on God for power in daily living. Salvation in Christ makes one a "new creature" (II Cor. 5:17), and the believer needs to realize that "all things are of God" (v. 18). God's leadership and power are provided for the believer in the death and resurrection of Jesus Christ and effected by the Holy Spirit who has been given to us.

The Scope of God's Judgment

God's sentence of judgment included the Israelites as well as the Egyptians: "All the firstborn in the land of Egypt shall die, from the firstborn of Pharaoh that sitteth upon his throne, even unto the firstborn of the maidservant that is behind the mill; and all the firstborn of beasts" (Ex. 11:5). This sentence of condemnation was designed particularly for the Egyptians, but even the Israelites could not escape the judgment unless a lamb was killed and its blood applied to the doorposts of their dwelling.

Israel could not escape this judgment simply because they were a righteous people or because they were a chosen people. They had to make personal application of the blood if they were to escape the sentence of judgment. The Israelites were direct descendants of Abraham, with whom God had made a covenant, but this special relationship alone did not exempt them from the judgment God was about to bring on all Egypt.

Many today think that because they have been reared in a godly home and have attended a good church they will escape condemnation. But these things in themselves do not deliver a person from condemnation. There must be a personal relationship with Jesus Christ—there must be a personal application of His blood in order for that individual to be delivered from condemnation. One born into a godly home is no different than one born into an ungodly home. This truth is evident from Romans 3:22,23: "For there is no difference: for all have sinned, and come short of the glory of God." This sentence of universal condemnation proceeds from the righteousness of God.

The words of Romans 3:23 cannot be emphasized too strongly: "All have sinned, and come short of the glory of God." Romans 6:23 states the results of serving sin: "For the wages of sin is death." However, verse 23 does not end with that statement. It goes on to say, "But the gift of God is eternal life through Jesus Christ our Lord."

Justice Satisfied; Mercy Expressed

God cannot clear the guilty unless the standards of His holiness are met. God wants to be merciful to us, but He cannot be merciful until His justice has been completely satisfied. The good news is that God's justice was completely satisfied in the death of His Son. Romans 3:24,25 tells us, "Being justified freely by his grace through the redemption that is in Christ Jesus: whom God hath set forth to be a propitiation through faith in his blood, to declare his righteousness for the remission of sins that are past, through the forbearance of God."

Because the Lord Jesus Christ satisfied the righteous demands of the Heavenly Father, it was possible for God to uphold His righteous standards and yet be able to forgive those who trusted Jesus Christ for salvation. This fact is expressed in Romans 3:26: "To declare, I say, at this time his righteousness: that he might be just, and the justifier of him which believeth in Jesus."

Justice and mercy were reconciled because justice was satisfied by the offering of the shed blood of Jesus. Every demand of justice was satisfied; every claim of holiness was fully met. All of this was possible by means of a substitute. Just as a lamb was offered as a sacrifice in Old Testament

times, so Jesus Christ was the Lamb of God who took away
the sin of the world (see John 1:29).

When God gave instructions to the Israelites prior to the
Exodus from Egypt, He told Moses, "Speak ye unto all the
congregation of Israel, saying, In the tenth day of this month
they shall take to them every man a lamb, according to the
house of their fathers, a lamb for an house: and if the household be too little for the lamb, let him and his neighbour
next unto his house take it according to the number of the
souls; every man according to his eating shall make your
count for the lamb. Your lamb shall be without blemish, a
male of the first year: ye shall take it out from the sheep, or
from the goats" (Ex. 12:3-5). A lamb without blemish died
and was accepted by God as a substitute for the firstborn.

The difference between the Egyptians and the Israelites
was not a moral one because all were under sin. The difference was only the blood of the lamb. The Israelites experienced the mercy of God because they put their faith in the
substitute, allowing God's justice to be satisfied so He could
extend mercy. The meeting of justice and mercy was beautifully expressed by the psalmist: "Mercy and truth are met
together; righteousness and peace have kissed each other"
(Ps. 85:10). The meeting of justice and mercy is possible only
because of shed blood. The Passover lamb was a type of
Christ who shed His blood on the cross, thus becoming the
Passover Lamb for the world.

Concerning Christ, the Lamb of God, the Bible says that
the Father "hath made him to be sin for us, who knew no
sin; that we might be made the righteousness of God in him"
(II Cor. 5:21). Romans 8:32 adds, "He that spared not his
own Son, but delivered him up for us all, how shall he not
with him also freely give us all things?" All of this is available
to us as believers because "we were reconciled to God by the
death of his Son" (5:10).

No one is saved by prayer, although prayer is a way of
accepting salvation or expressing our desire for it. Neither is
anyone saved by fasting. Rather, salvation is only by substitu-
tion—trusting Jesus Christ as Saviour because He is the One
who died in the place of every person. People are saved not
because of any righteousness they have in themselves but

because of trusting in Jesus Christ, who then becomes their righteousness.

Application of the Blood

So, also, the Israelites were not spared judgment in Egypt because they prayed or because they fasted or because of their own merits but only because they applied the shed blood as God instructed. They were in houses behind the blood which had been applied to the doorposts; thus, their firstborn were spared from death.

In order for the firstborn to be spared, a lamb had to be killed and its blood applied to the doorposts. Death would be inflicted either on the firstborn or on the substitute for the firstborn. But the death of the lamb alone would not do; its blood had to be applied as God instructed. God said, "They shall take of the blood, and strike it on the two side posts and on the upper door post of the houses" (Ex. 12:7). Nothing was left to chance or to man's ingenuity. Salvation was, and is, totally of God.

Hebrews 9:22 says, "Without shedding of blood is no remission [forgiveness]." But in Exodus 12:7 God instructed that the blood be sprinkled on the doorposts. Do these terms refer to the same action? No, shedding and sprinkling are not synonymous. The shedding of blood refers to propitiation, or satisfaction. Sprinkling of blood refers to appropriation, or application.

Although Christ shed His blood for the sins of the world (I John 2:2), no one is saved from condemnation unless he personally trusts Christ as Saviour (John 1:12). Receiving Christ as Saviour is appropriating to oneself what Christ has made available. Not until the blood has been applied does it actually provide safety. It is not enough to know that the blood of Jesus Christ was shed for the forgiveness of sin—one must personally trust Him as Saviour.

Just as none of the Israelites were delivered from death simply by the shedding of the lamb's blood, so no one is delivered from eternal condemnation just by the shedding of Christ's blood. In both cases the blood must be applied. There must be "faith in his blood" (Rom. 3:25). Forgiveness and reconciliation are attained by faith only—"For by grace are ye saved through faith; and that not of yourselves: it is the gift of God: not of works, lest any man should boast" (Eph. 2:8,9).

Notice that the sprinkling of blood by the Israelites was not to be a secretive thing—it was to be sprinkled on the doorposts, indicating public, or open, confession. The New Testament says that "if thou shalt confess with thy mouth the Lord Jesus, and shalt believe in thine heart that God hath raised him from the dead, thou shalt be saved" (Rom. 10:9).

The Israelites were not to sprinkle the blood on the threshold where it might be trampled on but on the doorposts as a public confession. This was also God's seal for them, which promised that they would be spared the judgment of death on the firstborn.

God made it unmistakably clear to the Israelites what it would take for them to escape judgment: "When I see the blood, I will pass over you, and the plague shall not be upon you to destroy you, when I smite the land of Egypt" (Ex. 12:13). Unless the Israelites met God's conditions, they would experience the loss of their firstborn just as the Egyptians would. So it was necessary for each family to apply the shed blood of a lamb to the doorposts. The applied blood was the only means of safety. It revealed that deliverance had already been accomplished in the death of the substitute. God's eye was not on the house as such nor on those in it but on the blood which had been applied to the house.

Feelings and God's Promises

Have you ever wondered how those in the house might have felt during this time? Even after they had sprinkled the blood on the doorposts, could they be sure that they would escape God's judgment on the land of Egypt?

A similar question which many ask today is, How can a person be sure of his relationship with God? Each person should ask himself, What am I depending on for my salvation?

The only correct answer to both questions is, One can depend on the promises of God. It did not matter how the Israelites felt. Feelings had nothing to do with their deliverance. The crucial matter was whether they had taken God at His word and had applied the blood. If so, they could also count on His promise to deliver them from the judgment regardless of their feelings at the time.

So, too, when a person today applies the shed blood of Christ by trusting Him as personal Saviour, he can count on the promises of God to deliver him from coming judgment. A person must not rely on his family or church background or on anything else. Salvation is obtained only by applying the shed blood of Christ, which is done by receiving Him as personal Saviour. When this is done, one can then rely on Christ's promise: "He that heareth my word, and believeth on him that sent me, hath everlasting life, and shall not come into condemnation; but is passed from death unto life" (John 5:24). Notice that the one who has trusted Christ as Saviour will never come into condemnation. What a tremendous promise!

The assurance of salvation is not based on some special feeling; rather, it is to be based on God's promises. We are to take God at His word. Satan tries to get a person to trust his feelings, because he knows that the person will probably doubt his salvation as soon as his feelings change. But if you have trusted Jesus Christ as your personal Saviour, you are a child of God—you have forgiveness of sin and eternal life whether you feel like it or not!

When the lamb had been slain and the blood applied to the doorposts, no one could condemn the Israelites. So, also, because Christ had been crucified for the world, and when His blood is applied by individually receiving Him as Saviour, a person is delivered from condemnation (John 5:24). These are promises that God Himself has made, and it is "impossible for God to lie" (Heb. 6:18).

When a person appropriates what God has done for him, no one can successfully bring a charge against him. The Bible says, "Who shall lay anything to the charge of God's elect? It is God that justifieth. Who is he that condemneth? It is Christ that died, yea rather, that is risen again, who is even at the right hand of God, who also maketh intercession for us" (Rom. 8:33,34). Christ has accomplished all that we need for salvation, and He is at the right hand of God this very moment interceding for those who have trusted Him as Saviour.

Concerning the importance of the sacrifice of the Lord Jesus Christ, Hebrews 10:14 says, "For by one offering he hath perfected for ever them that are sanctified." The Old Testament offerings had to be made over and over again, but the offering of Christ for sin was made once for all.

Since Christ was the offering for sin, anyone who places his faith in Jesus Christ as his Saviour is delivered from condemnation. However, even though we are saved by faith (Eph. 2:8,9), we are not to think that faith *itself* saves. It is actually the object of our faith—the Lord Jesus Christ—that saves us. Faith itself has not paid the penalty for sin. Only Jesus Christ has paid this penalty; faith is the means by which we appropriate what He accomplished.

If no blood was on the doorposts of the houses of the Israelites, no amount of believing that it was there would deliver the occupants from judgment. They actually had to put their confidence in God's word and then act accordingly. Just believing that Jesus Christ lived long ago and died for our sin does not save anyone from condemnation; an individual must personally trust Jesus Christ as his Saviour in order to be saved. Once this decision for Christ has been made, a person is saved regardless of his feelings or uncertainties, just as the Israelites were delivered from judgment by applying the blood regardless of how many questions they may have had.

It is important to distinguish between security and assurance. A person who trusts Christ as Saviour has security whether he realizes it or not (John 10:28,29). Assurance is that peace of heart that comes from taking God at His word concerning one's security. Assurance is related to peace about one's relationship with the Lord.

Satan loves to destroy a person's peace concerning his security in Christ. But the Christian who has confidence in God's Word will have assurance about his salvation because he is resting on the promises of God, not on feelings. Although peace may be destroyed, security depends on the promises of God. Assurance is the response of a person's heart, acknowledging by faith that what God has said is true.

Instructions to the Israelites

Consider the various aspects of the instructions God gave the Israelites prior to the Exodus. The blood made them safe; the word made them sure. The feast which they were instructed to eat made them strong; the dress (they were instructed to eat fully clothed) made them ready for departure. These truths are seen in Exodus 12:8-11.

All of this has a modern-day parallel. It is not enough that Christ has died on the cross—we must appropriate by faith what He has done for us. By faith He becomes our life, and by faith we receive strength from Him. Such was alluded to by Jesus Himself, as recorded in John 6:51,54: "I am the living bread which came down from heaven: if any man eat of this bread, he shall live for ever: and the bread that I will give is my flesh, which I will give for the life of the world. . . . Whoso eateth my flesh, and drinketh my blood, hath eternal life; and I will raise him up at the last day."

Concerning the eating of the lamb, God instructed the Israelites, "Thus shall ye eat it; with your loins girded, your shoes on your feet, and your staff in your hand; and ye shall eat it in haste: it is the Lord's passover" (Ex. 12:11). The lamb was to be eaten for strength and in a posture that was ready for departure. The Israelites were to shake off the yoke of Egypt and forsake the sin of the land. They were citizens of another country and were to be ready to leave immediately for that land.

This reminds us of Hebrews 13:12-14: "Wherefore Jesus also, that he might sanctify the people with his own blood, suffered without the gate. Let us go forth therefore unto him without the camp, bearing his reproach. For here have we no continuing city, but we seek one to come."

Second Corinthians 6:14 also instructs believers, "Be ye not unequally yoked together with unbelievers: for what fellowship hath righteousness with unrighteousness? And what communion hath light with darkness?" So even though the believer is *in* the world he is not to be part *of* the world— he is to be separated to God even while living in the world.

From Exodus 12:34-37 we learn more details about the activities of Israel: "So the people took their dough before it was leavened, with their kneading bowls bound up in the clothes on their shoulders. Now the sons of Israel had done according to the word of Moses, for they had requested from the Egyptians articles of silver and articles of gold, and clothing; and the Lord had given the people favor in the sight of the Egyptians, so that they let them have their request. Thus they plundered the Egyptians. Now the sons of Israel journeyed from Rameses to Succoth, about six hundred thousand men on foot, aside from children" (NASB).

Just as the Israelites were to move out at once from Egypt, so the person who knows Jesus Christ as Saviour should immediately begin a journey away from the things of the world. This present world should not be considered home by believers. The Bible says, "For here have we no continuing city, but we seek one to come" (Heb. 13:14).

Abraham was an example to the believer in the way he should fix his eyes on eternal, not temporal, blessings. The Bible says concerning Abraham, "By faith he sojourned in the land of promise, as in a strange country, dwelling in tabernacles with Isaac and Jacob, the heirs with him of the same promise: for he looked for a city which hath foundations, whose builder and maker is God" (11:9,10). Philippians 3:20 tells believers, "For our conversation [citizenship] is in heaven; from whence also we look for the Saviour, the Lord Jesus Christ."

God does not expect the believer to leave this world, but He expects him to be separated from it while he is here. In His high-priestly prayer the Lord Jesus said, "I pray not that thou shouldest take them out of the world, but that thou shouldest keep them from the evil [one]" (John 17:15).

So we see that the first step of God's redemption was to save them by blood. However, the Israelites also needed to be delivered from slavery to the Egyptians. This was the second step in God's redemptive plan for them.

Chapter 4

Saved by Power

As the Israelites began their march, God began to deal with them in the second phase of His redemptive plan, a step that involved power. Although these were distinct steps in Israel's deliverance, the steps involving blood and power take place simultaneously today when an individual becomes a Christian. When one receives Jesus Christ as his Saviour, the blood of Christ is applied to his life—the benefit of what Christ accomplished is applied to him. At the same time, God gives the believer power to live a life separated from the world.

Having clearly instructed the Israelites to apply the blood to the doorposts, God began to lead them through the wilderness. Exodus 12:37 says, "And the children of Israel journeyed from Rameses to Succoth, about six hundred thousand on foot that were men, beside children." Inasmuch as wives and children were not counted in these 600,000, it is estimated that the total group may have been between two and three million people.

They journeyed "from Rameses to Succoth." This was a journey of about 15 miles and was on a well-traveled trade route that would lead them directly to Canaan. It was about 200 miles from where they had lived in Egypt to the land of Canaan, and this trade route could be traveled in about eight or ten days. Traders who traveled the road could make the distance in about three days, but a huge group like the Israelites would take much longer.

This part of the journey was initiated by the people themselves under the leadership of Moses. Succoth made a

29

good meeting place for them before proceeding further to Canaan.

The Bible says, "They baked unleavened cakes of the dough which they brought forth out of Egypt, for it was not leavened; because they were thrust out of Egypt, and could not tarry, neither had they prepared for themselves any victual" (v. 39). This verse reveals how quickly the Israelites left Egypt.

Note the statement, "And a mixed multitude went up also with them" (v. 38). This mixed multitude that went along with the Israelites later proved to be one of the wiles of the Devil, who operates both as a roaring lion and as a cunning serpent. In Egypt he had worked as a roaring lion through the oppression of Pharaoh and his attempts to keep the Israelites in Egypt. But when Satan was unable to keep the Israelites in Egypt, he tried to hinder their clean separation from Egypt by an infiltration of those who were not really believers.

Later on, there were possibly intermarriages of this mixed multitude with the Israelites. Those who were not really believers proved to be a thorn in Israel's side because they became dissatisfied and influenced the Israelites to grumble time and again. This mixed multitude reminds us of the unconverted who attend church services today. If they are allowed a voice of authority in the church, they most certainly will direct the church in a way that is not honoring to God.

The mixed multitude apparently had been drawn to the Israelites because of the demonstration of divine power, yet they had not really experienced a change of heart. They saw that something was happening to the Israelites, and they wanted to be a part of it even though they did not have a proper relationship with the Lord.

God's Route

The Israelites traveled from Rameses to Succoth, but then God chose a different route for them. The Bible says, "And it came to pass, when Pharaoh had let the people go, that God led them not through the way of the land of the Philistines, although that was near; for God said, Lest peradventure the people repent when they see war, and they return to Egypt: but God led the people about, through the way of the wilderness of the Red sea: and the children of Israel went up harnessed out of the land of Egypt" (Ex. 13:17,18). The route God chose was not by an easily traveled road but was a detour through the wilderness. The other road led through a populated area; it was easier and much more traveled, but in His wisdom, God chose the long road for the Israelites.

On this long route there were no highways, no bridges, no resources to supply their needs and no signs to direct their paths. In fact, it took them two years to reach Kadesh-barnea, which was on the southern extremity of the land of Canaan. But even this teaches us that God chooses the way His people should go. There is a very important lesson to be learned from this incident. We should not only realize that God chooses the way, but we should recognize that it is for our best if we respond to His direction.

Jeremiah said, "O Lord, I know that the way of man is not in himself: it is not in man that walketh to direct his steps" (Jer. 10:23). Proverbs 20:24 says, "Man's goings are of the Lord; how can a man then understand his own way?"

Realizing that we do not have the wisdom to know for sure the way we should walk, it is important that we rely on the counsel of God's Word. "Trust in the Lord with all thine heart; and lean not unto thine own understanding. In all thy ways acknowledge him, and he shall direct thy paths. Be not wise in thine own eyes: fear the Lord, and depart from evil" (3:5-7).

Notice also Psalm 37:23: "The steps of a good man are ordered by the Lord: and he delighteth in his way." Psalm 119:105 says, "Thy word is a lamp unto my feet, and a light unto my path." The New Testament assures, "For as many as are led by the Spirit of God, they are the sons of God" (Rom. 8:14).

By blood the Israelites had been delivered from the judgment on the firstborn. By the power of God they had been delivered from slavery in Egypt. Now they were being led by God, not on the easily traveled, short route, but on the difficult, long road.

Chapter 5

The Long Road

"It came to pass, when Pharaoh had let the people go, that God led them not through the way of the land of the Philistines, although that was near; for God said, Lest peradventure the people repent when they see war, and they return to Egypt: but God led the people about, through the way of the wilderness of the Red sea: and the children of Israel went up harnessed out of the land of Egypt" (Ex. 13:17,18).

Preparation for Warfare

In a sense, the Israelites were God's infant children, and from the standpoints of traveling and warfare they had many things to learn. And through the experiences of the nation of Israel, God has many things to teach those of us who live today. The New Testament says, "Now all these things happened unto them for ensamples [examples]: and they are written for our admonition, upon whom the ends of the world are come" (I Cor. 10:11).

This same passage tells us, "There hath no temptation taken you but such as is common to man: but God is faithful, who will not suffer [permit] you to be tempted above that ye are able; but will with the temptation also make a way to escape, that ye may be able to bear it" (v. 13). This verse is not only true concerning us, but it was also true concerning the Israelites. God was not going to submit them to a test more difficult than they could bear. God knows how much we can take; therefore, He knows how many tests to allow to come into our lives in order to help us to mature.

God completely understands us, so He knows our feelings when we face difficult situations. Psalm 103 expresses this so well, and over the years I've gone back to this psalm hundreds of times. Especially notice verses 13 and 14: "Like as a father pitieth his children, so the Lord pitieth them that fear him. For he knoweth our frame; he remembereth that we are dust."

Abraham is a prime example of biblical characters who passed through tests. God allowed him to pass through many tests of faith until He brought him to the last and greatest test—the offering of his son. The rest of the tests were mild in comparison to that, but they grew more severe as God sought to mature Abraham in the faith.

Although God may never ask us to literally sacrifice a son, He does bring greater and greater tests into our lives in order to mature us and to conform us "to the image of his Son" (Rom. 8:29).

Israel was not yet ready for warfare, yet later they would be fighting the Canaanites. So it was necessary for God to allow the nation to be tested in order to prepare them for battle.

The Christian is involved in spiritual warfare, and God has supplied all of his needs for that. Ephesians 1:3 tells of God's supply: "Blessed be the God and Father of our Lord Jesus Christ, who hath blessed us with all spiritual blessings in heavenly places in Christ." But God is concerned that we apply what He has made available for us. This passage goes on to say, "According as he hath chosen us in him before the foundation of the world, that we should be holy and without blame before him in love: having predestinated us unto the adoption of children by Jesus Christ to himself, according to the good pleasure of his will, to the praise of the glory of his grace, wherein he hath made us accepted in the beloved" (vv. 4-6).

The Book of Ephesians climaxes by telling of the warfare in which the maturing Christian will be engaged: "Finally, my brethren, be strong in the Lord, and in the power of his might. Put on the whole armour of God, that ye may be able to stand against the wiles of the devil. For we wrestle not against flesh and blood, but against principalities, against powers, against the rulers of the darkness of this world, against spiritual wickedness in high places" (6:10-12).

In spiritual warfare it is very important for us to learn that God never asks us to bear more than we are able, just as He never called on the Israelites to bear more than they were able.

God intended the long road by which He led the Israelites to be a means of blessing them rather than a means of withholding blessing. We often assume that the shortcut always holds the blessing rather than the long road, but this only reveals that we look at things from the human standpoint rather than from God's viewpoint. Sometimes detours are more beautiful than the main road. But even if no physical beauty is involved, there is beauty of soul when God accomplishes His purpose in an individual life.

It is important to remember that God led the Israelites— He selected the way. Nothing was left to chance or to poor reasoning. God had brought Israel into existence by His own choice; now He was leading the people in the way they should go.

Concerning Christians today, the New Testament reveals: "We are his workmanship, created in Christ Jesus unto good works, which God hath before ordained that we should walk in them" (Eph. 2:10). We are created for good works, and God works in our lives in order to lead us on to spiritual maturity (1:4,5).

The blessing in God's leading Israel Himself can be seen as one considers that these people had been slaves in Egypt. They were undisciplined in the art of warfare and survival—all they knew was the hard work of slavery.

God wanted the nation of Israel to have a walk of faith, not a walk based only on sight. The only way He could teach them this was by means of the long road. They had to learn to wait on God; they had to learn to be patient; they had to learn to trust God completely.

Although we cannot always understand God's providential workings, we can learn to believe and trust Him. This comes from realizing that God, in His wisdom, makes no mistakes and that the final outcome will be for our good and His glory.

Five Purposes of the Long Road

There were at least five purposes of the long road for Israel. First, it was used to reveal God's power as He led them through the Red Sea, not around it. The people had to experience the great power of God in doing spectacular things for them. By opening the Red Sea for them, God revealed His tremendous power so that they could trust Him for anything in the future.

Second, the long route was used to destroy the power of the enemy. When the Israelites had passed through the Red Sea, the water closed in on the Egyptians, their enemy. At that time Israel recognized the wonderful power of God.

Third, while on the long road Israel received the Law. In God's program of the ages there was a specific time and a specific place for the Mosaic Law to be given. The Israelites were the specific people to receive it, and God wanted them in the place of His choice for this purpose.

Fourth, the Israelites had time to become properly organized. The children of Israel needed to be organized into a commonwealth prior to their entrance into Canaan.

Fifth, Israel was humbled and proved on the long road. The desert was the only place large enough that would provide a place where the Israelites could be completely separated to God.

Later, in speaking to the children who had come through the wilderness experience, Moses told them, "Thou shalt remember all the way which the Lord thy God led thee these forty years in the wilderness, to humble thee, and to prove thee, to know what was in thine heart, whether thou wouldest keep his commandments, or no. And he humbled thee, and suffered thee to hunger, and fed thee with manna, which thou knewest not, neither did thy fathers know; that he might make thee know that man doth not live by bread only, but by every word that proceedeth out of the mouth of the Lord doth man live" (Deut. 8:2,3).

Israel needed to learn God's way of working with His people. They needed to learn what was later stated in Romans 8:28: "We know that all things work together for good to them that love God, to them who are the called according to his purpose." The reason for God's working this

way is seen in the following verse: "For whom he did fore-
know, he also did predestinate to be conformed to the image
of his Son" (v. 29). God wants believers to be conformed to
the image of Jesus Christ.

Even though the Israelites did not have the New Testament, they had sufficient information about God to realize
that He knew best and that only when they followed Him
would things work out to their good and for His glory.

The Israelites also needed to learn something about the
way God deals with His own in chastisement. This is a
method God uses to train His children and mature them.
Concerning chastening Hebrews 12:5-7 says, "Despise not
thou the chastening of the Lord, nor faint when thou art
rebuked of him: for whom the Lord loveth he chasteneth,
and scourgeth every son whom he receiveth. If ye endure
chastening, God dealeth with you as with sons; for what son
is he whom the father chasteneth not?" So when God
chastens an individual, it reveals that the person really
belongs to Him. This is God's way of dealing with His own
children in order to train them and lead them on to spiritual
maturity.

There is no indication that the chastening of the Lord is
enjoyable; in fact, the opposite is true. Hebrews 12:11 says,
"Now no chastening for the present seemeth to be joyous,
but grievous: nevertheless afterward it yieldeth the peaceable
fruit of righteousness unto them which are exercised
thereby." This is what Israel had to learn, and this is what we
have to learn also.

Knowing Themselves and Knowing God

The Israelites definitely needed to understand two other
matters—they needed to know themselves and they needed to
know God.

God led them 40 years in the wilderness for the purpose
of helping them to know themselves. There He humbled
them and proved them so they would know what was in their
hearts (Deut. 8:2).

After the Apostle Paul learned what was in his heart, he
wrote: "For I know that in me (that is, in my flesh,) dwelleth
no good thing: for to will is present with me; but how to

perform that which is good I find not" (Rom. 7:18). Paul had no confidence in the flesh. Most of us have to learn this lesson the hard way; Israel learned it in the wilderness.

The purpose of the Law that was later given to Israel was to reveal their sinfulness in order to emphasize how far they were from the standards of God. The ceremonial law revealed God's grace, however, for it made provision for sin.

God's leading and the instructions He gave the Israelites were to enable them to know themselves better. Out in the desert they were completely alone with God and were forced to see themselves as they really were. They had to learn to depend on Him to supply their needs.

In addition to learning to know themselves, the Israelites also needed to learn to know God. They needed to personally experience how God can take care of His own. Moses reminded the Israelites of the way God worked with them when he said, "He humbled thee, and suffered thee to hunger, and fed thee with manna, which thou knewest not, neither did thy fathers know; that he might make thee know that man doth not live by bread only, but by every word that proceedeth out of the mouth of the Lord doth man live" (Deut. 8:3).

In order for the Israelites to really know God, they had to follow Him. They had seen how God had miraculously worked at the Passover, but they had many other things to experience in the wilderness that would prove God's ability to take care of His own. In the wilderness they were to see how God would provide food and water, protect them from the enemy and reveal His Law to them. All these things were necessary for them to really learn to know God.

These were not things that Israel could learn on the easy road; the path of least resistance never teaches the valuable lessons that one needs to know. Too many Christians are unwilling to let God deal with their souls because they do not realize the good that can result. Perhaps they even want to know God better, but they are unwilling to be really exercised about spiritual matters.

The Long Road Brings Blessing

In the wilderness God revealed Himself to the Israelites so they would have a firsthand knowledge of Him. Even though the longer way may have seemed harder to the Israelites, it was really the way of comfort and advantage. Notice the significant words in Exodus 13:18: "God led the people about." God led them through the trackless wilderness to make them totally dependent on Himself.

This is an important lesson for us to learn. God often leads His children through the deep, dark valleys to teach them His ways and to enable them to fully experience His blessing. The Apostle Paul realized this, and he stated his heart's desire in these words: "That I may know him, and the power of his resurrection, and the fellowship of his sufferings, being made conformable unto his death" (Phil. 3:10). What a tremendous statement! If we desire power like this, we must ask ourselves if we also desire the fellowship of His suffering that goes along with it.

David realized the way the Lord works in a believer's life and expressed it in these words: "Yea, though I walk through the valley of the shadow of death, I will fear no evil: for thou art with me; thy rod and thy staff they comfort me" (Ps. 23:4). Although some think that David wrote this psalm when he was a young shepherd, he seems to be looking back over his life and reflecting on how many times God had led him through the valley of the shadow of death. He had faced death on many occasions, but God had delivered him. Before he became king, Saul tried to put David to death, but God preserved David's life. Seeing God work in his behalf caused David to have a different perspective on living the rest of his days.

So the wilderness and the valley experiences prepare us for the road ahead. The Bible says that the Israelites "took their journey from Succoth, and encamped in Etham, in the edge of the wilderness" (Ex. 13:20). At this point they were still journeying on a well-traveled road, but from here the caravan road turned to the northeast and went along the Mediterranean Sea. The desert was south of them, and Etham was right at the edge of the desert. It was here that God definitely took over and ordered that they travel south instead of following the well-known road.

The Lord told Moses, "Speak unto the children of Israel, that they turn and encamp before Pi-hahiroth, between Migdol and the sea, over against Baal-zephon: before it shall ye encamp by the sea. For Pharaoh will say of the children of Israel, They are entangled in the land, the wilderness hath shut them in" (14:2,3).

All the green vegetation faded away into waste and sand as the Israelites turned southward. That's exactly what God wanted because He knew what Pharaoh would think—that the Israelites were hopelessly entangled in the wilderness and that he could easily overtake them. But God had a plan in mind that was far beyond anything that Pharaoh could even imagine!

Chapter 6

Led by a Cloud

The method God used to lead the Israelites is indicated in Exodus 13:21,22: "The Lord went before them by day in a pillar of a cloud, to lead them the way; and by night in a pillar of fire, to give them light; to go by day and night: he took not away the pillar of the cloud by day, nor the pillar of fire by night, from before the people."

The Pillar of Cloud and Fire

We are not told how this pillar was shaped—perhaps it looked like a huge umbrella with a point, extending down to the people. Whatever shape it had, it served God's purpose in guiding the people both day and night. It protected them from the hot sun during the day, and it gave light to them at night. What a wonderful provision God made for His own!

As sinners the Israelites needed a savior; as captives they needed a deliverer; but as pilgrims they needed a guide. The predominant function of the pillar of cloud was to guide the Israelites through the barren desert as they journeyed from Egypt to Canaan.

God has also provided a guide for believers today, although it is not a pillar of cloud. The guide God has provided is the Holy Spirit. Before Jesus left His disciples, He told them, "I will pray the Father, and he shall give you another Comforter, that he may abide with you for ever; even the Spirit of truth; whom the world cannot receive, because it seeth him not, neither knoweth him: but ye know him; for he dwelleth with you, and shall be in you" (John 14:16,17). Jesus also told His disciples concerning the Holy

Spirit, "When he, the Spirit of truth, is come, he will guide you into all truth: for he shall not speak of himself; but whatsoever he shall hear, that shall he speak: and he will shew you things to come" (16:13).

For the Israelites the pillar of cloud was a visible sign of the Lord's presence with them. Regardless of the circumstances during their journey, the cloud—the evidence of God's presence—remained with them. How reassuring this must have been!

Fire is a symbol of the presence of the Lord, the One who neither sleeps nor slumbers. God gave abundant evidence of His presence—the pillar of cloud by day and the pillar of fire by night. At no time were the Israelites left without an evidence of His presence.

God's special care of Israel in the wilderness is indicated by what Moses said after the wilderness wanderings: "For the Lord's portion is his people; Jacob is the lot of his inheritance. He found him in a desert land, and in the waste howling wilderness; he led him about, he instructed him, he kept him as the apple of his eye. As an eagle stirreth up her nest, fluttereth over her young, spreadeth abroad her wings, taketh them, beareth them on her wings: so the Lord alone did lead him, and there was no strange god with him" (Deut. 32:9-12).

The appearance of the cloud to the Israelites in the desert marked a turning point in their journey. Exodus 13:20 says, "They took their journey from Succoth." The emphasis in this clause seems to be on what the Israelites did on their own. However, the following verse says, "The Lord went before them by day in a pillar of a cloud, to lead them the way" (v. 21). This indicates the intervention of the Lord in specifically leading the people in the way He wanted them to go.

When God began to lead them by a pillar of cloud by day and a pillar of fire by night, Israel's walk of faith really began. They were to move when the cloud moved, and they were to stay when the cloud remained stationary. They were to depend totally on the Lord for leadership.

Just as the cloud went before the Israelites, the Lord goes before those who are His own. The Bible says, "When he putteth forth his own sheep, he goeth before them, and the sheep follow him: for they know his voice" (John 10:4).

Inasmuch as God provided a pillar of fire at night for the Israelites, anyone who was not walking in the light evidenced that he was outside the realm of fellowship with the Israelites and with God. A parallel to this is seen in the New Testament: "God is light, and in him is no darkness at all. If we say that we have fellowship with him, and walk in darkness, we lie, and do not the truth: but if we walk in the light, as he is in the light, we have fellowship one with another, and the blood of Jesus Christ his Son cleanseth us from all sin" (I John 1:5-7).

Other writers in the Bible knew of the way God led the Israelites and wrote of it. Nehemiah wrote: "Moreover thou leddest them in the day by a cloudy pillar; and in the night by a pillar of fire, to give them light in the way wherein they should go" (Neh. 9:12). As we have indicated, God's guiding the Israelites by light is a reminder to us of His giving the Holy Spirit to guide believers "into all truth" (John 16:13).

The fact that God provided guidance for Israel revealed that they were His own people. He does not provide guidance for those who are not His own. So, also, Church-Age believers are told, "For as many as are led by the Spirit of God, they are the sons of God" (Rom. 8:14).

The Trumpets

In God's program of providing guidance for Israel, He later designated that trumpets be used for certain signals. God instructed, "Make thee two trumpets of silver; of a whole piece shalt thou make them: that thou mayest use them for the calling of the assembly, and for the journeying of the camps. And when they shall blow with them, all the assembly shall assemble themselves to thee at the door of the tabernacle of the congregation" (Num. 10:2,3). So in addition to the moving of the cloud, the Israelites had trumpets to signal them in their march through the wilderness.

Whereas the cloud reminds us of the leadership of the Holy Spirit, the trumpets remind us of the guidance of God's Word. The psalmist said, "Thy word is a lamp unto my feet, and a light unto my path" (Ps. 119:105). He also wrote:

"The entrance of thy words giveth light; it giveth understanding unto the simple" (v. 130). So the Word of God is to be used as a guide—God never leads in a way that is contrary to His revealed Word.

Trumpets are mentioned frequently in scripture—Israel was guided by trumpets, and one trumpet in particular is mentioned for the Church. Referring to the latter, the Bible says, "For the Lord himself shall descend from heaven with a shout, with the voice of the archangel, and with the trump [trumpet] of God: and the dead in Christ shall rise first: then we which are alive and remain shall be caught up together with them in the clouds, to meet the Lord in the air: and so shall we ever be with the Lord" (I Thess. 4:16,17).

Referring to the same event, I Corinthians 15:51,52 says, "Behold, I shew you a mystery; We shall not all sleep, but we shall all be changed, in a moment, in the twinkling of an eye, at the last trump [trumpet]: for the trumpet shall sound, and the dead shall be raised incorruptible, and we shall be changed."

For Israel the cloud and the trumpets went together. They were not led just by the cloud nor just by the trumpets but by both. Of course, both would be in harmony if the trumpets were blown according to God's direction.

Guidance of the Holy Spirit and God's Word

Some today want to be guided only by the cloud—the leadership of the Holy Spirit. But it is evident that the impressions they have do not always originate with the Holy Spirit. Others want to be guided only by the trumpets—the Word of God. They open the Bible at random and find a verse on which they base a major decision. We must remember, however, that the cloud and the trumpets go together—there must be the leading of both the Holy Spirit and the Word of God. It is important to realize, however, that the Holy Spirit never leads in a way that is contrary to what God has revealed in His Word. As we study the Word, the Holy Spirit will communicate to us what we ought to do.

The cloud God provided for Israel served as a covering for the people. The psalmist said of God, "He spread a cloud for a covering" (Ps. 105:39). From Exodus 14:19,20 we also learn that the cloud served as a guard: "The angel of God, which went before the camp of Israel, removed and went behind them; and the pillar of the cloud went from before their face, and stood behind them: and it came between the camp of the Egyptians and the camp of Israel; and it was a cloud of darkness to them, but it gave light by night to these: so that the one came not near the other all the night."

On the one hand the cloud was a visible evidence of God's presence, but on the other hand it protected Israel from its enemies. The time referred to in this passage is when the Egyptians were pursuing the Israelites immediately after Moses had led them out of the land. But the conflict here was not so much between Israel and Egypt as it was between Jehovah and Egypt.

All the Israelites had to do was to remain in their place while God protected them. God put Himself between His own people and the enemy. God provided security for His own, even as we read in Ephesians 4:30 that we are sealed by the Holy Spirit for the day of redemption.

It is assuring to know that the child of God is under the protecting hand of God. This does not mean that the believer will be free from difficulty, however. "In the world," Jesus said, "ye shall have tribulation: but be of good cheer; I have overcome the world" (John 16:33). Jesus also promised, "I will never leave thee, nor forsake thee" (Heb. 13:5). Because of this great promise, believers can "boldly say, The Lord is my helper, and I will not fear what man shall do unto me" (v. 6).

The Israelites experienced the gracious provision of God—He never took away the pillar of cloud by day nor the pillar of fire by night (Ex. 13:22). In spite of all of the grumbling of Israel, God did not take away the visible signs of His presence. Concerning these experiences Nehemiah wrote: "Yet thou in thy manifold mercies forsookest them not in the wilderness: the pillar of the cloud departed not from them by day, to lead them in the way; neither the pillar of fire by night, to shew them light, and the way wherein they should go" (Neh. 9:19). Although God had to chasten the Israelites and even judge them at times, He never forsook them.

In Old Testament times it was possible for God to remove the Holy Spirit from people. This is why, after his sin, David prayed, "Take not thy holy spirit from me" (Ps. 51:11). This did not mean that the Old Testament believer lost his salvation. It meant only that God was removing the Holy Spirit from him for empowering him for a particular service. However, during the Church Age the Holy Spirit is never taken from the believer. Jesus promised that He would send the Holy Spirit "that he may abide with you for ever" (John 14:16).

The cloud that God provided for Israel's guidance is mentioned nearly 50 times in the Pentateuch alone and is frequently mentioned throughout other portions of the Bible. So the provision of the cloud was considered by Old Testament writers to be a highly significant matter in Israel's history. How wonderful it is to recognize that God leads His own people! He does not leave them to flounder on their own.

Chapter 7

Passing Through the Sea

Israel had congregated at a place called Succoth, which was located on a well-traveled route to Canaan. They were on their way to Etham, but somewhere between Succoth and Etham God took over the leadership and provided a cloud that stayed with them during the rest of their journey. But God's route took them a different direction than they had intended to go. They must have intended to go northeast on the well-traveled route, but God took them southeast into the wilderness. But as we have seen, God had reasons for taking them in this direction, for it was for their good and His glory.

What a beautiful sight it must have been as Israel traveled under the pillar of cloud by day and the pillar of fire by night! In the wilderness the Israelites had to depend completely on God's guidance and provision. They were able to see Him work in a way they otherwise never would have.

In all of this we see how God's preparation of His servant Moses paid off. How could any man lead so many people to and through the desert had not his faith in God been thoroughly settled? Moses showed that he had no doubts concerning God's ability to do what He purposed to do.

Hemmed in by Trials

Even as God had the Israelites turn south into the wilderness, He knew what Pharaoh would think: "For Pharaoh will say of the children of Israel, They are entangled in the land, the wilderness hath shut them in. And I will harden Pharaoh's heart, that he shall follow after them; and I will be honoured

46

upon Pharaoh, and upon all his host; that the Egyptians may know that I am the Lord" (Ex. 14:3,4). Although Satan is wise, he is not as wise as God is, and time and time again Satan oversteps himself. This is what happened in Pharaoh's case. Pharaoh thought he could easily overtake the Israelites, so he and his army immediately pursued them (vv. 5-9). As the Egyptians came in behind them, the Israelites were terribly frightened, but they were about to see a great display of God's power.

We must remember that the Israelites were hemmed in on all sides. In front of them was the Red Sea, on the sides were mountains and the desert, and behind them were the pursuing Egyptians.

Have you had those times in your life when it seemed as if you had no place to turn except to God? Notice what the Bible says about trials that believers experience. First Peter 1:5-7 says that believers "are kept by the power of God through faith unto salvation ready to be revealed in the last time. Wherein ye greatly rejoice, though now for a season, if need be, ye are in heaviness through manifold temptations: that the trial of your faith, being much more precious than of gold that perisheth, though it be tried with fire, might be found unto praise and honour and glory at the appearing of Jesus Christ." Notice especially the words "the trial of your faith." To God it is very important that our faith be tested in order to prove its genuineness. We are not tested to see whether or not we have faith, but to reveal to us that the faith we have in Christ Jesus is the answer to our need.

The New Testament Epistle of James also tells about trials which believers undergo: "My brethren, count it all joy when ye fall into divers [various] temptations; knowing this, that the trying of your faith worketh patience. But let patience have her perfect work, that ye may be perfect and entire, wanting nothing. If any of you lack wisdom, let him ask of God, that giveth to all men liberally, and upbraideth not; and it shall be given him. But let him ask in faith, nothing wavering. For he that wavereth is like the wave of the sea driven with the wind and tossed" (1:2-6). If you wonder about the reason for your trials, turn to God and He will give you wisdom concerning what He is endeavoring to accomplish in your life.

God's reason for leading Israel by way of the long road
was that He knew they would become discouraged if they got
into war with the Philistines, and they would probably want
to return to Egypt. Actually, the Israelites seemed to complain and wanted to return to Egypt every time things got
difficult, but God knew it would have been worse had they
gone the other way. How regrettable that the Israelites did
not have enough confidence in God to realize that He would
not test them beyond what they were able to bear (see I Cor.
10:13).

As we consider all that God allowed Israel to experience,
it is understandable to ask the question, Why? The answer is
given in I Corinthians 10:11: "All these things happened
unto them for ensamples [examples]: and they are written
for our admonition, upon whom the ends of the world are
come." The experiences of Israel are typical of an individual
Christian's experience, so the more a believer learns about the
life of the nation of Israel, the more he will know about
handling the difficulties that come into his own life.

Identification With God's Power

God made a unique display of His power when He
opened the Red Sea and allowed the Israelites to pass
through. So great was this demonstration of power that when
Old Testament writers wanted to refer to God's tremendous
power, they would cite the incident of the Red Sea. In the
New Testament God's tremendous power was displayed in
the resurrection of Jesus Christ, and the New Testament
writers frequently referred to this incident when citing God's
power.

The opening of the Red Sea and the resurrection of
Christ are events which are appealed to as standards of
measurement for the great power of God. Referring to the
resurrection, Ephesians 1:19,20 says, "And what is the
exceeding greatness of his power to us-ward who believe,
according to the working of his mighty power, which he
wrought in Christ, when he raised him from the dead." God
raised Jesus from the dead in spite of the resistance of Satan
and all the powers of hell who tried to keep Christ in the
grave.

The New Testament also refers back to the Red Sea incident as a display of God's power. The Apostle Paul wrote: "Moreover, brethren, I would not that ye should be ignorant, how that all our fathers were under the cloud, and all passed through the sea; and were all baptized unto Moses in the cloud and in the sea" (I Cor. 10:1,2). The basic meaning of the word "baptized" here is "identified." The Israelites were delivered because they were identified with Moses in the Red Sea.

Baptism for the believer is an outward act which reveals his identification with Jesus Christ. Upon receiving Jesus Christ as Saviour, the Holy Spirit places the person into the Body of Christ. This is known as the baptism of the Holy Spirit (I Cor. 12:13).

Teaching concerning our identification with Christ through baptism is seen in Romans 6:4,5: "Therefore we are buried with him by baptism into death: that like as Christ was raised up from the dead by the glory of the Father, even so we also should walk in newness of life. For if we have been planted together in the likeness of his death, we shall be also in the likeness of his resurrection." Water baptism is simply a picture of what is taught in Romans 6 concerning our identification with Christ in His death, burial and resurrection.

When the Israelites marched through the Red Sea onto the victory side, the sea then closed in on the Egyptians who were following them. By this judgment of God, the power of the Egyptians over the Israelites was broken!

When a person receives Jesus Christ as Saviour, which is the application of Christ's shed blood, the individual is freed from the power of sin by his identification with the death and resurrection of Christ. So Israel's delivery from Egypt is a beautiful illustration of the believer's deliverance from the power of sin.

First Corinthians 10 is a significant chapter because it was written to believers and uses incidents from Israel's history to illustrate what is needed in believers' lives. This chapter was written to challenge believers to live victoriously. The chapter argues for a life that is lived on the basis of one's identification with Christ in His death, burial and resurrection. Galatians 2:20 expresses this identification: "I am crucified with Christ: nevertheless I live; yet not I, but Christ liveth in me: and the life which I now live in the flesh I live by the faith of the Son of God, who loved me, and gave himself for me." We have already seen this same truth expressed in Romans 6:4,5.

As we consider the parallels between Israel and the individual believer, the Passover represents salvation from the penalty, or condemnation, of sin. Deliverance through the Red Sea, however, represents deliverance from the power and slavery of sin.

It is important that those who know Jesus Christ as Saviour not only realize that they are saved from the condemnation of sin but that they are also saved from the power of sin—they no longer have to let sin dominate them. The Israelites were saved before they left their homes in Egypt, but their emancipation was not complete until the Red Sea took care of their enemies. As long as the Israelites were in enemy territory, they were subject to bondage.

Emancipation From Sin

Have you ever wondered why many people are still living in spiritual Egypt even though they have received Jesus Christ as Saviour? They are still living in defeat, although Christ has made it possible for them to live a life of victory. No believer will experience a life of victory until he realizes that he is identified with Christ.

God has provided a passport to victory, but it must be used, or relied on. It is not enough to know about it; we must live accordingly by appropriating this privilege in Christ. The recognition of our identification with Christ as set forth in Romans 6 leads to victory over sin.

Israel's march through the Red Sea serves as an example of complete emancipation from sin. God opened the sea, Israel marched through and Egypt marched after them. But when Israel stepped onto the victory side, the enemy was completely destroyed. The Israelites were then free from the slavery of Egypt.

In considering our relationship with Christ, we potentially died with Him when we trusted Him as Saviour. Also, since He had broken the power of the Devil (Heb. 2:14), we became identified with Him in victory. But although this victory is ours potentially, we must, by faith, act on what we know in order to make it ours experientially.

Romans 6:2-5 tells what actually took place from God's viewpoint. Verses 6-13 tell of the practical application as believers, by faith, appropriate what Christ accomplished in their behalf. It is important to realize that this is a position attained by faith. To be redeemed from death by the blood is great, but to remain in Egypt would be slavery, oppression and defeat. But that's where many Christians are living today—in spiritual Egypt.

Four key words in Romans 6 deserve special notice—know, reckon, yield and obey. When we know what has been accomplished in our behalf (v. 6) and reckon ourselves to be dead to sin, or accept it as a fact (v. 11), then we need to yield to the Lord (v. 13). Yielding is acting upon our faith. Our desire then will be to obey Him in everything (v. 17).

Pharaoh is an example of the enemy of the believer. After Pharaoh lost his slaves through blood redemption, he tried to recapture them in order to bring them under his domination. And after Satan loses people from his control when they receive Christ as Saviour, he also tries to bring them back under his domination. Satan will use all the devices he can in order to keep a believer in bondage so he will not be able to effectively serve Christ.

Reaction to the Enemy

Israel became terrified by the advances of the enemy and expressed fear in irrational ways. They accused Moses of false motives, thinking he had led them into the wilderness to die (Ex. 14:11), and spoke as if their salvation wasn't really worth it all (v. 12). They doubted that God could lead them to freedom, so they thought it was better to remain in slavery in Egypt.

It's also possible for new believers, like small children, to be frightened because they do not yet know God's power. But once a person tastes the life that God has for him, he will have no desire to return to what the world offers.

If you have trusted Jesus Christ as your Saviour, at what place in the Christian life are you? Are you a young Christian still looking back at the things of the world, or have you seen the full, rich life that is yours because of your personal relationship with Christ?

Like the disciples in the storm, we sometimes cry out, "Carest thou not that we perish?" (Mark 4:38) as if the Lord is unconcerned about us. The Israelites reacted in this way. God had brought them out of Egypt and through the Red Sea, but whenever they faced new trials, they thought surely the Lord did not care anything about them. This is why their faith needed to be tested—they needed to learn that God is sufficient for every need. They also needed to realize that they were not sufficient by themselves—and this is the lesson we need to learn.

Christians often quote Philippians 4:19: "My God shall supply all your need according to his riches in glory by Christ Jesus." But sometimes one wonders if they have really experienced the promise of this verse. God is sufficient to meet every need we have as we live according to His will.

Walking in accordance with God's will, however, sometimes means that we will go through severe testing (I Pet. 1:6,7). This testing is needed to give us a greater concept of who God is and what He wants to do in our lives. God also tests us so that we can learn what it is to be completely emancipated from the power of sin.

It is wonderful to be free from the power of sin and to be completely secure in the hand of God. The believer's security is seen clearly in the words of Jesus: "My sheep hear my voice, and I know them, and they follow me: and I give unto them eternal life; and they shall never perish, neither shall any man pluck them out of my hand. My Father, which gave them me, is greater than all; and no man is able to pluck them out of my Father's hand" (John 10:27-29). Our salvation is completely God's undertaking. This is why no one is able to pluck us out of His hand.

Romans 8:32 assures us, "He that spared not his own Son, but delivered him up for us all, how shall he not with him also freely give us all things?" And especially notice the triumphant statement of the following verses: "Who shall lay anything to the charge of God's elect? It is God that justifieth. Who is he that condemneth? It is Christ that died, yea rather, that is risen again, who is even at the right hand of God, who also maketh intercession for us" (vv. 33,34).

Our security in the Lord is also seen from Ephesians 1:13,14: "In whom ye also trusted, after that ye heard the word of truth, the gospel of your salvation: in whom also after that ye believed, ye were sealed with that holy Spirit of promise, which is the earnest of our inheritance until the redemption of the purchased possession, unto the praise of his glory."

Elements of Deliverance

In the plan of deliverance that God revealed to Israel, three distinct elements were mentioned in Exodus 14:13: "Moses said unto the people, Fear ye not, stand still, and see the salvation of the Lord."

First, notice the requirement of a right heart attitude— "fear ye not." Over and over again, God's Word instructs people not to fear. So often these instructions come, when, humanly speaking, there seems to be great reason to fear. Study the different people who were told not to fear, such as Abraham (Gen. 15:1), Joshua (Josh. 8:1), Gideon (Judg. 6:23), Daniel (Dan. 10:12) and the disciples (Luke 12:32).

God calls for fearless boldness such as was expressed by David: "Yea, though I walk through the valley of the shadow of death, I will fear no evil" (Ps. 23:4). Fearless boldness is also expressed in Psalm 118:6: "The Lord is on my side; I will not fear: what can man do unto me?"

As we consider how God worked with the nation of Israel, we learn many valuable principles concerning the way He works with the individual believer today. It is important that believers get a good foundation in these matters so that they can progress in the Christian life as God intends.

The Apostle Paul emphasized that the only foundation that can really be laid is Jesus Christ, and one needs to be careful how he builds on that foundation. Paul said, "According to the grace of God which is given unto me, as the wise masterbuilder, I have laid the foundation, and another buildeth thereon. But let every man take heed how he buildeth thereupon. For other foundation can no man lay than that is laid, which is Jesus Christ" (I Cor. 3:10,11).

If you have received Jesus Christ as your personal
Saviour, then you have the proper foundation laid in your
own life, but it is important that you build properly on that
foundation in order to go on to spiritual maturity. That is
why we are giving much attention to the spiritual lessons God
taught Israel through Moses.

As Israel was fleeing from Egypt, the people became
hemmed in on all four sides. They began to panic, for there
was seemingly no way out of their dilemma. When they
became convinced that the situation was hopeless, then God
instructed the people through Moses: "Fear ye not, stand
still, and see the salvation of the Lord, which he will shew to
you to day: for the Egyptians whom ye have seen to day, ye
shall see them again no more for ever" (Ex. 14:13). Notice
those significant words, "Stand still, and see the salvation of
the Lord." But notice that first of all God told them, "Fear
ye not."

The Israelites were certainly in the valley of the shadow
of death, and at this point they lacked the ability to say, "I
will fear no evil," as David later wrote (Ps. 23:4).

The words of Moses to Israel, "Stand still" (Ex. 14:13),
had the meaning of "Take your stand." Moses wanted the
people to stand firm and wait on the Lord for deliverance.

God is determined to help those who will allow Him to
do so. He is looking for those who are standing firm and have
their eyes fixed on Him. The Bible says, "For the eyes of the
Lord run to and fro throughout the whole earth, to shew
himself strong in behalf of them whose heart is perfect
toward him" (II Chron. 16:9).

The Example of Jehoshaphat

In this regard, Jehoshaphat's testimony is extremely
encouraging. Jehoshaphat and his small army were surrounded and greatly outnumbered, but his confidence in God
never waned. Jehoshaphat said, "O our God, wilt thou not
judge them? For we have no might against this great
company that cometh against us; neither know we what to
do: but our eyes are upon thee" (II Chron. 20:12). And
notice the way God responded to this kind of confidence in
Him. He told Jehoshaphat, "Ye shall not need to fight in this

battle: set yourselves, stand ye still, and see the salvation of the Lord with you, O Judah and Jerusalem: fear not, nor be dismayed; to morrow go out against them: for the Lord will be with you" (v. 17).

When we fix our eyes on the Lord and place our confidence in His ability to solve our problems, He will show Himself strong in our behalf. Notice, however, that God told Jehoshaphat and his army, "To morrow go out against them." On the one hand, we should realize the danger of going out in our own strength, or self-effort, but on the other hand we should beware of the other extreme—passivity. God nowhere condones the attitude which is expressed, or at least implied, by some believers who think they should remain idle and let the Lord do it all.

The Lord does not fight when the believer remains strictly passive. God promised victory to Jehoshaphat, but Jehoshaphat had the responsibility of leading his army out in order to participate in the victory God was going to give him.

As the believer goes into a spiritual battle, he needs to be constantly reminded that his confidence should never be in himself but in the Lord. As Isaiah 30:15 says, "In quietness and in confidence shall be your strength."

As Moses instructed the Israelites what to do in their desperate situation, he told them to stand still and "see the salvation of the Lord" (Ex. 14:13). The Israelites needed physical deliverance, but Moses was concerned that they also have spiritual sight to see the Lord work in their behalf. Although the circumstances and the enemy were against them, Moses did not want them to give an inch but to stand firm and see the salvation God was going to give them. In this way they would learn to know God as they had not known Him before.

It is important that the believer know God as far as salvation is concerned, but he should also know Him through seeing Him work in his daily life. In this regard, II Peter 1:3 contains tremendous truth: "According as his divine power hath given unto us all things that pertain unto life and godliness, through the knowledge of him that hath called us to glory and virtue." Note especially the words "unto life and godliness"; that is, eternal life and godly living.

Do you know Christ as your Saviour? If so, do you also know Him as the One who is able to provide all that you need for Christian living? When we get to know the Lord in this way, there's a quietness and confidence in our Christian walk.

Even when circumstances are against the believer, and even though unbelievers may be persecuting him, he can take confidence in Paul's words: "For our light affliction, which is but for a moment, worketh for us a far more exceeding and eternal weight of glory; while we look not at the things which are seen, but at the things which are not seen: for the things which are seen are temporal; but the things which are not seen are eternal" (II Cor. 4:17,18).

Although the Israelites had their eyes fixed on that which is temporal, Moses had his eyes fixed on that which is eternal—on God Himself. This is why Hebrews 11:27 says that Moses was "seeing him who is invisible." Moses had an understanding of God's program, and he wanted the people to have their spiritual eyes open to see it also. Moses wanted the people to realize that God would fight their battles if only they would stand firm and have confidence in Him.

This is why Moses told the people, "The Lord shall fight for you, and ye shall hold your peace" (Ex. 14:14). Moses made it clear to the people that the battle was the Lord's, not theirs.

The New Testament also reveals how the Lord fights for the believer. Galatians 5:17 says, "For the flesh lusteth against the Spirit, and the Spirit against the flesh: and these are contrary the one to the other: so that ye cannot do the things that ye would." This verse reveals that even though the sinful nature, or flesh, seeks to dominate the believer, the Holy Spirit strives against the flesh in behalf of the believer. Through the strength of the Holy Spirit, the believer can live above the pull of the flesh.

The Apostle Paul told of the conflict he had in his life as he sought to do what he knew was right and yet did not have the ability in himself to do it (Rom. 7:15-25). As he relied on the Holy Spirit, however, Paul was able to experience victory. This is why he said, "The law of the Spirit of life in Christ Jesus hath made me free from the law of sin and death. For what the law could not do, in that it was weak through the flesh, God sending his own Son in the likeness of sinful flesh, and for sin, condemned sin in the flesh: that the righteousness of the law might be fulfilled in us, who walk not after the flesh, but after the Spirit" (8:2-4).

The Holy Spirit frees the believer from the entanglements of the flesh. What a tremendous realization this is! God does all the fighting *for* the believer before he has become established in the faith. But even after he is more mature, the Holy Spirit does the fighting *through* the believer.

Actively Claiming Victory

Even though the Israelites were told to "stand still" (Ex. 14:13), God also told them to "go forward" (v. 15). This reveals that the "stand still" did not mean they were to be completely passive; rather, they were to stand firm and put confidence in the Lord for the victory He could and would give them as they moved ahead. It is important to realize that God gives us the victory He promises only as we move ahead to take it. A key verse on this subject is Joshua 1:3. God had promised the Israelites the land, but He told Joshua, "Every place that the sole of your foot shall tread upon, that have I given unto you, as I said unto Moses." Although the Lord had promised the land to the Israelites, they needed to move in, by faith, and take it.

God makes the victory available to us, but He expects us to be obedient in moving forward and taking the victory.

Before the command was given by God to the Israelites concerning moving forward, He promised them that they would not see the Egyptians any more forever (Ex. 14:13). The invisible God promised them the victory before the people were commanded to go forward and take the victory. They knew the promise, and they were to move ahead according to it and claim it.

In Israel's case, we see that God leads forward, not backward. And in their situation, God did not even lead around but through. God told Moses, "But lift thou up thy rod, and stretch out thine hand over the sea, and divide it: and the children of Israel shall go on dry ground through the midst of the sea" (v. 16). Although, humanly speaking, they could see no way out, God promised to take them through the barrier before them.

Moses' Rod

As the Lord was instructing Moses concerning opening the Red Sea, He told him, "Lift thou up thy rod, and stretch out thine hand" (Ex. 14:16). What a helpless, hopeless action this would normally be! There was no magical power in Moses' rod. He was about as helpless in this situation as was the lame man to whom Jesus said, "Take up thy bed, and walk" (John 5:11). But God always gives the ability to do what He commands. This was true with the Israelites and with the people Jesus healed, and it is true with us. We need to learn to live one day at a time, even one step at a time. As we take one step, depending on God, He will provide the strength we need, and then we will be ready for the next step.

God was trying to teach Israel valuable lessons so the people would be ready to meet the obstacles they would face in the future. They had to fight battles on the way to Canaan, the Jordan River had to be crossed and Jericho had to be taken—but in each case God would be with them and enable them to have victory if they would only trust Him. God would go before them as a good shepherd goes before his sheep (John 10:4,27); their responsibility was to follow Him.

Not only did God command the Israelites to go forward but He also instructed them how to go forward. He told Moses to divide the sea by taking his rod and stretching out his hand over the sea so the Israelites could go through on dry ground (Ex. 14:16). The rod Moses had was that of a shepherd, but yielded to God, it was the rod of God. God did many miracles with that rod in the hand of Moses as he was obedient and used it to God's glory.

Humanly speaking, it was foolish to think that Moses could divide the Red Sea with the rod he held in his hand. However, we must not forget the principle that God uses what the world considers foolish to demonstrate the foolishness of what the world considers wise (I Cor. 1:26-28). The reason God works this way is so that "no flesh should glory in his presence" (v. 29) and to teach us the lesson of verse 31: "He that glorieth, let him glory in the Lord."

Escape for Israel; Destruction for Egypt

God was not yet through with the Egyptians. He told Moses, "Behold, I will harden the hearts of the Egyptians, and they shall follow them: and I will get me honour upon Pharaoh, and upon all his host, upon his chariots, and upon his horsemen" (Ex. 14:17).

God allowed Pharaoh and his army to follow Israel so that in one event Israel was saved and Egypt was destroyed. The opening of the Red Sea was the means of escape for the Israelites, but it was the means of destruction for the power of Egypt.

So also, God allowed Satan to stir up anger against the Lord Jesus Christ in order to have Jesus crucified. But the death of Jesus Christ not only provided salvation for all who would believe in Him, it also destroyed Satan's power (Col. 2:15; Heb. 2:14).

Notice God's purpose for allowing the Egyptians to pursue the Israelites: "The Egyptians shall know that I am the Lord, when I have gotten me honour upon Pharaoh, upon his chariots, and upon his horsemen" (Ex. 14:18). After the incident of the Red Sea there would be no doubt that God had acted in behalf of His people and that He had brought to nothing the greatest power on earth.

The Bible also reveals that God brought glory to Himself even through the death of Jesus Christ. Philippians 2:9-11 says, "Wherefore God hath highly exalted him, and given him a name which is above every name: that at the name of Jesus every knee should bow, of things in heaven, and things in earth, and things under the earth; and that every tongue should confess that Jesus Christ is Lord, to the glory of God the Father." Even those who reject Jesus Christ as Saviour will someday have to acknowledge that He is Lord of all.

This reveals how important it is that each person seriously consider his relationship with Jesus Christ and receive Him as Saviour and Lord before it is eternally too late.

As the Egyptians pursued the Israelites, "the angel of God, which went before the camp of Israel, removed and went behind them; and the pillar of the cloud went from before their face, and stood behind them: and it came between the camp of the Egyptians and the camp of Israel; and it was a cloud and darkness to them, but it gave light by night to these: so that the one came not near the other all the night" (Ex. 14:19,20).

God had already promised Israel the victory; now He provided protection for them. In Egypt God had provided the lamb to save the Israelites from death when He passed over the land; now He provided a cloud to protect them from death by the Egyptians.

This reveals the principle that God not only provides for salvation but also for daily living. This is clearly stated in Romans 5:8-10: "But God commendeth his love toward us, in that, while we were yet sinners, Christ died for us. Much more then, being now justified by his blood, we shall be saved from wrath through him. For if, when we were enemies, we were reconciled to God by the death of his Son, much more, being reconciled, we shall be saved by his life." If God provided what we needed in salvation, surely we can expect Him to provide what we need to bring glory to Him in our daily lives.

God and Circumstances

The Israelites often made the mistake of interpreting God in the light of their circumstances, and most believers have this same tendency today. But just as God caused a cloud to move between the Israelites and the Egyptians, so God puts Himself between the believer and circumstances.

As adverse situations develop in our lives, we should not feel defeat; rather, we should ask ourselves what God wants to accomplish in our lives through the circumstances. We must fix our spiritual eyes on God and realize that He is in control of circumstances. When we recognize this, we will not be defeated by adverse situations; we will respond positively to them and try to discover what God has in them for us.

The Bible records an incident which emphasizes the different way people respond to circumstances. As the Israelites were on their way to Canaan, they came to Kadesh-barnea where 12 men were sent into Canaan to spy out the land (Num. 13). Ten of the men returned with a report that revealed they were looking only at the circumstances and not at God. As a result, their recommendation was, "We be not able to go up against the people; for they are stronger than we" (v. 31). But two of the spies, Joshua and Caleb, had their eyes fixed on God rather than on the circumstances. Caleb's recommendation was, "Let us go up at once, and possess it; for we are well able to overcome it" (v. 30).

When one concentrates on the circumstances, God becomes small; when one concentrates on God, the circumstances become small. This is what we need to realize, and this is what Israel needed to realize as they were fleeing from the Egyptians.

The Bible reveals that it was God, not Israel, who actually fought the Egyptians. Exodus 14:24,25 says, "And it came to pass, that in the morning watch the Lord looked unto the host of the Egyptians through the pillar of fire and of the cloud, and troubled the host of the Egyptians, and took off their chariot wheels, that they drave them heavily: so that the Egyptians said, Let us flee from the face of Israel; for the Lord fighteth for them against the Egyptians." What a statement! Even the unbelieving Egyptians realized God was fighting against them.

Just as God provided protection for the Israelites, so also He provides protection for the individual believer. This does not mean that we will always be delivered from testings or difficult circumstances, but it means that God will be with us and fight for us in those situations. Ephesians 1:13,14 assures believers, "Ye were sealed with that holy Spirit of promise, which is the earnest of our inheritance until the redemption of the purchased possession, unto the praise of his glory." Ephesians 4:30 tells us we are sealed with the Holy Spirit "unto the day of redemption." And the Lord assures the believer, "I will never leave thee, nor forsake thee" (Heb. 13:5). With promises like these there is no reason for us to fear circumstances.

Note another way the Lord protected Israel: "The children of Israel went into the midst of the sea upon the dry ground: and the waters were a wall unto them on their right hand, and on their left" (Ex. 14:22). There was no way the enemy could get to them—a cloud was between them and the enemy, and the walls of water protected them on each side. And while they were protected from the sides and from the rear, the Israelites were able to go ahead in full light as God led the way.

The water of the Red Sea had symbolized death to the Israelites, but now it had no power over them. Instead, it was actually a defense for them. The very sea which they had so feared had now become their means of deliverance! And that which became salvation for the Israelites became death to their enemy.

God Fights the Enemy

Exodus 14:24,25 reveals how God hindered the enemy of the Israelites. He "troubled the host of the Egyptians, and took off their chariot wheels, that they drave them heavily: so that the Egyptians said, Let us flee from the face of Israel; for the Lord fighteth for them against the Egyptians."

God's resistance of Israel's enemy is a reminder of the way He is resisting Satan's program right now. God is preventing Satan from accomplishing his desires with us, because He is restraining sin by means of the Holy Spirit actively working in the lives of believers. Second Thessalonians 2:6,7 tells of this restraining work: "And you know what restrains him now, so that in his time he may be revealed. For the mystery of lawlessness is already at work; only he who now restrains will do so until he is taken out of the way" (NASB). The Holy Spirit, working through believers, will restrain sin until the Rapture of the Church, when believers will be removed from earth to heaven. After this, the Holy Spirit will continue His work on earth in much the same way that He did before Pentecost.

After the Rapture of the Church the entire earth will experience a seven-year period of tribulation. How wonderful it is to realize that God protects His own. The Bible says, "No weapon that is formed against thee shall prosper; and every tongue that shall rise against thee in judgment thou shalt condemn. This is the heritage of the servants of the Lord, and their righteousness is of me, saith the Lord" (Isa. 54:17).

Psalm 91 also assures the believer of the protective hand of the Lord. "He who dwells in the shelter of the Most High will abide in the shadow of the Almighty. I will say to the Lord, 'My refuge and my fortress, my God, in whom I trust!' For it is He who delivers you from the snare of the trapper, and from the deadly pestilence. He will cover you with His pinions, and under His wings you may seek refuge; His faithfulness is a shield and bulwark. You will not be afraid of the terror by night, or of the arrow that flies by day" (vv. 1-5, NASB).

As the believer looks around him today and sees many things that might cause him to be frightened, he is instructed by the Lord through His Word not to be afraid because God will be with him no matter what happens. Psalm 91 also says, "A thousand may fall at your side, and ten thousand at your right hand; but it shall not approach you. You will only look on with your eyes, and see the recompense of the wicked. For you have made the Lord, my refuge, even the Most High, your dwelling place. No evil will befall you, nor will any plague come near your tent. . . . Because he has loved Me, therefore I will deliver him; I will set him securely on high, because he has known My name. He will call upon Me, and I will answer him; I will be with him in trouble; I will rescue him, and honor him. With a long life I will satisfy him, and let him behold My salvation" (vv. 7-10, 14-16, NASB).

As God did all of the fighting and protecting of the Israelites, the result was the overthrow of Egypt. "Moses stretched forth his hand over the sea, and the sea returned to his strength when the morning appeared; and the Egyptians fled against it; and the Lord overthrew the Egyptians in the midst of the sea. And the waters returned, and covered the chariots, and the horsemen, and all the host of Pharaoh that came into the sea after them; there remained not so much as one of them" (Ex. 14:27,28).

Egypt's chief strength and glory was its king and its army. While the Egyptians had previously suffered great judgment, the triumphant army had not been weakened in its power.

But God completely overthrew Egypt and broke its power once and for all. As a nation, Egypt continued to exist, but it was never again such a mighty world power.

Just as Egypt's power to hold Israel captive and enslave God's people was broken, so also Satan's power to enslave was broken by the death of the Lord Jesus Christ. Hebrews 2:14 says, "Forasmuch then as the children are partakers of flesh and blood, he [Jesus Christ] also himself likewise took part of the same; that through death he might destroy him that had the power of death, that is, the devil." (See also Col. 2:15.)

As the power of Egypt over the Israelites was broken, so also the power of sin over the believer was broken by Christ's death. Romans 8:3 says, "For what the law could not do, in that it was weak through the flesh, God sending his own Son in the likeness of sinful flesh, and for sin, condemned sin in the flesh."

Israel's Complete Emancipation

The final verses of Exodus 14 reveal that the emancipation of Israel was completed: "But the children of Israel walked upon dry land in the midst of the sea; and the waters were a wall unto them on their right hand, and on their left. Thus the Lord saved Israel that day out of the hand of the Egyptians; and Israel saw the Egyptians dead upon the sea shore. And Israel saw that great work which the Lord did upon the Egyptians: and the people feared the Lord, and believed the Lord, and his servant Moses" (vv. 29-31).

The dead bodies of the Egyptians on the seashore were the evidence of Israel's complete emancipation. This sight brought great fear on Israel; they believed God, and Moses was completely vindicated in their eyes. They saw that their redemption was completely of God, working through Moses after they had shed the blood of the lamb and applied it to their doorposts. So also, our redemption is completely of God through a Person—Jesus Christ. Only as we apply His shed blood by receiving Him as Saviour can we benefit from what He accomplished for us on the cross. Just as Israel had complete emancipation from the power of Egypt and its slavery, so we who trust Christ are completely emancipated from Satan's power to enslave us in sin.

It is especially important that a believer realize the total emancipation God has provided for him. The Christian who does not realize this will not progress in the Christian life as God intends. Having accepted the total victory that God has accomplished for us, we then need to walk, or live, on the basis of it.

The incident of God delivering Israel through the Red Sea is specifically referred to in I Corinthians 10:1,2: "Moreover, brethren, I would not that ye should be ignorant, how that all our fathers were under the cloud, and all passed through the sea; and were all baptized unto Moses in the cloud and in the sea." Verse 11 says, "Now all these things happened unto them for ensamples [examples]: and they are written for our admonition, upon whom the ends of the world are come." The things that happened to Israel were literally types in that they prefigure that which takes place in an individual believer's life.

The crossing of the Red Sea indicates that God made a way through death for His people. Thus, the Red Sea was the boundary line of the Egyptians' power over the Israelites. As a parallel, Christ's death on the cross marks the boundary line of Satan's power over those who trust in Christ.

Death and Resurrection

It is important to realize that there is resurrection as well as death in Christ. The Bible says, "For if we have been planted together in the likeness of his death, we shall be also in the likeness of his resurrection" (Rom. 6:5).

The person who has received Jesus Christ as Saviour has participated in His death, and he has also participated in His resurrection—believers have been raised to sit together with Christ in the heavenlies (Eph. 2:5,6).

After God's judgment on the Egyptians at the Red Sea, Israel was dead to Egypt and all that was connected to it. Egypt no longer had any power over the Israelites. The cloud and the sea were to the Israelites what the cross and the grave of Christ are to us. The cloud gave them security from the enemy; the sea separated them from Egypt. The cross of

Christ shields us from that which is against us; the grave, the place of death, reveals that in Christ we are dead to the world. We stand on heaven's side, or the resurrection side, of the empty tomb of Jesus.

After the Israelites had passed through the Red Sea, the waters of death flowed between them and the place of bondage, cutting them off from Egypt's power. The Israelites were on resurrection ground and were to begin their journey through the wilderness to taste of the heavenly manna and water from the spiritual rock. All of this and more the Israelites were to benefit from as they marched toward the land of rest. But it took them a long time to reach the place of their destination. So also, it takes many Christians a long time to recognize that they have been separated from bondage and that they are actually free to do the will of God.

Just as the crossing of the Red Sea completed the deliverance of Israel from Egypt in order that they could begin their journey toward the Promised Land, so also when a person trusts Christ and has complete salvation, he is to progress in his Christian walk.

As the Israelites were identified with Moses in the Red Sea (I Cor. 10:2), so the believer is united with Christ in His death and resurrection. Paul alluded to this union with Christ when he said, "I am crucified with Christ: nevertheless I live; yet not I, but Christ liveth in me: and the life which I now live in the flesh I live by the faith of the Son of God, who loved me, and gave himself for me" (Gal. 2:20). (See also Rom. 6:5 and Eph. 2:5,6.)

The crossing of both the Red Sea and the Jordan River illustrate what was accomplished for the believer in the death of Christ. At the Red Sea there was separation from Egypt; at the Jordan River there was an entering into the place of rest. The place of rest for the believer is referred to in Hebrews 4:9,10: "There remaineth therefore a rest to the people of God. For he that is entered into his rest, he also hath ceased from his own works, as God did from his."

For the believer the death of Christ not only separates him from this present evil world, but it also makes him spiritually alive and seats him with Christ. What a glorious truth this is! We are on the resurrection side. We have much more than the forgiveness of sin; we have been associated with the risen Christ so that we may be united with Him forever and live the heavenly life. He who was dead is now alive! And this same Jesus indwells the bodies of believers in order to live His life in them (I Cor. 6:19,20). What a glorious privilege is ours!

Completed Promises of God

The fact that God was able to bring the Israelites out of Egypt was an assurance that He also had the ability to bring them into the land. This is precisely what He had promised the Israelites. God had said, "I will bring you out from under the burdens of the Egyptians" (Ex. 6:6). But He had also promised, "I will bring you in unto the land" (v. 8).

So also, God has not only redeemed us, but He also has the ability to complete the work He has begun. "Being confident of this very thing, that he which hath begun a good work in you will perform it until the day of Jesus Christ" (Phil. 1:6).

In order that we might have an indication that God is going to complete His work, He has given us the Holy Spirit. Paul reminded the Ephesian believers, "In whom ye also trusted, after that ye heard the word of truth, the gospel of your salvation: in whom also after that ye believed, ye were sealed with that holy Spirit of promise, which is the earnest of our inheritance until the redemption of the purchased possession, unto the praise of his glory" (Eph. 1:13,14).

It is wonderful to know that we are sealed with the Holy Spirit "unto the day of redemption" (4:30). God has given the Holy Spirit to the believer as an earnest, or an evidence, that He will complete what He has promised.

God has made available to us the same power that raised Jesus Christ from the dead. The Apostle Paul was concerned that all believers might know "what is the exceeding greatness of his power to us-ward who believe, according to the working of his mighty power, which he wrought in Christ, when he raised him from the dead, and set him at his own right hand in the heavenly places, far above all principality, and power, and might, and dominion, and every name that is named, not only in this world, but also in that which is to come" (1:19-21).

Someday those of us who know Jesus Christ as Saviour will be displayed as trophies of His grace, as is indicated in Ephesians 2:6,7: "And hath raised us up together, and made us sit together in heavenly places in Christ Jesus: that in the ages to come he might shew the exceeding riches of his grace in his kindness toward us through Christ Jesus."

No wonder the Bible says that Jesus Christ "is able also to save them to the uttermost that come unto God by him" (Heb. 7:25). The reason He is able to save us to the uttermost is seen in the last phrase of this same verse: "Seeing he ever liveth to make intercession for them."

Having begun the work of salvation, God is not going to let us down before it is completed. God has made available to us all that we need for salvation and also for the Christian life. That is why the Bible says, "We know that all things work together for good to them that love God, to them who are the called according to his purpose" (Rom. 8:28). This enables us to be "more than conquerors through him that loved us" (v. 37). What tremendous encouragement this is to walk in the way He has so richly provided in Christ!

Chapter 8

The Song of Assurance and Praise

Exodus 14 reveals a people under the pressure of their circumstances—self was extremely prominent. Exodus 15 reveals a people with pressures removed—self was forgotten.

A nation of slaves, fleeing from their masters, had suddenly become a nation of free men. They stood on the shores of a new land, completely emancipated from their slave owners. The proud nation of Egypt, which for generations had inflicted indescribable grief on them, had suffered a humiliation so great that they would never completely recover from it.

Praise and Worship

As the early morning light broke, the Israelites stood on the seashore and viewed the dead bodies of their enemies. As the people of God realized the glorious victory and release they had just experienced, they burst into a song of extraordinary praise and worship to God.

In the Israelites' song recorded in Exodus 15, the word "Lord" occurs 11 times, and various personal pronouns referring to Him occur more than 30 times. So it is clear that the song was sung *to* Him and *about* Him. All the honors of the victory were reverently laid at His feet.

In this song of assurance and praise, Moses is not mentioned once. This indicates that the Israelites now had complete confidence in the trustworthiness of God. The last verse of Exodus 14 says that the people "believed the Lord, and his servant Moses" (v. 31), but Moses is not mentioned in the song. Those who really understand spiritual realities know they should focus attention on the Lord, not on the servant.

When self is forgotten and our eyes are turned totally to the Lord, praise must come forth. The normal result of worship is praise. If we are not expressing praise to the Lord and about the Lord, the indication is that we are not really occupied with the Person of Christ as we ought to be.

Each believer would do well to ask himself, What does the indwelling Christ really mean to me? To some, He is only theology. But He is to be much more than that to the believer; He is an inner, spiritual, living experience and reality. When we have our eyes opened to Christ's great work for us and in us through our identification in His death, burial and resurrection, we will gladly praise Him.

Although every believer has eternal life in Christ (I John 5:12), Christ wants to be much more than salvation to us. He wants us to be gripped with the reality of His indwelling and the outworking of His life in us. Do you experientially know the reality of His abiding, indwelling presence and the outworking of His life?

The Lord Jesus Christ is everything to the believer— "Christ in you, the hope of glory" (Col. 1:27). Knowing the reality of that caused the Apostle Paul to say, "Whereunto I also labour, striving according to his working, which worketh in me mightily" (v. 29). (See also Gal. 2:20.) As we recognize the reality of Christ's continued presence and of His working in us, our faith is strengthened. This is also the basis for spiritual victory.

The Lord Jesus Christ will not fail us; He will see us through to the end (see Rom. 8:29,30,32,35-39; Phil. 1:6). However, we must learn to believe God even when circumstances are against us. Israel expressed such confidence as they saw themselves as victors over all their enemies. In their song of assurance and praise, it is evident that the Israelites realized the victory they had just experienced was an indication of victory that would be theirs in the future. They believed all of God's promises listed in Exodus 6:6-8, from emancipation to the entering of Canaan.

Notice some of the great words of their song: "Who is like Thee among the gods, O Lord? Who is like Thee, majestic in holiness, awesome in praises, working wonders? Thou didst stretch out Thy right hand, the earth swallowed them. In Thy lovingkindness Thou hast led the people whom Thou hast redeemed; in Thy strength Thou has guided them to Thy holy habitation. The peoples have heard, they tremble; anguish has gripped the inhabitants of Philistia. Then the chiefs of Edom were dismayed; the leaders of Moab, trembling grips them; all the inhabitants of Canaan have melted away. Terror and dread fall upon them; by the greatness of Thine arm they are motionless as stone; until Thy people pass over, O Lord, until the people pass over whom Thou hast purchased. Thou wilt bring them and plant them in the mountain of Thine inheritance, the place, O Lord, which Thou hast made for Thy dwelling, the sanctuary, O Lord, which Thy hands have established. The Lord shall reign forever and ever" (15:11-18, NASB).

Confidence for the Future

Although the Israelites were right in their viewpoint at this time, they faltered later when tests came. But even though the Israelites faltered and failed, God remained true to His promises. It is interesting to note, however, that the Israelites sang their victory song even before they took the first step into the wilderness. They were aware of God's promises, so at this time they were confident of victory even though they later faltered.

God has also made many promises to the believer today (see Rom. 8:38,39; Eph. 1:13,14; I Pet. 1:4-7). We, too, need to be assured of the trustworthiness of God if we are to progress in the Christian life by growing to spiritual maturity. How wonderful it is to recognize that God knows the end as well as the beginning. So we may, like Israel, sing the song of victory even before we take the first step into the wilderness of future experiences in our daily walk.

Having confidence in God even before one meets obstacles is what faith is all about. Hebrews 11 tells of many heroes of the faith who had an unshakable confidence in the trustworthiness of God.

The fact that Israel experienced many failures later as they were tested is a reminder to us that the hope and joy we experience in Christ at the height of some previous experi-

Chapter 9

Entering the Desert Experience

Moses was a person of tremendous faith. He demonstrated this by taking about three million people into a desert where there was no water, no food, no shelter, no roads—nothing. Yet he had confidence that God could and would sustain them physically since He had ordered them to go into the desert.

Moses knew the desert well, for he had spent 40 years there learning spiritual lessons from God before he was commissioned to return to Egypt to lead the Israelites out. Of course, the object of Moses' faith was much more important than the amount or greatness of his faith. To learn this is to learn one of the greatest lessons of all—our faith must not be in our faith, it must be in God.

What concept of God do you have? Is He a little God as far as you are concerned? Does He have only a small amount of power? Or is He a great God to you? Does He have the ability to accomplish whatever He pleases? Only when you recognize Him as all-powerful and all-wise will you be able to have the song of assurance and praise that Moses and the Israelites had.

Dependent on God's Provision

The Israelites had been redeemed by blood from the judgment that fell on Egypt, and they had been redeemed by the power of God from the slavery of Egypt. But now they needed to learn how to walk in God's path.

So, too, when a person today receives Jesus Christ as Saviour and is delivered from the condemnation and power of sin, he needs to learn how to walk with God in the way He leads.

Just as Israel needed a training period, so every believer today needs a training period. In the wilderness the Israelites were shut out from the world around them and were completely alone with God—they had to depend on Him for everything. The training they received was to help them see the futility of the self-life.

Everyone, because of their sinful nature, is basically selfish. Only when a person receives Jesus Christ as Saviour is he given a new perspective so that he can have a genuine concern for others. But sometimes even a believer needs to go through difficult tests in order to learn not to rely on self. That is what happened to Israel—God brought tests into their lives to teach them to rely on Him for everything.

The Bible records: "So Moses brought Israel from the Red sea, and they went out into the wilderness of Shur; and they went three days in the wilderness, and found no water" (Ex. 15:22). Imagine—about three million people and no water! But this was precisely the kind of predicament God wanted Israel to experience so they would have no alternative but to trust Him completely. God was for the nation, not against it, so they really had no reason to fear as long as they were obedient to Him.

The spiritual lessons the Israelites had learned so far were associated with birth and babyhood experiences. Now that they were a free people, although still very much under God's watchful care, they were to experientially grow in stature so that as mature people they might enter, conquer and possess the Promised Land. At this point, the Israelites weren't ready for what was coming in Canaan, so God had to train them and prepare them for that crucial time.

The Israelites had learned from experience that God alone had accomplished their redemption and emancipation from Egypt. They simply accepted what God had done for them. During the next two years of Israel's history, the people were to see a demonstration of God's provision for their every need. This was a fulfillment of what God had promised through Moses: "I will take you to me for a people, and I will be to you a God: and ye shall know that I am the

Lord your God, which bringeth you out from under the burdens of the Egyptians" (6:7).

The next two years were to be filled with many learning experiences for the Israelites. As far as they knew at the time they fled from Egypt, they would be in the land of Canaan within a few weeks. But additional time was needed in order to teach them valuable spiritual lessons. They were taught to follow, to believe and to obey God. God could not take them any faster through these experiences because it took them so long to learn the lessons.

The Israelites had already become acquainted with the cloud which was God's visible means of leadership, light and protection. They were soon to experience God's providing manna, meat, water and many other necessities for their journey.

God provided for the Israelites because of the nation's relationship to Him. So, too, all that is provided for the individual believer is due to his perfect position in Christ. Those who know Christ as Saviour need to seriously consider and establish in their minds the significance of this position.

Jesus said, "He that heareth my word, and believeth on him that sent me, hath everlasting life, and shall not come into condemnation; but is passed from death unto life" (John 5:24). The person who knows Christ as Saviour can also claim the promise of Romans 8:1: "There is therefore now no condemnation to them which are in Christ Jesus." Ephesians 1:13,14 tells the believer that the Holy Spirit has been given to him as an earnest, or pledge, that God will complete what He has begun. Philippians 1:6 specifically states this: "Being confident of this very thing, that he which hath begun a good work in you will perform it until the day of Jesus Christ."

The believer is not to trust in himself. He is to realize that all of his sufficiency is found in Jesus Christ. As the Apostle Paul said, "Not that we are sufficient of ourselves to think any thing as of ourselves; but our sufficiency is of God" (II Cor. 3:5). The believer's completeness in Christ is noted in Colossians 2:9,10: "For in him dwelleth all the fulness of the Godhead bodily. And ye are complete in him, which is the head of all principality and power." How wonderful it is to realize that God has provided us with "all things that pertain unto life and godliness" (II Pet. 1:3). We receive a new nature when we accept Jesus Christ as Saviour. Because of this we even have a change in our desires—we want to please Him and to serve Him rather than desiring to please ourselves and to serve sin.

Progressing to Maturity

The way a believer is to live the Christian life is stated in Colossians 2:6: "As ye have therefore received Christ Jesus the Lord, so walk ye in him." A person receives Christ as Saviour by grace through faith (Eph. 2:8), so he is to live by the same principle. No one is able to work for his salvation, so we do not go on to spiritual maturity by works.

We become spiritually mature as we learn to exercise faith in God for every step of the way. Colossians 2:7 reveals that we are to be "rooted and built up in him, and stablished in the faith, as ye have been taught, abounding therein with thanksgiving." As we learn more about God and His way and have a greater confidence in Him and His provisions for us, we, too, will be "rooted and built up in him."

Someone might ask, How do we become spiritually mature? A partial answer is found in Hebrews 5:12-14. Verses 12,13 say, "For when for the time ye ought to be teachers, ye have need that one teach you again which be the first principles of the oracles of God; and are become such as have need of milk, and not of strong meat. For every one that useth milk is unskilful in the word of righteousness: for he is a babe." But how does a believer develop to the point that he is able to take strong meat? The answer is in verse 14: "But strong meat belongeth to them that are of full age, even those who by reason of use have their senses exercised to discern both good and evil." We become spiritually mature as we exercise our spiritual senses. When we apply the Word of God to daily life situations, the result will be spiritual growth.

Having told the Hebrew Christians of the need for spiritual maturity and how to accomplish it, the writer of Hebrews said, "Therefore leaving the principles of the doctrine of Christ, let us go on unto perfection [maturity]; not laying again the foundation of repentance from dead works, and of faith toward God, of the doctrine of baptisms, and of laying on of hands, and of resurrection of the dead, and of eternal judgment" (6:1,2). In other words, we are to leave the foundational things and go on to maturity. Notice that we are not to lay again the foundation but to build upon it as we go on to maturity.

The Apostle Paul said, "For other foundation can no man lay than that is laid, which is Jesus Christ" (I Cor. 3:11). When a person receives Jesus Christ as Saviour, the true foundation has been laid in his life. He never again needs to lay the foundation, but he does need to build on that foundation with quality materials, as indicated by Paul in verses 12-15. Those who have built with "gold, silver, precious stones" will be rewarded, but there will be no reward for those who have built with "wood, hay, stubble."

The Israelites had their foundation laid when they were delivered from Egypt by means of the Passover and when the nation was emancipated from Egypt's slavery as it passed through the Red Sea. These experiences never needed to be repeated, but it was important that the people go on in their walk with God and build on the foundation that had been laid.

It is important for those who know Jesus Christ as Saviour to know about the perfect position they have in Him. But it is also important that they learn to apply all the strength that is available as a result of their union with Him. This is what Paul referred to when he said, "I am crucified with Christ: nevertheless I live; yet not I, but Christ liveth in me" (Gal. 2:20). By faith we are to apply, or appropriate, the strength of God made available to us by putting on the whole armor of God (Eph. 6:10-13).

The road ahead for the three million Israelites in a barren desert was a human impossibility. However, God was about to demonstrate His power in a way which the world had never seen before.

So, too, it is impossible to live the Christian life in this world of sin in the power of human strength alone. This is why the Lord Jesus told us: "Abide in me, and I in you. As the branch cannot bear fruit of itself, except it abide in the vine; no more can ye, except ye abide in me. I am the vine, ye are the branches: he that abideth in me, and I in him, the same bringeth forth much fruit: for without me ye can do nothing" (John 15:4,5).

Just as the Israelites had to be brought to the end of themselves, so every believer must have the same experience. In Romans 7 Paul expressed how he came to the end of himself, and in Romans 8 he sounded the glorious note of having found victory through the Holy Spirit's strength which was made available to him as he, by faith, appropriated what he needed.

Israel's Needs Supplied

In the desert Israel was completely shut in to God. The people had to depend on God to supply everything through His man, Moses. Moses was their well-trained and mature leader who was competent to help them know God and His way intimately. We can begin to understand why God took so much time in training Moses—there was an overwhelming task ahead of him. God had to prepare Moses so he would not give in to the Israelites under pressure. Moses' faith had to be deeply rooted in God so he would have complete confidence in God, even in the face of seeming impossibility. Moses did not know how or where God was going to lead or what God was going to do, but he was sure God knew what He was doing. This was the tremendous confidence Moses had in God.

God provided leadership for the Israelites in the person of Moses. The believer today has also been given a leader—the Holy Spirit. Before Jesus ascended to heaven, He told His disciples, "I will pray the Father, and he shall give you another Comforter, that he may abide with you for ever; even the Spirit of truth; whom the world cannot receive, because it seeth him not, neither knoweth him: but ye know him; for he dwelleth with you, and shall be in you" (John 14:16,17).

According to Hebrews 7:25 and 8:1 Jesus Christ is enthroned and is interceding for us, yet the life and power that He is and has indwells us by means of the Holy Spirit. When Jesus Christ was on earth, He lived a perfect life through the power of the Holy Spirit. Now, by the same Holy Spirit, the life of Jesus Christ is available to us and is produced in us. Our strength and ability is derived from Jesus Christ by means of the Holy Spirit.

In the desert Israel had no water or food; these things were supplied only by direct miracles of God. This was the way that God chose to prove Himself to Israel. Israel found no natural springs in the desert to quench their thirst; they had to rely totally on God to satisfy their needs.

So, too, the basic needs of the Christian cannot be supplied by the world. Only God can provide that which deeply satisfies the spiritual needs of the believer. Just as Israel found no natural springs in the desert to satisfy their thirst, so the believer finds no earthly springs that can satisfy his spiritual thirst. The Israelites were not desert people—they were not *of* the desert, they were just passing through. So also the believer is not of this world, he is only passing through.

This reminds us of Abraham, of whom it was said, "By faith he sojourned in the land of promise, as in a strange country, dwelling in tabernacles [tents] with Isaac and Jacob, the heirs with him of the same promise: for he looked for a city which hath foundations, whose builder and maker is God" (Heb. 11:9,10).

Philippians 3:20 reveals that believers are actually citizens of the heavenly country: "For our conversation [citizenship] is in heaven; from whence also we look for the Saviour, the Lord Jesus Christ." In encouraging Christians to witness concerning the crucifixion, Hebrews 13:13,14 says, "Let us go forth therefore unto him without the camp, bearing his reproach. For here have we no continuing city, but we seek one to come." The testimony of the songwriter should be the testimony of every Christian: "This world is not my home, I'm just a-passing through."

It is almost impossible to comprehend all that would be involved in taking care of the needs of the Israelites in the desert. A Christian military officer once stationed in that area of the world calculated that it would take approximately 4000 tons of food a day to feed the three million Israelites. He also calculated that it would take two freight trains, each a mile long, to haul that amount of food. He made many other interesting calculations, but the important thing to realize is that there was no way, humanly speaking, that the needs of the Israelites could be taken care of.

The Purpose of Testing

Exodus 15:22 states that the Israelites started on their journey through the wilderness after passing through the Red Sea. They had been redeemed by blood from condemnation; they had been redeemed by the power of God from the slavery of the Egyptians. They probably expected that they would have a smooth journey from there on. Perhaps they thought, Aren't we the chosen people of God? Surely God is obligated to bring us into the Promised Land without more difficulty. But immediately after their song of assurance and praise for what God had done, they experienced severe testing. They "found no water" (v. 22).

This often happens—after a time of victory comes a time of testing. We see this principle even in the life of the Lord Jesus Christ. At His baptism there was the glorious announcement: "This is my beloved Son, in whom I am well pleased" (Matt. 3:17). But immediately afterward came the testing from Satan (4:1-11).

The Israelites needed to experience testing in order to check their true acquaintance with God and to check their own hearts. The purpose of the testing and discipline of the wilderness was not to furnish the Israelites with a title to Canaan which they had merited by their own works. Rather, the purpose of these experiences was to acquaint them with God and to reveal to them what their own hearts were like. They had to learn what power was available to them because of their relationship with God. They needed to enlarge their capacity for the enjoyment of Canaan when they actually arrived there.

The purposes of the wilderness experience were specifically mentioned by Moses later when the nation had arrived on the east side of the Jordan River, just before entering the land. Moses told the people, "Thou shalt remember all the way which the Lord thy God led thee these forty years in the wilderness, to humble thee, and to prove thee, to know what was in thine heart, whether thou wouldest keep his commandments, or no. And he humbled thee, and suffered thee to hunger, and fed thee with manna, which thou knewest not, neither did thy fathers know; that he might make thee know that man doth not live by bread only, but by every word that proceedeth out of the mouth of the Lord doth man live" (Deut. 8:2,3).

Travelers and Wanderers

The Israelites might have reasoned that since they were following the cloud, which was an indication of God's presence, they should have an easy road. Many Christians think the same way today. Some believe that if you are in the will of God, you will not experience any difficulty. Therefore, as soon as difficulty comes, they reason that one is not in the will of God. They do not realize, however, that God allows tests in order to mature us in the Christian life (I Pet. 1:6,7).

How sad it is that some who are saved and dedicated to the Lord are completely unprepared to accept the testings that occur through the "wilderness" of life. As believers we must remind ourselves that we are to journey through the wilderness and not just to wander around in it. As long as we are going through the wilderness of this world, we can expect tests along the way, even though we are in the will of God at the time.

Each believer needs to ask himself whether he is a traveler or a wanderer in the Christian life. A traveler goes from one point to another, but a wanderer has no particular goal or sense of direction. He makes his home wherever he is and is unconcerned about progress. Those of us who know Jesus Christ as Saviour need to have a sense of direction as we journey toward heaven. We must not be wanderers, making this world our home and living as if we're going to be here forever.

Faith, or confidence, in God is the determining factor in the way a person lives in this life. If the believer does not think God has great things in mind for him, he will be content to wander in this life without having his eyes fixed on the future. But the believer who has confidence in God will be like Abraham who "looked for a city which hath foundations, whose builder and maker is God" (Heb. 11:10).

Abraham, and the others mentioned in Hebrews 11, lived by faith, as is evident from verse 13: "These all died in faith, not having received the promises, but having seen them afar off, and were persuaded of them, and embraced them, and confessed that they were strangers and pilgrims on the earth." Those of us who know Christ as Saviour should recognize that we, too, are "strangers and pilgrims on the earth."

What a shame that many Christians aimlessly wander in this life with no spiritual purpose at all. In contrast notice the Apostle Paul who had a specific goal in mind. When addressing the Ephesian elders concerning what might happen to him when he went to Jerusalem, Paul said, "But none of these things move me, neither count I my life dear unto myself, so that I might finish my course with joy, and the ministry, which I have received of the Lord Jesus, to testify the gospel of the grace of God" (Acts 20:24). Notice Paul's goal: "That I might finish my course with joy, and the ministry, which I have received of the Lord Jesus."

At the time that Paul spoke these words much of his ministry was still ahead of him. Did he accomplish what he set out to do? The answer is found in the last recorded letter he wrote. Paul wrote: "I am now ready to be offered, and the time of my departure is at hand. I have fought a good fight, I have finished my course, I have kept the faith" (II Tim. 4:6,7).

If you know Jesus Christ as your Saviour, do you have a goal in life? Or are you like a motorboat whose engine is running while the anchor is dropped? Some Christians are anchored to the world and go nowhere spiritually. They may engage in much motion, or activity, but because they are anchored to the world and the desires of the old life, they do not honor Christ in their daily walk.

Those who have trusted Jesus Christ as their personal Saviour have become new creatures and possess new desires (II Cor. 5:17). However, they are not following their new desires if they are going after the things of the world. This in itself is the reason that Christians must be tested—to teach them about themselves as well as the faithfulness of God.

How sad it is to be an unused Christian. It is tests that often change a Christian from uselessness to usefulness. The

Bible reminds us: "Now no chastening for the present seemeth to be joyous, but grievous: nevertheless afterward it yieldeth the peaceable fruit of righteousness unto them which are exercised thereby" (Heb. 12:11).

Purposes of the Wilderness Experience

For Israel, the wilderness experience served two purposes: to teach them about God and His methods and to teach them about themselves.

God had told the Israelites, "I will take you to me for a people, and I will be to you a God: and ye shall know that I am the Lord your God, which bringeth you out from under the burdens of the Egyptians" (Ex. 6:7).

God desires that we today know Him in an intimate way also. We must learn to trust Him in spite of the circumstances and apparent conflicts. The Apostle John wrote: "We know that the Son of God is come, and hath given us an understanding, that we may know him that is true" (I John 5:20). It is important that those who are heaven-bound really know the God of heaven. Do we really know *Him* or do we only know *about* Him?

To some people, heaven is only a beautiful place where the streets are paved with gold. But even that signifies a difference between earthly and heavenly priorities. What is considered most valuable here on earth is used in heaven only as paving on which to walk. The most important part of heaven will be the fact that we will be in the very presence of God and will have fellowship with Him. We must not let the values of this life influence our thinking concerning what will be important in heaven. When we stand in the very presence of God, everything else will be secondary.

God planned for the Israelites to learn to know themselves through the testings they experienced. The testing of the wilderness manifested the evil that was in their hearts, the incurable corruption of the flesh. Although God performed miracle after miracle for them, as soon as they faced the next test, they grumbled and complained as if they had never seen God work in their behalf.

Our testings can also show us what our hearts are really like. We need to be humbled and to prove by experience that entrance into the abundant life is solely a matter of sovereign grace; it is not based on our merits. We need to realize that we are not to have any confidence in our old nature, or flesh, for it can produce nothing good (Rom. 7:18).

The tests we face will be like the wilderness tests of Israel in that they will expose our weaknesses and failures, but they will also magnify the power and longsuffering of God who bought us and then brought us to the place of testing.

To the natural man the world offers much that is attractive and alluring, but to the spiritual man what the world has to offer is only "vanity and vexation of spirit" (Eccles. 1:14). The world offers much to satisfy the lust of the flesh, the lust of the eyes and the pride of life (I John 2:16), but it offers nothing whatever to satisfy the desires of the new nature. Each believer should be able to say with the Apostle Paul, "God forbid that I should glory, save in the cross of our Lord Jesus Christ, by whom the world is crucified unto me, and I unto the world" (Gal. 6:14).

Chapter 10

Bitter Waters

After the Israelites had passed through the Red Sea, "they went out into the wilderness of Shur; and they went three days in the wilderness, and found no water" (Ex. 15:22).

Imagine what a desperate situation it was for all the Israelites to be without water. How glad they must have been when they came to Marah and saw water! But their delight soon ended, because "when they came to Marah, they could not drink of the waters of Marah, for they were bitter" (v. 23).

Even though the Israelites had been miraculously delivered through the Red Sea, they thought now that they were all going to perish for lack of water. The Bible says, "The people murmured against Moses, saying, What shall we drink?" (v. 24). The people thought that the Lord had forgotten all about them and that they would die in the barren wilderness. A short time before they had been praising God for His mighty deliverance; now they had no hope whatsoever that the problem before them could be solved.

You have probably experienced this kind of discouraging situation even as we have. I remember in particular when Mrs. Epp and I had first come to Lincoln, Nebraska, in 1939 to begin the Back to the Bible ministry. We had three small children at the time. About the first week of July our situation was desperate—letters weren't being received, so money wasn't being received either.

I remember walking the floor and trying to find something from the Word of God that would strengthen me and encourage my soul. The only verse which the Lord seemed to keep pounding home to my soul was, "I shall yet praise him" (Ps. 42:5). But I didn't know how I could possibly do that. My attitude was one of murmuring and complaining, and I even expressed to the Lord that I didn't see how I could praise Him for that day. I was really downcast.

My wife, however, recognizing the condition I was in, said, "Well, we can't both be down on the same day." So she went to the Word to find what promise the Lord would give her. She found a promise in Job that she claimed that day: "Though he slay me, yet will I trust in him" (Job 13:15).

All this took place on July 5. A month later we received a letter from a missionary friend in Africa. Enclosed was an American $5 bill. There was only a brief note saying, "God laid it on my heart to send you this money for the radio." When I looked at the date on the letter, I noticed that it had been written on July 5! I praised the Lord that day because it settled an important issue in my life. It proved that God would take care of those who committed their way to Him.

Murmuring and Complaining

The Israelites felt sorry for themselves in the desert, for even though they had water, it was so bitter they couldn't drink it. However, the clue to what God was doing through this test is found in the last words of Exodus 15:25: "There he proved them." This first test which the Israelites experienced after they had passed through the Red Sea was designed to teach them (and through them to teach us) that nothing the world had to offer would satisfy their most basic needs. The Israelites had to learn to trust God to supply their needs, and we have to learn the same lesson.

The believer needs to realize that the waters of this world are bitter and totally unsatisfactory when it comes to meeting his most basic spiritual needs. In His discussion with the woman at the well, Jesus kept emphasizing that those who drink of the waters of this world will thirst again but that those who drink of the water He has to offer will never thirst again (John 4:13,14). Jesus invited all to drink of the water He has to offer: "If any man thirst, let him come unto me, and drink" (7:37).

Many believers do not realize that they will experience
tests and trials in their lives after redemption. God does not
want us to settle down and be content in this world; in fact,
Jesus made it clear that in this world there would be severe
problems. He said, "Peace I leave with you, my peace I give
unto you: not as the world giveth, give I unto you. Let not
your heart be troubled, neither let it be afraid" (14:27).
Jesus told believers, "If the world hate you, ye know that it
hated me before it hated you. If ye were of the world, the
world would love his own: but because ye are not of the
world, but I have chosen you out of the world, therefore the
world hateth you" (15:18,19). He also said, "In the world ye
shall have tribulation: but be of good cheer; I have overcome
the world" (16:33).

So we see that only God has something to offer us that
really satisfies. And He wants to teach us through the tests
we face to depend only on Him to fully meet our needs. He
wants to teach us His ways and His values. We need to learn
to trust God not only when times are good but also when
there seems to be no solution to the problem. We need to
realize that even though we do not know how God is going to
solve the problem, "all things work together for good to
them that love God, to them who are the called according to
his purpose" (Rom. 8:28). This means that we must recognize His sovereignty and ability to accomplish what He
knows is best both for us and for Him.

Even the Apostle Paul had to learn these lessons in his
own life. Yet, he was eventually able to say, "Not that I
speak in respect of want: for I have learned, in whatsoever
state I am, therewith to be content. I know both how to be
abased, and I know how to abound: every where and in all
things I am instructed both to be full and to be hungry, both
to abound and to suffer need. I can do all things through
Christ which strengtheneth me" (Phil. 4:11-13).

Only three days after the Red Sea experience the
Israelites were grumbling against Moses and against God.
Three days before they had been singing, now they were
complaining. The people had said, "The Lord is my strength
and song, and he is become my salvation: he is my God, and I
will prepare him an habitation; my father's God, and I will
exalt him. . . . Who is like unto thee, O Lord, among the

gods? Who is like thee, glorious in holiness, fearful in praises, doing wonders? . . . Thou in thy mercy hast led forth the people which thou hast redeemed: thou hast guided them in thy strength unto thy holy habitation" (Ex. 15:2,11,13).

What went wrong? Why such a change of attitude in just three days? They had overlooked the fact that the cloud had led them in this direction, and since God was leading them, He would supply their needs.

When the people murmured against Moses (v. 24), they were actually murmuring against God, because Moses was God's representative to lead them. Every complaint against circumstances, every grumbling about the daily trials of life is directed against the One who "worketh all things after the counsel of his own will" (Eph. 1:11). Although the Israelites did not have this verse at the time, they had seen enough of God's work to know that He did not make mistakes and that He could perform anything necessary to provide for them. And remember, what happened to Israel is to serve as an example to us (I Cor. 10:11).

Notice what Moses' reaction was when the people murmured against him: "He cried unto the Lord" (Ex. 15:25). While the people were blaming him for their situation, Moses was calling out to the Lord. What a great example this is for us, demonstrating that we should turn everything over to God.

Concerning this matter I have especially appreciated Psalm 37:5: "Commit thy way unto the Lord; trust also in him; and he shall bring it to pass." Notice also I Peter 5:7: "Casting all your care upon him; for he careth for you." Psalm 55:22 conveys the same thought: "Cast thy burden upon the Lord, and he shall sustain thee: he shall never suffer the righteous to be moved."

How important it is that we keep "looking unto Jesus the author and finisher of our faith" (Heb. 12:2). Our confidence must be in Him, not in ourselves.

The Tree

As Moses called out to God in his need, God revealed what Moses should do. "The Lord shewed him a tree, which when he had cast into the waters, the waters were made sweet" (Ex. 15:25). This place was called Marah, meaning "bitter," but now it had become "sweet." Our Marahs, or testings, are for the purpose of driving us to Jesus Christ, even as God used this Marah to prove the Israelites (v. 25). Even though the bitter waters were a bad experience at first, it was used to draw the people closer to the Lord. So also, even though chastening is difficult for us to bear, the results are good (Heb. 12:11).

Romans 5 shows the method by which God works in the lives of believers: "We glory in tribulations also: knowing that tribulation worketh patience; and patience, experience; and experience, hope: and hope maketh not ashamed; because the love of God is shed abroad in our hearts by the Holy Ghost which is given unto us" (vv. 3-5).

How can anyone glory in tribulation? The answer is given in Romans 5:1,2: "Therefore being justified by faith, we have peace with God through our Lord Jesus Christ: by whom also we have access by faith into this grace wherein we stand, and rejoice in hope of the glory of God." When we recognize that our position is secure in Christ, we will be willing to endure tribulation. We can then realize that it will give us a greater understanding of who God is and of the way He wants to work in our lives.

Notice that God instructed Moses to throw a tree into the bitter waters to make them sweet (Ex. 15:25). This tree is a reminder of the cross of the Lord Jesus Christ. All that we have is related to what Christ accomplished for us. He suffered, He died on the cross (tree), He was buried, He rose from the dead and He ascended to the Father. The Bible says, "Who his own self bare our sins in his own body on the tree, that we, being dead to sins, should live unto righteousness: by whose stripes ye were healed" (I Pet. 2:24). We are also told, "Christ hath redeemed us from the curse of the law, being made a curse for us: for it is written, Cursed is every one that hangeth on a tree" (Gal. 3:13).

So the tree that Moses threw into the bitter waters to make them sweet points us to all that Jesus Christ accomplished for us in relation to the cross. There He accomplished a work for us, but now He is working in us. No wonder Paul said, "God forbid that I should glory, save in the cross of our Lord Jesus Christ" (6:14).

Suffering for God

As those of us who know Christ glory in the cross and all that is related to it, we will realize that our lives will involve suffering. In fact, suffering weans us from dependence on the world.

Paul desired to really know God, and he realized that this involved suffering: "That I may know him, and the power of his resurrection, and the fellowship of his sufferings, being made conformable unto his death" (Phil. 3:10). Paul recognized that any suffering the believer endured in this life could not be compared with the rewards to come. He said, "If children, then heirs; heirs of God, and joint-heirs with Christ; if so be that we suffer with him, that we may be also glorified together. For I reckon that the sufferings of this present time are not worthy to be compared with the glory which shall be revealed in us" (Rom. 8:17,18).

Paul had much to say about suffering. To Timothy he wrote: "Therefore I endure all things for the elect's sakes, that they may also obtain the salvation which is in Christ Jesus with eternal glory. It is a faithful saying: For if we be dead with him, we shall also live with him: if we suffer, we shall also reign with him: if we deny him, he also will deny us" (II Tim. 2:10-12). The denying that Paul referred to was not denying Jesus Christ as Saviour but denying His way, His methods and His purpose. If we refuse to accept these matters, God will deny us rewards that would result from suffering for Him.

If those who know Christ as Saviour murmur and complain against man and God as the Israelites did, the result will be a spiritually stunted life. They will only prove their immaturity.

God always works in our lives to bring about spiritual growth and maturity. It is not enough to know information; one must act upon it. God revealed to Moses that a nearby tree should be thrown into the bitter waters, but the waters would have remained bitter had Moses not acted on God's instructions. Notice that Moses did not provide the cure, he only applied it. This reminds us again of Romans 6. God has provided the cure for the sin problem both before and after we become His children, but we must apply it by faith in order to benefit from it. Victory comes in Christian living only as we take God at His Word and live accordingly. Of course, the basis for all of our victory is that we have been "justified by faith" (Rom. 5:1).

A Place of Refreshing

After the incident at Marah, the Israelites "came to Elim, where were twelve wells of water, and threescore and ten palm trees: and they encamped there by the waters" (Ex. 15:27).

From this verse we see the principle that blessing follows testing. The Israelites were tested at Marah, where God revealed His power to take care of every need they had. Then they found an abundance of water and shelter at Elim. Whereas Marah was a place of testing, Elim was a place of refreshing. Elim was a foretaste of what they would have once they entered Canaan. This foretaste was like earnest money given as an indication that the purchaser will follow through on his promise. The New Testament reveals that the Holy Spirit is the earnest for the believer—the indication that God will follow through on all He has promised (Eph. 1:13,14).

The Israelites had no unfulfilled needs or wants at Elim. They could have said as did David, "The Lord is my shepherd; I shall not want. He maketh me to lie down in green pastures: he leadeth me beside the still waters. He restoreth my soul: he leadeth me in the paths of righteousness for his name's sake" (Ps. 23:1-3).

Notice that David said, "He maketh me to lie down in green pastures." We might not always want to go where the Lord wants us to, but through the testing which He allows, He makes us come to the place of refreshing.

The person who relies on God for his daily needs and rejoices in the person of God is truly blessed. David told of the person who is blessed by God: "Blessed is the man that walketh not in the counsel of the ungodly, nor standeth in the way of sinners, nor sitteth in the seat of the scornful. But his delight is in the law of the Lord; and in his law doth he meditate day and night. And he shall be like a tree planted by the rivers of water, that bringeth forth his fruit in his season;

his leaf also shall not wither; and whatsoever he doeth shall prosper" (1:1-3). When we realize how good the Lord is to those who love Him and walk in His way, we can say with the psalmist, "O magnify the Lord with me, and let us exalt his name together" (34:3).

At this stage in Israel's history, God was just beginning His work to bring them to full strength—to bring them to the point of spiritual maturity that He desired. God also works in believers today to bring about that which pleases Him. In fact, God has given gifted men to the Church whose purpose it is to equip the saints to do the work of the ministry: "He gave some, apostles; and some, prophets; and some, evangelists; and some, pastors and teachers; for the perfecting [equipping] of the saints, for the work of the ministry, for the edifying of the body of Christ: till we all come in the unity of the faith, and of the knowledge of the Son of God, unto a perfect [mature] man, unto the measure of the stature of the fulness of Christ" (Eph. 4:11-13). Again, we can be assured that whatever process God begins, He will complete (Phil. 1:6).

Chapter 11

Manna From Heaven

After experiencing the blessing of the 12 wells of water
and the 70 palm trees, the Israelites "took their journey from
Elim, and all the congregation of the children of Israel came
unto the wilderness of Sin, which is between Elim and Sinai,
on the fifteenth day of the second month after their
departing out of the land of Egypt" (Ex. 16:1).

Moses' Great Faith

The Israelites were on their way toward Mt. Sinai where
the Law would be given by God through Moses. Moses
demonstrated great faith and courage as he led the Israelites
in this direction, which took them through the barren desert,
farther and farther from the supplies of the outside world.
For the first time, the real emptiness and privation of the
desert probably stared Moses and his people in the face. Until
then they had been near populated areas, but they were
leaving civilization for the barren, wind-swept desert. Their
journey took them farther and farther from any population
center, and humanly speaking, they seemed headed for
certain death.

Imagine—about three million people were led by Moses
into the howling waste of the desert! Remember, Moses was
not ignorant of conditions in the desert—he had spent time
there being prepared by God for the very task he was now
performing. But no matter what kind of leadership genius
Moses had, it would take constant provision by miracles of
God to sustain the Israelites in the desert. And Moses knew

93

this because he had spent 40 years there learning spiritual
lessons he would never forget.

Some believers go into situations that they do not know
about, and they must rely on God to lead them. But Moses'
faith was even greater because he knew the obstacles and
went anyhow. This reminds us of Abraham, of whom the
Bible says, "By faith Abraham, when he was called to go out
into a place which he should after receive for an inheritance,
obeyed; and he went out, not knowing whither he went"
(Heb. 11:8). Yet when famine came, Abraham went down to
Egypt (Gen. 12:10).

Moses knew his obstacles ahead of time and demonstrated unreserved faith in God. His experiences with Pharaoh
and of seeing God work now paid off.

Moses' Leadership Tested

Believers today must be spiritually strong in Christ so
they can face tests. The Bible instructs believers how they
ought to live: "As ye have therefore received Christ Jesus the
Lord, so walk ye in him: rooted and built up in him, and
stablished in the faith, as ye have been taught, abounding
therein with thanksgiving" (Col. 2:6,7). A person is saved by
faith and is to live by faith. Only then is the believer able to
face the tests that God allows to come into his life.

The Apostle Paul had undergone many severe tests, but
his testimony was: "Thanks be to God, which giveth us the
victory through our Lord Jesus Christ" (I Cor. 15:57).
Because of the victory that is always possible in Christ, Paul
went on to urge believers, "Therefore, my beloved brethren,
be ye stedfast, unmoveable, always abounding in the work of
the Lord, forasmuch as ye know that your labour is not in
vain in the Lord" (v. 58).

The test that Moses was about to undergo had to do with
his leadership. The Israelites grumbled against him and said,
"Would to God we had died by the hand of the Lord in the
land of Egypt, when we sat by the flesh pots, and when we
did eat bread to the full; for ye have brought us forth into
this wilderness, to kill this whole assembly with hunger" (Ex.
16:3). The Bible reveals, however, that the murmurings of
the Israelites were really directed against the Lord (v. 7).

Only a month had elapsed since the Israelites had left Egypt, and they were already questioning God's goodness and greatness. This reveals the total depravity of man. God had delivered them from Egypt by miracle after miracle, yet they grumbled and complained when they encountered a problem. And it wasn't that there were just a few people who grumbled—"the whole congregation of the children of Israel murmured" (v. 2). What a sad situation. How this must have grieved Moses, and how it especially must have grieved the heart of God!

The psalmist, in commenting on this incident, said, "They sinned yet more against him by provoking the most High in the wilderness. And they tempted God in their heart by asking meat for their lust. Yea, they spake against God; they said, Can God furnish a table in the wilderness?" (Ps. 78:17-19). So the divine commentary on the incident in Exodus is that the people, though they grumbled against Moses, were actually speaking against God. They questioned God's ability to take care of them.

The sin of the Israelites was even worse in that they took an oath, as indicated by the expression "Would to God we had died" (Ex. 16:3). This amounted to taking the name of the Lord in vain.

In their rebellion and unbelief the Israelites lied about their former situation. They said that in Egypt they "sat by the flesh pots" and ate "bread to the full" (v. 3). How a little bit of time had affected their memories!

The Israelites had forgotten that they were actually slaves in Egypt. Their gathering of gold, silver and jewelry before they left Egypt was a matter of picking up their back wages. Their situation as slaves had not been good at all, but they had forgotten this.

What about their song of victory, recorded in Exodus 15? At that time they were so thankful to the Lord, but a month later they had forgotten their hard taskmasters in Egypt and the goodness of the Lord in delivering them from Egypt. At the Red Sea they had realized that God was not only leading them out of Egypt but that He was also leading them into the land (v. 13).

What the Israelites needed to do at this time was to count their blessings. Since God had delivered them many times before, would He now forsake them? They should have known God better than that. But murmurers and complainers are shortsighted. The cloud had not left them; they were still under it. It not only provided them with the guidance of God but also gave them shade from the hot sun. But they thought God had completely forsaken them. They were right where God wanted them, and they should have realized that even though they did not understand what God was doing, it was for their best.

How fickle people can be. The Israelites were singing songs of praises on one day and complaining to God on the next. Remember, when we murmur at the circumstances God brings into our lives, we are actually murmuring against Him.

Moses' Reactions

Moses did not try to defend himself; he simply went to the Lord and then faithfully delivered to the people the instructions he received from the Lord. What an interesting study it is to observe the reactions of Moses at times like this. He loved his people dearly and was giving his life to lead them from Egypt to Canaan, yet they frequently complained against him. But their murmurings only drew him closer to the Lord. How about us? When others complain against us, are we driven to the Lord for counsel and direction? Because Moses had seen God work so mightily in the past, he was willing to trust God now without question.

Let us not be like the Israelites who complained against the Lord. We often tend to feel sorry for ourselves and to question God's goodness, but we should instead remind ourselves of all that He has done for us. Jesus Christ has paid the penalty for our sins so we can be delivered from eternal condemnation, and He has provided all we need to live a life of victory. So in times of discouragement, let us stop and count our blessings before we question the goodness of God.

The reactions of Moses proved what a gentle and great man he really was. No wonder the Bible says, "(Now the man Moses was very meek, above all the men which were upon the face of the earth)" (Num. 12:3).

As the people grumbled against Moses, God took up his case and fought in his behalf. Having trusted in Jesus Christ as Saviour, we can rely on Him to take care of any situation. Paul expressed it in these words: "I know whom I have believed, and am persuaded that he is able to keep that which I have committed unto him against that day" (II Tim. 1:12). Is this the kind of confidence you have in God? Each believer can have the assurance that God will work to defend the believer who seeks to glorify Him.

Consider what trials accomplish in our lives. Before Job had experienced severe testing, he did not have nearly as great a concept of God as he did later. After experiencing his trials, Job said, "I have heard of thee by the hearing of the ear: but now mine eye seeth thee. Wherefore I abhor myself, and repent in dust and ashes" (Job 42:5,6). Think of some of the other statements Job made: "He knoweth the way that I take: when he hath tried me, I shall come forth as gold" (23:10); "Though he slay me, yet will I trust in him" (13:15).

Consider what a test David went through when he and the men under his leadership discovered that their wives and children had been taken captive. David was blamed for negligence in letting them be captured; in fact, the men were even considering stoning David to death. But the Bible says, "David encouraged himself in the Lord his God" (I Sam. 30:6). No matter what the test, that's what the Lord wants each of us to do—to encourage ourselves in Him.

Notice the reaction of the psalmist when he was tested: "Be merciful unto me, O God: for man would swallow me up; he fighting daily oppresseth me. Mine enemies would daily swallow me up: for they be many that fight against me, O thou most High. What time I am afraid, I will trust in thee. In God I will praise his word, in God I have put my trust; I will not fear what flesh can do unto me. Every day they wrest my words: all their thoughts are against me for evil" (Ps. 56:1-5).

Perhaps you think that you would never murmur against God as the Israelites did, but think of some of the statements you may have made or thoughts you may have had under adverse circumstances. I've heard believers say, "Why did God take my husband?" or "Why did God take my wife?" or "Why did God take my child?" While such questions can be asked simply as a result of the frustration of the moment, some ask such questions in bitterness of soul, actually questioning God's wisdom and goodness.

Bread from Heaven

But how good God is, even to those who blame Him for difficult circumstances! When the Israelites grumbled against God, He told Moses, "Behold, I will rain bread from heaven for you; and the people shall go out and gather a certain rate every day, that I may prove them, whether they will walk in my law, or no" (Ex. 16:4).

Surely this was amazing grace—that God would perform a miracle to bring bread from heaven to feed complainers! It's more logical to think that He would rain fire from heaven to destroy them rather than bread from heaven to feed them. How wonderfully great and amazing is the mercy of the Lord! "Who is a God like unto thee, that pardoneth iniquity, and passeth by the transgression of the remnant of his heritage? He retaineth not his anger for ever, because he delighteth in mercy" (Mic. 7:18).

A word that stands out in the psalms of David is "mercy." David delighted in the mercy of God because he knew what it was to experience God's grace and forgiveness.

Comparing the nation of Israel to an individual, Israel was a new man with a heavenly nature and had need of heavenly food. Ephesians 1:3 tells us, "Blessed be the God and Father of our Lord Jesus Christ, who hath blessed us with all spiritual blessings in heavenly places in Christ." God has made available all the heavenly food that we will ever need.

In Israel's case food actually descended from heaven for them to gather. In commenting on this incident later, the psalmist referred to the manna as "angels' food" (Ps. 78:25).

Manna is a beautiful type of the food which God provides for our souls. The Word of God—both the living, incarnate Word and the written Word—provides food for our souls. Of course, even the written Word is living, as indicated in Hebrews 4:12: "For the word of God is quick [living], and powerful, and sharper than any twoedged sword, piercing even to the dividing asunder of soul and spirit, and of the joints and marrow, and is a discerner of the thoughts and intents of the heart."

The flesh pots that the Israelites remembered in Egypt belonged to earth, but manna belonged to heaven. Sometimes the Israelites were faced with the question of which they enjoyed most, the food of earth or the food of heaven. It is good for each believer to reflect on what he enjoys most—the things of the world or the things of heaven.

Remember, the provision of the manna was for the purpose of proving, or testing, Israel (Ex. 16:4). The Israelites had been delivered physically from Egypt, but God was concerned about their heart, or desires, being delivered from Egypt also. Later, not everyone appreciated the manna God sent from heaven (Num. 11:4-6). Though they appreciated it at first because it kept them from starvation, they grew weary of this miraculous provision from heaven.

Just as the extent of enjoyment the Israelites had in the manna determined whether the desires of their hearts were fixed on God or Egypt, so the believer's attitude toward God reveals whether his attention is fixed on Christ or on the things of the world. Each believer needs to ask himself, Does Christ truly satisfy me? Am I taken up with Him? Do I have to have other things in addition to Christ to be satisfied?

When referring to Himself as the Bread of Life, Jesus compared Himself and His Word to the manna that came down from heaven (John 6:22-59). Jesus is the Word, and He said, "I am the living bread which came down from heaven: if any man eat of this bread, he shall live for ever: and the bread that I will give is my flesh, which I will give for the life of the world" (v. 51).

Christ is the living Word, but He is revealed to us in the written Word. We know of Him and we assimilate truths about Him as we study the written Word. The written Word tells of the living Word who was made flesh and dwelt among men (1:14). So we need to feed on the written Word because it reveals to us the incarnate, living Word, Jesus Christ Himself.

So the manna of the Old Testament prefigured Jesus Christ as revealed in the New Testament. This is why Jesus explained, "Moses gave you not that bread from heaven; but my Father giveth you the true bread from heaven. For the bread of God is he which cometh down from heaven, and giveth life unto the world" (6:32,33). When His listeners asked for His bread, Jesus said, "I am the bread of life: he that cometh to me shall never hunger; and he that believeth on me shall never thirst" (v. 35). Let us feed on the written Word of God in order that we may feed on the living Word.

Two Natures

The person who knows Jesus Christ as Saviour has two natures. He has the old nature, or Adamic nature, which he had when he was born into this life. This nature is referred to in the Bible as the flesh. This nature enjoys the things of the world and is particularly concerned about fitting into the world system and all that it has to offer. But the believer also has a new nature, which he received when he trusted Jesus Christ as personal Saviour. This new nature is satisfied only with heavenly food. The worldly Christian is one who, although a believer, desires the things of the world system. Worldliness is more an attitude toward the world than a particular behavior pattern.

Because the believer has two natures, he must decide to which nature he will yield. Both natures are vying for his attention, but he can yield to only one at a time, so he must make a choice. Paul told believers, "Neither yield ye your members as instruments of unrighteousness unto sin: but yield yourselves unto God, as those that are alive from the dead, and your members as instruments of righteousness unto God" (Rom. 6:13). He asked, "Know ye not, that to whom ye yield yourselves servants to obey, his servants ye are to whom ye obey; whether of sin unto death, or of obedience unto righteousness?" (v. 16). Perhaps some wonder how they are to yield themselves to God and to righteousness. Paul explained, "I speak after the manner of men because of the infirmity of your flesh: for as ye have yielded your members servants to uncleanness and to iniquity unto iniquity; even so now yield your members servants to righteousness unto holiness" (v. 19).

God promised to take care of the spiritual needs of the Israelites. He was going to "rain bread from heaven" for them (Ex. 16:4). Notice it was bread "from heaven." Its origin was not in this world, even as the bread which the believer today is to feed on is not of this world. The living Word, Jesus

Christ, is God, so He is eternal. Although He entered this world by being born of flesh, He did not have His origin in this world. Neither is the origin of the written Word in this world. Second Timothy 3:16 reveals its origin: "All scripture is given by inspiration of God [is God-breathed]." Although God uses human authors to write the Scriptures, He is the One who superintended so that they chose precisely the words He wanted them to choose. So as we study the written Word in order to feed on the living Word, we are actually gaining spiritual strength from that which originates outside the world.

Referring to the manna, Moses told the Israelites, "In the morning, then ye shall see the glory of the Lord" (Ex. 16:7). The manna was a type of Jesus Christ, who referred to Himself as "the bread of life" (John 6:35). To grow spiritually, a believer must feed on Jesus Christ, who is the living Word, and He is revealed only in the written Word, the Bible. It is impossible to know more about Christ unless one knows more about the Bible.

The Israelites gathered manna in the morning and had the glory of the Lord revealed to them, just as a believer will see the glory of the Lord as he reads and meditates on the Word of God each day. Although it is not essential to have a devotional time in the morning, many Christians find that this is the best part of the day for this special time with the Lord. What a difference it will make in our lives as we daily read and meditate on God's Word and see His glory revealed to us!

Think of the abundant provision God made for the Israelites in the manna. The Israelites were to gather "an omer for every man" (Ex. 16:16). An omer equaled about six pints. Assuming there were about 3 million people, this would mean that they gathered more than 18 million pints of manna a day. Think of this tremendous quantity! And God provided this not only for one day or for several days but for 40 years. They thought they would starve in the desert, but God took care of them abundantly.

Gathering and Using the Manna

Notice that the manna was found wherever the cloud was located. As long as the Israelites stayed where God wanted them to be, their needs were taken care of. Any individual who left the accompanying cloud and traveled on his own would not have his needs taken care of. But wherever the cloud, which was the indication of God's presence with the people, was found, there was sustenance.

Notice also that the Israelites did not have to go a long distance to get groceries. The manna fell near them. So also, the Word is constantly available to us. Not only is the living Word everywhere present, but we also have the written Word available on every hand. Most homes in North America have more than one copy or translation of the Bible, so the written Word is easily accessible to all. The Israelites either had to gather the manna or trample it underfoot. What a parallel this is to us concerning the Word of God! We either read and obey it, or we trample its truths underfoot. What are you doing with the Word of God?

The manna came in the form of "a small round thing" (Ex. 16:14). So also, the written Word is not a big library—all 66 books are contained in a relatively small volume. Yet more truth is contained in this one small volume than in the greatest of libraries. In this one small volume God has revealed all we need to know in order to bring us into right relationship with Himself and to enable us to live a life of victory.

The Bible reveals that the manna the Israelites were provided with was white (v. 31). This color is the symbol of purity, and certainly the Word of God is pure. The psalmist said, "The words of the Lord are pure words: as silver tried in a furnace of earth, purified seven times" (Ps. 12:6). Also the purity of the Word is seen in the words "holy scriptures" (II Tim. 3:15). There is no mixture of falsehood, or error, with truth. The original writings contained no mistakes, no contradictions, no blemishes. What a wonderful revelation God has given us!

God gave the Israelites manna to eat. It did them no good if they only looked at it or considered it something to be admired. So also, the written Word of God has been given to us for more than intellectual admiration; it is spiritual food to us as we assimilate its truths. It is one thing to know information from or about the Word of God on an intellectual level, but it's quite another thing to apply those truths to one's life. Only when it is applied does the person come into right relationship with Jesus Christ and grow to spiritual maturity.

Although we should study the Bible for the doctrine it contains, we should look beyond the doctrine to see the person it reveals, the Lord Jesus Christ. We must see Christ as more than a mere historical person. We must see Him as the Scriptures reveal Him—as God, as Redeemer and as life itself.

The Bible itself has much to say about the Word of God. Sometime try using Psalm 119 during your devotional time and consider the various ways that the Word of God is referred to in this psalm. The entire psalm has 176 verses which are divided into segments of eight verses each. When originally written in Hebrew, the first eight verses began with the first letter of the Hebrew alphabet, the second eight verses began with the second letter of the alphabet, and so on. In your devotional time consider eight verses each day. As you meditate on the verses, you will see the many references to the Word of God and will realize more than ever how important it is to the believer's life.

When we study the Scriptures, we recognize that Jesus Christ is far more than just a person who lived long ago; He is more than the "historical Jesus." In reality Jesus Christ is eternal life itself. The Bible says, "This is the record, that God hath given to us eternal life, and this life is in his Son. He that hath the Son hath life; and he that hath not the Son of God hath not life" (I John 5:11,12). Since Jesus Christ is life, we not only receive eternal life by trusting Him as personal Saviour, but we gain spiritual strength as we feed on the written Word which reveals Him to us.

In regard to spiritual food, three words sum up what a believer needs to do: appropriate, masticate and assimilate.

Appropriating

It is obvious that the Israelites had to gather the manna as it came from heaven. God did not force it down their throats; rather, the Israelites had to take the responsibility of gathering it. Benefiting from the manna involved a condition; it had to be gathered.

Both the provision and condition concerning salvation are seen in John 3:16. The provision is, "For God so loved the world, that he gave his only begotten Son." The condition involved is seen in the words, "that whosoever believeth in him should not perish, but have everlasting life." As the Israelites had to gather the manna, so a person has to receive Christ as Saviour. "As many as received him, to them gave he power to become the sons of God, even to them that believe on his name" (1:12).

Joshua 1:3 also reveals both God's part and Israel's part in claiming the Promised Land: "Every place that the sole of your foot shall tread upon, that have I given unto you, as I said unto Moses." God had given the land to the Israelites, but they had to go in and actually take it.

To appropriate the Word of God is to take it to ourselves; it is to make it our own. We come to the Word of God with all of our needs, and then we apply what the Bible says to our needs. When we believe God and obey His Word, we are appropriating it. The believer feeds on Christ as he lives by His promises (Col. 2:6,7).

Masticating

Having appropriated spiritual food, we then need to masticate it. That is, we need to meditate on it; we must determine to make it our own. This involves more than just a quick reading of the Word or even taking time in the Word; it involves reflecting on the truths we see in the Word and applying them to our personal needs.

The psalmist had much to say about meditating on God's Word. Concerning the man who is blessed, the psalmist said, "His delight is in the law of the Lord; and in his law doth he meditate day and night. And he shall be like a tree planted by the rivers of water, that bringeth forth his fruit in his season; his leaf also shall not wither; and whatsoever he doeth shall prosper" (Ps. 1:2,3).

Notice the following statements in Psalm 119: "Open thou mine eyes, that I may behold wondrous things out of thy law" (v. 18); "How sweet are thy words unto my taste! Yea, sweeter than honey to my mouth!" (v. 103); "The entrance of thy words giveth light; it giveth understanding unto the simple" (v. 130).

It is regrettable that today the art of meditation on God's Word seems to have been lost. Believers are too busy; they are involved in too many other things. But it is tremendously important that we spend time in God's Word and meditate on its truths. Satan will do everything he can to keep the believer from having time for God's Word. He realizes that time spent meditating on the truths of God's Word is the believer's secret to spiritual power. If Satan cannot keep a person from Christ, he will endeavor to keep him immature by discouraging him from studying and meditating on God's Word, the basis for spiritual growth.

One way to have the Word of God readily available for meditation is to memorize it. The psalmist said, "Thy word have I hid in mine heart, that I might not sin against thee" (v. 11). You may memorize God's Word by the verse or by the chapter; but memorize it. You will discover progress in your spiritual life as you have it available at all times for meditation.

Another way to meditate on God's Word is to write out the verses you are studying. Perhaps you will want to combine writing down verses with memorizing them. You can write them on cards, which will help to fix the verses in your mind, and then you can carry the cards with you to memorize, review and meditate on when you find available time. I often meditate on verses during my morning walk. Sometimes I don't get past one verse for a whole mile because I find so much in it, and God uses it to speak to my heart. At other times I'll review and meditate on several verses during this same time. But the important thing is that we meditate, whatever our method.

Assimilating

In addition to appropriating and masticating the Word of God, we also need to assimilate it. We do this as we comprehend the Word. This takes time, just as it takes time for physical food to be assimilated and to strengthen the body. This is the whole purpose of appropriating and masticating—that one may have spiritual strength and growth.

Jeremiah referred to this whole process when he said, "Thy words were found, and I did eat them; and thy word was unto me the joy and rejoicing of mine heart" (Jer. 15:16). Assimilating the Word of God is not only the means of spiritual nourishment, but it is also a safeguard against temptation and error. This is why the psalmist said, "Thy word have I hid in mine heart, that I might not sin against thee" (Ps. 119:11).

We need to assimilate God's Word not only for salvation but also for our daily walk. Christ saves us from condemnation, but He does much more than that; He also sustains us spiritually. To know Christ for salvation and to grow in Him are two distinct matters, although both are accomplished by faith (Col. 2:6,7).

What are you feeding on today? Is it God's Word or is it television programs or books that dishonor Him? Of course, even activities that do not dishonor Him may rob you of time that you should be spending in His Word. Each of us needs to be very careful in our use of time.

Notice that the Israelites were to gather the manna every day (see Ex. 16:4). What they gathered on one day would not keep until the next. They could not hoard enough or store enough to last a week or a month. If they tried to store it, it would breed worms (vv. 19,20).

Moses instructed the Israelites, "Let no man leave of it till the morning" (v. 19). However, there are always those who refuse to follow instructions, and this was the case concerning the Israelites. But notice what happened to the manna they stored up: "It bred worms, and stank" (v. 20).

It was necessary for the Israelites to gather the manna every morning, for it came with the dew of the morning and melted when the sun became hot (vv. 14,21).

This should be a lesson to us—we must use the Word of God as we gather it. Some Christians seem to want only to take in information about the Word of God without applying it to their lives. But this is not using the Word as it is gathered. Such people may become intellectual giants, but they lack the spiritual insight that God wants them to have and which they attain as they apply the Word to daily life situations.

The Lord Jesus Christ had to tell the Church of Ephesus: "Nevertheless I have somewhat against thee, because thou hast left thy first love. Remember therefore from whence thou art fallen, and repent, and do the first works; or else I will come unto thee quickly, and will remove thy candlestick out of his place, except thou repent" (Rev. 2:4,5). This local church had left its first love. They didn't lose it; they left it. It is an accident when we lose something, but it is either by intent or neglect that we leave something. Many Christians, through neglect, have left their first love because they have not studied the Word of God as they should have. As a result, God takes the testimony away from the believer.

Just as we should not expect one meal to last us all week, neither should we expect time and meditation spent in the Word of God on Monday to last us for several days. We are not to rely on the past but are to daily appropriate, masticate and assimilate the Word of God.

Manna in the Morning

Notice especially that there was a precise time when the Israelites were to gather the manna. The Bible says, "When the dew that lay was gone up, behold, upon the face of the wilderness there lay a small round thing, as small as the hoar frost on the ground" (Ex. 16:14). This verse reveals that the manna came early in the morning.

Did they have all day to gather the manna? The answer is found in verse 21, which says, "When the sun waxed hot, it melted." Both of these verses imply that the manna was to be gathered in the morning.

So also, it is important that the believer's daily devotional period be early in the morning before his mind becomes cluttered with the things of the day.

The usual objection to having the devotional period in the morning is lack of time. It is true that you probably do not have enough time to do a lengthy study in God's Word, such as reading several chapters or a book of the Bible, in the morning. However, remember that the quality of the devotional period is more important than the quantity. Even if you don't have much time, if you determine to do so, you can find sufficient time to read and meditate on a chapter, or at least several verses, in order to get some truth that you can take with you throughout the day. Having seen some truth that you can especially apply to your life, you can then spend time in prayer, asking God to make the truth a reality in your life. Pray also for His guidance and spiritual strength throughout the day. Longer periods of study can be reserved for later in the day.

Just as the manna was fresh in the morning, so we find that the Word of God is fresh for us in the morning and speaks to our hearts in a way that is often not possible later in the day when we are mentally tired or our minds are cluttered with other things. It is not good to read God's Word just to fulfill a requirement; read His Word with a hungry heart to learn more about Him and what you can do to please Him.

In my devotional time I read a chapter, or perhaps two or three chapters. But the important thing is that I read until God draws my attention to a truth or to a verse that I especially need. Sometimes I then write the verse on a card so that I may later memorize it or at least have it available to read and meditate on during the day.

It is important that those of us who know Jesus Christ as Saviour have Him in first place in our lives. If our priorities are not in the right order, we will not be in His Word as we ought to be and our hearts will grow colder. Our lives will become feeble and barren. Remember, the written Word reveals to us the living Word.

The only way to have time for a devotional period is to determine that you will make time for it in your schedule. Just as we set aside time to eat and to do other things, we need to set aside time for the most important matter—fellowship with God.

Concerning the importance of meeting God in the morning in a devotional period, the following poem entitled "The Secret" has been of much encouragement to me:

> I met God in the morning,
> When my day was at its best;
> And His presence came like sunrise
> With a glory in my breast.

All day long His presence lingered,
All day long He stayed with me;
And we sailed in perfect calmness
O'er a very troubled sea.

Other ships were blown and battered,
Other ships were sore distressed,
But the winds that seemed to drive them,
Brought to us, both peace and rest.

Then I thought of other mornings,
With a keen remorse of mind,
When I, too, had loosed the moorings,
With the Presence left behind.

So I think I know the secret,
Learned from many a troubled way;
You must seek Him in the morning,
If you want Him through the day.

—Ralph Cushman

Our Attitudes in Devotions

The Scriptures indicate that the manna fell on the ground
(Ex. 16:14). It is doubtful that there were any trees or even
bushes for it to fall on, so the Israelites had to stoop to
gather it. Even this is a reminder of how we worship the Lord
in our devotional time. Either we actually kneel as we pray,
or at least we bow in reverence before Almighty God. What a
beautiful picture of how we worship God and glean spiritual
food from the Bible. We are to depend totally on the Holy
Spirit to take the things of God and to make them real to us.

Jesus told His disciples concerning the Holy Spirit, "I
have yet many things to say unto you, but ye cannot bear
them now. Howbeit when he, the Spirit of truth, is come, he
will guide you into all truth: for he shall not speak of
himself; but whatsoever he shall hear, that shall he speak: and
he will shew you things to come. He shall glorify me: for he
shall receive of mine, and shall shew it unto you" (John
16:12-14).

How does the Holy Spirit reveal these things to us? Usually, it is not by some vision or special experience but by the Word of God. As we study the Bible, the Spirit of God takes the Word and reveals the significance of its truths to us. This, of course, is difficult for the world to understand. The unregenerate person usually is motivated by the desire to analyze and criticize the Bible rather than believe it. But the person who has been regenerated by receiving Jesus Christ as Saviour comes with an open heart, eager to learn more about God. Unless one accepts the Bible as the Word of God, he cannot glean the truths from it that God intends.

We must be very careful that we do not adopt the world's viewpoint and insist on having an intellectual understanding of the Bible before believing it. Knowing that it is God's Word, we are to accept what it says whether we can understand it or not. One's approach to the Scriptures is vitally important to his spiritual life. Schooling often greatly affects one's approach to the Scriptures. This is why I highly recommend Bible school training before university training. This was the order in which our children received their training, and we believe God has richly rewarded because of it. Some think a person needs a college education in order to understand the Bible, but that is not the case. It is important that a person be deeply grounded in the Word of God before he faces the humanistic, and even atheistic, philosophy of the world. It is better to have a knowledge of the Bible without a college education than a college education without a knowledge of the Bible.

Personal Responsibility

As the manna fell in the wilderness for the Israelites, each person was to gather what he needed. The Lord instructed, "Gather of it every man according to his eating, an omer for every man, according to the number of your persons; take ye every man for them which are in his tents" (Ex. 16:16). The Bible records that the Israelites "gathered every man according to his eating" (v. 18). From these statements we see that there was personal responsibility to gather the food that each one needed; some gathered more, others gathered less, but each was to gather according to his particular need.

Think of the parallel this has for our feeding on God's Word. Each one must gather spiritual food for himself. A believer cannot live on another person's experience. Testimonies are interesting, and it is wonderful to have a pastor who preaches good messages, but a believer cannot live on those things alone. Each Christian must gather his own spiritual food according to his own need. If each one is feeding himself individually, then the testimonies and messages of others will be of encouragement to him, and he will be of much encouragement to others.

How much appetite for the Word of God do you have? Do you come to the Word with a hungry heart to learn all you can in order that you might know God better? The more we learn about Him, the more we will want to learn. Since Christians are at different stages of spiritual growth, it is especially important that each one gather spiritual food according to his own need. As we come to God with open and believing hearts, He will provide spiritual food. He told the Israelites, "Open thy mouth wide, and I will fill it" (Ps. 81:10). Just as a mother bird feeds her young, so the Lord feeds us as we open our spiritual mouths for Him.

Have you wondered how long God kept providing manna for the Israelites? The answer is found in Exodus 16:35: "The children of Israel did eat manna forty years, until they came to a land inhabited; they did eat manna, until they came unto the borders of the land of Canaan." It is baffling to consider the quantity of manna it took to feed nearly three million people for one day alone. Yet God supplied this quantity every day for 40 years! This is another indication of God's inexhaustible supply. As Isaiah 40:8 says, "the grass withereth, the flower fadeth: but the word of our God shall stand for ever."

The Israelites continued to eat the manna until they came into the land of Canaan. Joshua 5:11,12 says, "They did eat of the old corn of the land on the morrow after the passover, unleavened cakes, and parched corn in the selfsame day. And the manna ceased on the morrow after they had eaten of the old corn of the land; neither had the children of Israel manna any more; but they did eat of the fruit of the land of Canaan that year."

Manna had served a special purpose during a given time in the life of the nation Israel, but after they came into the land, it was no longer needed. The Scofield Reference Bible has a significant note concerning the manna: "The manna is a type of Christ in humiliation, known 'after the flesh,' giving his flesh that the believer might have life (John 6. 49-51); while the 'old corn of the land' is Christ apprehended as risen, glorified, and seated in the heavenlies. Occupation with Christ on earth, 'crucified through weakness,' tends to a wilderness experience. An experience befitting the believer's place in the heavenlies demands an apprehension of the power of His resurrection (2 Cor. 5. 16; 13. 4; Phil. 3. 10; Eph. 1. 15-23). It is the contrast between 'milk' and 'meat' in Paul's writings (1 Cor. 3. 1,2; Heb. 5. 12-14; 6. 1-3)" (p. 263).

It is important that Christians progress from the milk stage of their spiritual lives to the meat stage. Hebrews 5:11-14 reveals that we grow spiritually stronger as we exercise our senses to discern good and evil. As we study God's Word and apply it to daily, life situations, we will mature in the Christian life.

Chapter 12

Water From the Rock

"And all the congregation of the children of Israel journeyed from the wilderness of Sin, after their journeys, according to the commandment of the Lord, and pitched in Rephidim: and there was no water for the people to drink" (Ex. 17:1).

Thirsty at Rephidim

Under the direction of God, Moses had led the Israelites into the wilderness where there was no food or water. Moses was persuaded that God could provide anything they needed. The testing that he had gone through earlier had persuaded him of God's ability to provide, so Moses gave unquestioned obedience when the Lord commanded the people to leave the wilderness of Sin and go to Rephidim. Notice that Exodus 17:1 says, "According to the commandment of the Lord." Moses was not acting on his own—he was under orders.

The Israelites had shown great confidence in Moses and in the Lord, as seen in Exodus 14:31, but this confidence soon waned when they faced the stark reality that there was no water. "Wherefore the people did chide with Moses, and said, Give us water that we may drink" (17:2). The people quarreled with Moses about the lack of water, but notice his response: "Why chide ye with me? Wherefore do ye tempt the Lord?" (v. 2). Moses immediately pointed to the real problem—the people were not trusting the Lord, even though earlier they had sung a song of assurance and praise to the Lord (Ex. 15).

Previously, the people had grumbled against Moses and against God because they had no food (16:3). Since God had miraculously provided at that time, one would hope they would have learned that God could and would provide any need they had. But when they faced a lack of water, they quarreled with Moses again.

The Israelites seemed to go through a certain cycle whenever they faced a difficult problem. They had a need, they grumbled, the need was miraculously met, but they seemed to lack thankfulness. As soon as the next need arose, they went through the same cycle again. Notice the divine commentary on the Israelites, as recorded in Psalm 78:11-20: "And they forgot His deeds, and His miracles that He had shown them. He wrought wonders before their fathers, in the land of Egypt, in the field of Zoan. He divided the sea, and caused them to pass through; and He made the waters stand up like a heap. Then He led them with the cloud by day, and all the night with a light of fire. He split the rocks in the wilderness, and gave them abundant drink like the ocean depths. He brought forth streams also from the rock, and caused waters to run down like rivers.

"Yet they still continued to sin against Him, to rebel against the Most High in the desert. And in their heart they put God to the test by asking food according to their desire. Then they spoke against God; they said, 'Can God prepare a table in the wilderness? Behold, He struck the rock, so that waters gushed out, and streams were overflowing; can He give bread also? Will He provide meat for His people?' " (NASB).

Rephidim was undoubtedly a barren place, and the Israelites desperately needed water. This serves as a reminder, however, that the believer also has needs which the world cannot supply. The Israelites were thirsting for actual water, but the believer's need is for the things of God. And Jesus promised to quench the believer's real thirst for spiritual truth: "Blessed are they which do hunger and thirst after righteousness: for they shall be filled" (Matt. 5:6). Isaiah exclaimed, "Ho, every one that thirsteth, come ye to the waters, and he that hath no money; come ye, buy, and eat; yea, come, buy wine and milk without money and without price" (Isa. 55:1). How refreshing it is to see a new Christian who is hungry and thirsty for the things of God.

Unfortunately, older Christians sometimes do not evidence this same desire, perhaps because the cares of this world have dulled this desire.

Questioning God

Moses made it clear that the Israelites were tempting God by arguing with him about water: "Moses said unto them, Why chide ye with me? Wherefore do ye tempt the Lord?" (Ex. 17:2). The people were not only questioning Moses as a leader, but they were also questioning God's goodness. "They tempted the Lord, saying, Is the Lord among us, or not?" (v. 7). This revealed the sad condition of their hearts. God had saved them from Egypt, had divided the Red Sea, had destroyed Egypt's power, had provided a cloud to guide and protect them and had given them manna to eat. Yet in the face of a new need they seemed to have forgotten all that God had previously done for them.

This teaches us the need of keeping our spiritual eyes fixed on Christ. When we face circumstances that seem impossible, we need to remind ourselves of all that Jesus Christ has done for us in the past. We need to be faithful in meditating on the Scriptures, which reveal the goodness and ability of God. Even though we don't know how our problem may be solved, we can be confident that there is a solution to the problem and that God will provide the answer. We should consider ourselves under the care of the Shepherd who is able to meet all of our needs. Such a concept of God led David to say, "The Lord is my shepherd; I shall not want" (Ps. 23:1).

God's supply of grace is sufficient for all of our needs. The Bible says, "God is able to make all grace abound toward you; that ye, always having all sufficiency in all things, may abound to every good work" (II Cor. 9:8). When there seems to be a lack, God may be testing us to see if we'll trust Him to supply what is needed.

Remember, God Himself led Israel to Rephidim; they were led there "according to the commandment of the Lord" (Ex. 17:1). Certainly God knew there was no water at Rephidim; this did not take Him by surprise. However, the Israelites blamed Moses and God as if neither one of them thought of this possibility.

When the believer faces some extremely difficult circumstances, he also has a tendency to blame others. Who do you blame at such times? The tendency is to say, or at least to think, "Why is God so hard on me?" or "Why did God let this happen to me?"

During Job's early experiences he was somewhat critical of God's ways, but he was finally able to say, "He knoweth the way that I take: when he hath tried me, I shall come forth as gold" (Job 23:10). Can you say that?

We need to realize, as did the writer of Proverbs, that "man's goings are of the Lord; how can a man then understand his own way?" (20:24). Even though we don't understand the circumstances we face, we should realize "that all things work together for good to them that love God, to them who are the called according to his purpose" (Rom. 8:28).

Moses' Reaction to Accusations

As the Israelites argued with Moses, he made it clear that they were arguing not just with him but also with God. That is why Moses said, "Why chide ye with me? Wherefore do ye tempt the Lord?" (Ex. 17:2). The word "tempt" means "to try" or "to test." They were trying God's patience by questioning His goodness and His faithfulness. Moses was God's appointed leader, and the Israelites were even accusing him of plotting to kill them by bringing them into the desert where there was no water (v. 3). Think of how this accusation must have crushed the heart of Moses. But anyone who is in the position of leadership must realize that he will be falsely accused at times by his followers.

When the Israelites accused Moses of plotting to kill them and their children, Moses did not try to defend himself. He "cried unto the Lord, saying, What shall I do unto this people? They be almost ready to stone me" (v. 4). Moses did not defend himself against the cruel accusations of the Israelites; he turned to God and sought His solution.

How refreshing it is to see the way Moses cast himself on the Lord rather than trying to defend himself. This is the biblical reaction prescribed for every believer when he is falsely accused. The Bible says, "Cast thy burden upon the Lord, and he shall sustain thee: he shall never suffer the righteous to be moved" (Ps. 55:22). How beautifully this ties in with the thought expressed in Psalm 37:5: "Commit thy way unto the Lord; trust also in him; and he shall bring it to pass."

Jesus Himself provided the example of how the believer should react: "Who, when he was reviled, reviled not again; when he suffered, he threatened not; but committed himself to him that judgeth righteously" (I Pet. 2:23). Although Jesus was an example to us, He is much more than that because He now indwells every believer and desires to express His characteristics through the believer. Believers are told, "Christ in you, the hope of glory" (Col. 1:27). Our hope of victory is in the indwelling Christ. As we live in fellowship with Jesus Christ, His characteristics will be revealed in and through our lives.

Moses' heart attitude toward God was revealed in that he "cried unto the Lord" (Ex. 17:4). Moses' acknowledgement of his own lack of ability is seen in his statement: "What shall I do unto this people?" (v. 4). But this statement also shows Moses' confidence in God's ability to solve the problem.

God's Response to Moses

How God responded to Moses is seen in verses 5,6: "And the Lord said unto Moses, Go on before the people, and take with thee of the elders of Israel; and thy rod, wherewith thou smotest the river, take in thine hand, and go. Behold, I will stand before thee there upon the rock in Horeb; and thou shalt smite the rock, and there shall come water out of it, that the people may drink." Moses' obedience is seen in the last statement of verse 6: "And Moses did so in the sight of the elders of Israel."

The need for water was about to be met because Moses went to God with the problem. The source of supply was God Himself.

God directed Moses to "the rock in Horeb" (v. 6). A rock was the last place that anyone would expect to find water, but God promised that water would come from the rock. But it wasn't just any rock; it might be called a "God-possessed rock" inasmuch as God said, "I will stand before thee there upon the rock in Horeb" (v. 6).

This rock clearly looked forward to the Lord Jesus Christ. This is evident from I Corinthians 10:4 which says that the Israelites "did all drink the same spiritual drink: for they drank of that spiritual Rock that followed them: and that Rock was Christ." In particular, the "rock in Horeb" (Ex. 17:6) represented the human nature of Christ, for He was smitten for our sins. Isaiah said, "Surely he hath borne our griefs, and carried our sorrows: yet we did esteem him stricken, smitten of God, and afflicted. But he was wounded for our transgressions, he was bruised for our iniquities: the chastisement of our peace was upon him; and with his stripes we are healed" (Isa. 53:4,5).

The source of help is God, as it was for the Israelites, but the channel is Jesus Christ.

The water which flowed from the rock suggests to us the Holy Spirit who came from the Father to indwell every believer. While Jesus was still on earth, He promised the disciples, "I will pray the Father, and he shall give you another Comforter, that he may abide with you for ever. . . . The Comforter, which is the Holy Ghost, whom the Father will send in my name, he shall teach you all things, and bring all things to your remembrance, whatsoever I have said unto you" (John 14:16,26). Jesus also told the disciples, "Nevertheless I tell you the truth; it is expedient for you that I go away: for if I go not away, the Comforter will not come unto you; but if I depart, I will send him unto you" (16:7). The Holy Spirit came from the Father to indwell believers after the Lord Jesus Christ had finished the work of redemption.

The Rock

Note the distinctions between the manna which God rained from heaven to provide food for the Israelites (Ex. 16:14) and the rock which was smitten to provide water (17:6). That both the manna and the rock point forward to Jesus Christ is evident from the New Testament (John 6:32,33; I Cor. 10:4). The manna points to the incarnation of Christ—His entering the world as a man (John 1:14). The smitten rock symbolizes His crucifixion—on the cross He was smitten of God for our sins (Isa. 53:4,5). Isaiah 53:10 says, "Yet it pleased the Lord to bruise him; he hath put him to grief: when thou shalt make his soul an offering for sin." Jesus Christ offered Himself as the sacrifice for sin so that anyone might have forgiveness of sin and eternal life by receiving Him as personal Saviour.

The water which flowed from the rock was a beautiful picture of the Holy Spirit who was given to believers after the Lord Jesus Christ was crucified and glorified. Jesus had promised that the Comforter would be sent (John 14:16), and on the Day of Pentecost the Holy Spirit came to indwell every believer (Acts 2:1-4). Just as Moses had to strike the rock before the water flowed, so the Lord Jesus had to be smitten for our sins and exalted at the right hand of the Father before the Holy Spirit was sent to indwell believers.

The Holy Spirit is often compared to water. Jesus said, "If any man thirst, let him come unto me, and drink. He that believeth on me, as the scripture hath said, out of his belly shall flow rivers of living water" (John 7:37,38). Jesus spoke these words before He ascended to heaven; thus, verse 39 says, "(But this spake he of the Spirit, which they that believe on him should receive: for the Holy Ghost was not yet given; because that Jesus was not yet glorified.)"

So we see that running water was used to illustrate the ministry of the Spirit. This was no doubt what Christ had in mind when He told the woman at the well, "If thou knewest the gift of God, and who it is that saith to thee, Give me to drink; thou wouldest have asked of him, and he would have given thee living water. . . . Whosoever drinketh of the water that I shall give him shall never thirst; but the water that I shall give him shall be in him a well of water springing up into everlasting life" (4:10,14).

Three of the five types of the death of Christ have now been presented in the Book of Exodus. The Passover told of redemption by blood from the penalty of sin. The passing through the Red Sea (a figure of participating in death) symbolized redemption by power from the slavery of sin. And the smitten rock illustrated the new life provided in Christ through the Holy Spirit. Thus, both Calvary and Pentecost are pictured in the Old Testament types, and these two events must always be thought of in relation to each other.

Characteristics of God's Provision

The water flowing from the rock indicates the provision for life. The psalmist said, "Behold, he smote the rock, that the waters gushed out, and the streams overflowed" (Ps. 78:20). The smitten rock pointed to the smitten Christ who paid the penalty of sin. The gushing streams of water picture the gracious supply of life through the Holy Spirit.

God smote His Son and raised Him from the dead, thereby sending forth the life-giving stream, but man must come and drink. Although Jesus Christ has paid the penalty of sin for all (I John 2:2), only those who personally receive Him as Saviour have forgiveness of sin and eternal life (John 1:12; 5:24).

When God provides, He provides abundantly. When God provided water for the Israelites, the psalmist said, "He opened the rock and the waters gushed out; they ran in the dry places like a river" (Ps. 105:41). Concerning the life which the Lord Jesus Christ provides, He said, "I am come that they might have life, and that they might have it more abundantly" (John 10:10). This coincides with the way Jesus compared the Spirit to the abundance of running water (John 4:14; 7:37,38). So the rock in the wilderness prefigured Jesus Christ.

The constant provision for the Israelites is emphasized in I Corinthians 10:4: "They drank of that spiritual Rock that followed them: and that Rock was Christ." Notice that the Rock "followed them." Their needs were taken care of by God's abundant provision.

Not only was the supply abundant, but it was also free. All the Israelites had to do was to partake of what had been provided. This is a reminder of Isaiah's statement: "Ho, every one that thirsteth, come ye to the waters, and he that hath no money; come ye, buy, and eat; yea, come, buy wine and milk without money and without price" (Isa. 55:1). Jesus emphasized to the woman at the well that the water He provided was free: "If thou knewest the gift of God, and who it is that saith to thee, Give me to drink; thou wouldest have

asked of him, and he would have given thee living water"
(John 4:10). The free access to the water is also emphasized
in Revelation 22:17: "And the Spirit and the bride say,
Come. And let him that heareth say, Come. And let him that
is athirst come. And whosoever will, let him take the water of
life freely."

It is also significant to observe that God's supply is
always near. The Israelites did not have to go a long distance
to receive water; God directed them to a source in their area.
So also, God's spiritual supply is always near. Romans 10:8
says, "The word is nigh thee, even in thy mouth, and in thy
heart: that is, the word of faith, which we preach." Verse 13
states, "For whosoever shall call upon the name of the Lord
shall be saved."

There was no excuse for the Israelites' not having
sufficient water, because as I Corinthians 10:4 indicates, the
Rock followed them. The supply was always accessible to
them. So also, even though the Lord Jesus Christ died for sin
nearly 2000 years ago, what He accomplished is just as
powerful and available now as it was immediately after His
death on the cross. The invitation for all to come and to
drink freely still stands (Rev. 22:17). And remember the
promise of the Lord Jesus: "All that the Father giveth me
shall come to me; and him that cometh to me I will in no
wise cast out" (John 6:37). All are invited to come. Jesus
said, "Come unto me, all ye that labour and are heavy laden,
and I will give you rest" (Matt. 11:28). And what a
wonderful promise we have in Isaiah 1:18: "Come now, and
let us reason together, saith the Lord: though your sins be as
scarlet, they shall be as white as snow; though they be red
like crimson, they shall be as wool."

First Corinthians 10:4 reveals that the Israelites all drank
of the Rock that followed them. This is a beautiful illustration of the fact that during the Church Age every believer
is made a partaker of the Holy Spirit. Believers are told, "For
by one Spirit are we all baptized into one body, whether we
be Jews or Gentiles, whether we be bond or free; and have
been all made to drink into one Spirit" (I Cor. 12:13). It is
important to realize that every believer has the Spirit of God.
It is not possible to maintain that a person can receive Christ
as Saviour at one point in time and not receive the Holy

Spirit until another point in time. The Bible reveals that every believer has the Spirit of God. Romans 8:9 says, "Ye are not in the flesh, but in the Spirit, if so be that the Spirit of God dwell in you. Now if any man have not the Spirit of Christ, he is none of his."

The Holy Spirit: Receiving and Filling

Receiving the Holy Spirit does not depend on our attainment, or work, but on Christ's finished work. That is why John 1:12 says, "As many as received him, to them gave he power to become the sons of God, even to them that believe on his name."

To drink of the one Spirit is the birthright and the heritage of every born-again person. It is important to realize, however, that although every believer has the Spirit of God, not every believer is filled with the Holy Spirit. Receiving the Spirit is the believer's heritage. Ephesians 1:13,14 says, "In whom [Christ] ye also trusted, after that ye heard the word of truth, the gospel of your salvation: in whom also after that ye [literally, having] believed, ye were sealed with the holy Spirit of promise, which is the earnest of our inheritance until the redemption of the purchased possession, unto the praise of his glory." From these verses and from Romans 8:9 we learn that every believer has the Holy Spirit because he is sealed with the Holy Spirit. Ephesians 4:30 reveals that the believer is sealed with the Holy Spirit "unto the day of redemption."

Whereas receiving the Holy Spirit is the believer's heritage, being filled with the Holy Spirit is both the believer's privilege and command. The Bible says, "Be not drunk with wine, wherein is excess; but be filled with the Spirit" (5:18). The filling here referred to is the control of the Holy Spirit. Every believer, because he has the Holy Spirit indwelling him, is exhorted to let the Holy Spirit control all of his life.

The life through the Holy Spirit is the same in all believers, but the manifestation of that life in terms of spiritual development and spiritual maturity is different in each believer.

Every person who has been born again by receiving Christ as Saviour has the life of Christ in him by means of the Holy Spirit. Therefore, such terms as "deeper life" or "higher life" are sometimes misleading because all believers have the same spiritual life. However, this life can, and does, develop differently in different believers. Every believer has a varying degree of spiritual maturity. Although a baby may be physically complete when it is born, it needs to grow to physical maturity. So also, a believer in Christ has complete life when he is born again, but he needs to grow to spiritual maturity.

Those Christians who are more concerned about pleasing themselves than about pleasing Christ are carnal Christians. Paul told the Corinthians, "And I, brethren, could not speak unto you as unto spiritual, but as unto carnal, even as unto babes in Christ. I have fed you with milk, not with meat: for hitherto ye were not able to bear it, neither yet now are ye able. For ye are yet carnal: for whereas there is among you envying, and strife, and divisions, are ye not carnal, and walk as men?" (I Cor. 3:1-3). The spiritual person allows the Holy Spirit to fill, or control, his life (Eph. 5:18-20).

There is no difference in character as far as life itself is concerned; the only difference is in the development and growth of that life, which is determined by the individual believer. The one who grows to maturity is the one who has his senses exercised by taking the Word of God and applying it to daily life situations (Heb. 5:13,14).

Thus, the need of each person who knows Jesus Christ as Saviour is to obey the injunction to "be filled with the Spirit" (Eph. 5:18) and to "walk in the Spirit, and ye shall not fulfil the lust of the flesh" (Gal. 5:16).

Chapter 13

Spiritual Conflict

After recording the incident of obtaining water from the rock, the Bible says, "Then came Amalek, and fought with Israel in Rephidim" (Ex. 17:8).

Israel's First Warfare

This was Israel's first involvement in warfare. After they had tasted of the heavenly food (manna) and after they had drunk from the rock, the warfare began. The same thing happens in a believer's life after Christ has His rightful place in that person's heart and the Holy Spirit has been given His rightful place of control. In other words, after the believer has tasted spiritual food and drunk of the spiritual Rock, spiritual warfare begins in his life also.

When warfare came to Israel, the people were resting in Rephidim. This is a reminder that when we are at rest in the Lord because of the salvation we have in Him through the power of the Holy Spirit, we need to watch for the Enemy. After the new and holy nature of Christ is implanted in our hearts, Satan is ready to do battle with us.

Some people are under the impression that receiving Jesus Christ as Saviour ends any conflict in their lives. However, it is really only the beginning. Before receiving Christ as Saviour, a person has only one nature—the old, or Adamic, nature. There is no conflict as long as a person has only one nature to satisfy. But upon trusting Christ as Saviour, a person receives a new and holy nature which is in immediate conflict with the old nature. This conflict is referred to in Galatians 5:17: "For the flesh [old nature]

124

lusteth against the Spirit, and the Spirit against the flesh: and these are contrary the one to the other: so that ye cannot do the things that ye would." However, the preceding verse shows the way of victory for the Christian: "Walk in the Spirit, and ye shall not fulfil the lust of the flesh" (v. 16).

Until the Israelites met Amalek, they had little conflict. They had not fought with Pharaoh in Egypt nor did they break the power of Egypt at the Red Sea by submerging Pharaoh and his army in the water. God had done all of this in their behalf, even though individual Israelites were not faithful in believing Him.

So also, Christ has won all the battles for us and has obtained our peace. In Him there is forgiveness of sin. He alone died on the cross, was laid in the tomb and arose from the dead to accomplish our justification. He overcame Satan and took away the sting of death. These things were all accomplished apart from any of our activity.

The Book of Hebrews tells of that which Christ accomplished for us: "When he [Christ] had by himself purged our sins, sat down on the right hand of the Majesty on high" (1:3). The defeat of Satan is mentioned in Hebrews 2:14: "Forasmuch then as the children are partakers of flesh and blood, he [Christ] also himself likewise took part of the same; that through death he might destroy him that had the power of death, that is, the devil."

Because of what Christ has accomplished for us, Ephesians 1:3 says, "Blessed be the God and Father of our Lord Jesus Christ, who hath blessed us with all spiritual blessings in heavenly places in Christ."

In Israel's case, all previous conflicts had been between Jehovah and the Enemy, Satan. All the Israelites had to do was to stand still and see and enjoy the fruits of victory. But now they were about to enter serious conflict.

The moment the believer discovers and appropriates the truth concerning the personality and power of the Holy Spirit (as symbolized by the water from the smitten rock), he suddenly becomes aware of the new Enemy symbolized by Amalek.

Amalek's fighting against Israel parallels the struggle an individual believer has because of his two natures. Were there only darkness (the old nature) there would be no conflict.

Were there only light (the new nature) there would be no conflict. But because the believer has both natures, there is a constant struggle between the two. The statement in Galatians 5:17 which says, "The flesh lusteth against the Spirit, and the Spirit against the flesh" means that the desires of these two natures are totally opposed to each other. That is why the Christian experiences a constant struggle in life. He must choose which desires he will yield to—the desires of the new nature or the desires of the old nature.

Exodus 17:8 indicates the first time that Israel was really engaged in conflict with an enemy: "Then came Amalek, and fought with Israel in Rephidim." They were experiencing something they had not known before. They may have thought that once they were delivered from Egypt they would never experience conflict, but what a lesson they had to learn!

Receiving the New Nature

In the case of the Christian, God does not change a person's nature. Many teach that God changes a person's nature so that after he receives Christ as Saviour he will always be a complete victor over sin. But a changed nature is not taught in scripture. God does not improve or overhaul the old nature. Nothing is done to the old nature—God leaves it as it is. What He does, however, is to give man a new nature when he is born again. God does not attempt to improve the weaknesses of the old nature; He gives the believer an entirely new nature. So God does not remove man's old nature; rather, He adds the new nature. This new nature is "born . . . of the Spirit" (John 3:5). Believers are "partakers of the divine nature" (II Pet. 1:4).

The new life is Christ Himself, not the old life made over. And the wonderful truth is, "He that hath the Son hath life," but the sobering truth is, "He that hath not the Son of God hath not life" (I John 5:12).

At the time of salvation a divine nature is communicated to the believer. This divine nature is created within the believer by the Holy Spirit through the Word of God. The Bible refers to Christians as "being born again, not of corruptible seed, but of incorruptible, by the word of God, which liveth and abideth for ever" (I Pet. 1:23). Thus we see that the word "seed" is used in reference to the new nature. First John 3:9 also uses the word "seed": "Whosoever is born of God doth not commit sin; for his seed remaineth in him: and he cannot sin, because he is born of God." This seed is pure and is not capable of sin.

Although a new nature is implanted in the believer at the time of salvation, the old nature, or sin nature, remains unchanged until death or until Christ returns to catch away the believer from the earth. The Apostle Paul told of this in I Corinthians 15:51-53: "Behold, I shew you a mystery; We shall not all sleep, but we shall all be changed, in a moment, in the twinkling of an eye, at the last trump: for the trumpet shall sound, and the dead shall be raised incorruptible, and we shall be changed. For this corruptible must put on incorruption, and this mortal must put on immortality."

So in every Christian there are two natures, one sinful and one sinless. One is born of the flesh (after Adam), the other is born of God. These two natures differ from each other in origin, character, disposition and in the activities they produce. The two natures have absolutely nothing in common and are in complete opposition to each other.

Illustrations of the Two Natures

It is important to identify exactly who Amalek was, because it is significant that the Lord used him to symbolize the believer's old nature. From Genesis 36:12 we learn that Amalek was the grandson of Esau. Esau was the twin brother of Jacob, and because Esau was born first, he had rightful claim to the birthright. But he sold his birthright for some pottage. The birthright involved not only physical aspects but also spiritual aspects. The property to be inherited was the physical part; the spiritual leadership the oldest son was to exercise was the spiritual part. There were no priests at the time Jacob and Esau lived; the oldest son in the family was to carry out this responsibility for his family. So we see the full significance of what Esau was willing to give up for food when he was desperately hungry. He, too, is a significant illustration of the flesh, or the old nature.

The New Testament refers to Esau as an example not to be followed. Hebrews 12:16,17 says, "Lest there be any fornicator, or profane person, as Esau, who for one morsel of meat sold his birthright. For ye know how that afterward, when he would have inherited the blessing, he was rejected: for he found no place of repentance, though he sought it carefully with tears." This is a picture of the corruptness of the old nature.

On the other hand, Jacob sought the things of God, especially the birthright. True, he went after it in a carnal way, but when God had won over his carnality, he became "Israel"—a prince with God. Thus, Esau represents the old nature, and Jacob represents the new nature. These two are in constant conflict.

Other people also illustrate the two natures—for instance, Abraham's two sons Ishmael and Isaac. Ishmael was born after the flesh. God had promised Abraham many descendants, but after waiting for some time, Abraham had no son. Abraham's wife, Sarah, suggested an alternate plan. She gave her handmaid to Abraham, and a child, who was named Ishmael, was conceived and born. As long as Ishmael was alone in the house, there was no struggle, but when Isaac, the son of promise, was later born to Abraham and Sarah, conflict arose in the family. The New Testament comments concerning the conflict between these two sons: "But as then he that was born after the flesh persecuted him that was born after the Spirit, even so it is now" (Gal. 4:29). These two could not live in harmony together because one was born of a bondwoman and the other was born of a freewoman. God's solution is seen in His instructions to Abraham: "Cast out the bondwoman and her son: for the son of the bondwoman shall not be heir with the son of the freewoman" (v. 30).

The conflict of the two natures is also seen in the life of the Apostle Paul. After presenting the significant truths of Romans 5 and 6, Paul explained in Romans 7 the turmoil he went through as he struggled with the conflict between the desires of the new nature and the desires of the old nature. Paul constantly referred to himself in this chapter—personal pronouns occur many times. This reveals that he tried to solve his inner battle by relying on self. The Holy Spirit is not mentioned once in Romans 7.

However, in Romans 8 Paul presented victory in the Holy Spirit. The Holy Spirit is mentioned 19 times in this chapter. Read Romans 5—8 and notice the development within the chapters.

The two names given to Jacob also remind us of the two natures of the believer. Jacob was his name when he lived after the flesh. Later, when he began to live for God, his name was changed to Israel, which means "prince with God." A play on these names is made in Isaiah 9:8: "The Lord sends a message against Jacob, and it falls on Israel" (NASB). Inasmuch as Jacob's name was changed to Israel, his sons and their descendants became known as the children of Israel.

Pharaoh and Amalek are also a reminder of two different powers that influence the Christian's life. Pharaoh is a reminder of Satan, because he tried to keep the Israelites in slavery, just as Satan tries to keep people enslaved to sin. Amalek, on the other hand, is a reminder of the flesh, or old nature, for just as Amalek fought to keep Israel from victory, so the flesh seeks to keep the Christian from victory.

Pharaoh hindered Israel's deliverance from Egypt, and Amalek hindered Israel's progress once they were delivered from Egypt. Satan seeks to keep people in bondage and tries to prevent them from receiving Jesus Christ as Saviour. Once a person receives Christ as Saviour, however, the flesh opposes spiritual victory.

Two Aspects of Victory

Remember, Israel did not attack Amalek, Amalek attacked Israel. The new nature delights in God—it loves to commune with Him and to feed on His Word. But the old nature gives no peace to the believer. It robs him of joy and opposes everything that is of the Spirit. But when the flesh battles against the believer as Amalek fought against the Israelites, the Holy Spirit takes up the battle in behalf of the believer.

As Amalek attacked the Israelites, God revealed a means of victory for His people: "Moses said unto Joshua, Choose us out men, and go out, fight with Amalek: to morrow I will stand on the top of the hill with the rod of God in mine hand. So Joshua did as Moses had said to him, and fought with Amalek: and Moses, Aaron, and Hur went up to the top of the hill. And it came to pass, when Moses held up his hand, that Israel prevailed: and when he let down his hand, Amalek prevailed. But Moses' hands were heavy; and they took a stone, and put it under him, and he sat thereon; and Aaron and Hur stayed up his hands, the one on the one side, and the other on the other side; and his hands were steady until the going down of the sun. And Joshua discomfited [overwhelmed] Amalek and his people with the edge of the sword" (Ex. 17:9-13).

Israel's source of victory had two aspects—warfare and intercession. The warfare took place in the valley, which reminds us of the valley of everyday life. The real warfare takes place as we stand on the side of Christ against the downward pull of the old nature. We must determine to put our lives at His disposal for His use, and we must determine that our lives will be godly and pleasing to Him.

Joshua, the man of the Spirit, took his stand against the enemy. Amalek, an illustration of the flesh, took his stand against God's people.

The Christian life is one of warfare, but it is a spiritual warfare. Ephesians 6:12-18 tells of this spiritual warfare. Verse 17 tells believers, "Take the helmet of salvation, and the sword of the Spirit, which is the word of God." In addition to taking the armor of God, the believer is to be "praying always with all prayer and supplication in the Spirit, and watching thereunto with all perseverance and supplication for all saints" (v. 18). The two aspects of the spiritual warfare are evident—Joshua with the sword (of the Spirit, or the Word) and Moses with uplifted hands of intercession and prayer.

Although there was warfare between Amalek and the Israelites in the valley, the real battle was on the hilltop where Moses interceded. As long as Moses' hands were extended in prayer toward heaven, the Israelites had the advantage in the battle. But when his hands became heavy and were lowered, the battle went in favor of Amalek and his army.

The respective actions of Moses on the hilltop and Joshua in the valley revealed the provisions God has made for us to combat the flesh. We have the comfort of knowing that we are pronounced victorious and truly established as victors even before we enter the field of conflict. May we by faith approach the battle, singing the victor's song and appropriate the victory He has already won for us. The following verses tell of this victory: "But thanks be to God, which giveth us the victory through our Lord Jesus Christ" (I Cor. 15:57). "Now thanks be unto God, which always causeth us to triumph in Christ, and maketh manifest the savour of his knowledge by us in every place" (II Cor. 2:14). (See also Eph. 6:13 and Rom. 8:37.) How wonderful it is to realize that Jesus Christ provides all that we need to be victorious in spiritual warfare through the Holy Spirit.

Source of Victory

From the battle between Amalek and the Israelites we can learn many spiritual lessons. Amalek is a type of the old nature. The old nature is not eradicated when a person receives Christ as Saviour, but it is to be totally subjected. It is brought into subjection, just as Israel had victory over Amalek, through warfare and through intercessory prayer.

Joshua fought in the valley—a picture of the everyday warfare of the Christian life—while Moses interceded on the hilltop. Previously the Israelites had eaten the manna (the symbol of the Word of God) and had drunk the water from the rock (a symbol of the Holy Spirit). So, too, the believer must meditate on the Word of God and rely on the Spirit before he can expect spiritual victory.

As Joshua fought with Amalek and his men, he used the sword mightily. The Bible says, "Joshua discomfited Amalek and his people with the edge of the sword" (Ex. 17:13). Joshua's use of the sword is a reminder that the believer wins spiritual victories by using the sword of the Spirit. The Bible tells believers, "Take the helmet of salvation, the sword of the Spirit, which is the word of God" (Eph. 6:17). But while the believer is engaged in spiritual warfare, he is also to be "praying always with all prayer and supplication in the Spirit" (v. 18).

The combination of Moses' intercession on the hilltop and Joshua's fighting in the valley resulted in victory for the Israelites. They had to fight before they could be pronounced victors, whereas believers are already pronounced victors over sin because of what Jesus Christ accomplished for them. Their responsibility is to appropriate by faith the victory that Christ has made available to them. Ephesians 6:13 says, "Wherefore take unto you the whole armour of God, that ye may be able to withstand in the evil day, and having done all, to stand." This verse views the believer as being victorious in spiritual warfare, and he is to stand as a victor.

Romans 8:37 assures believers, "We are more than conquerors through him that loved us." Jesus has already won the battle for us, so we must realize that we are already victors and appropriate this victory by faith. If we do not realize that we are already victors, we will flounder in the Christian life as Paul did (see Rom. 7). When we realize, however, that victory has been provided and the Holy Spirit will enable us to participate in it, we will be able to say with Paul, "For the law of the Spirit of life in Christ Jesus hath made me free from the law of sin and death" (Rom. 8:2).

Appropriating Victory

However, the believer is not to be completely passive in spiritual warfare. Some think they are to do nothing but are to let God do everything. Victory does come from God, but He expects the believer to be involved in appropriating the victory. It is not sufficient that Moses interceded on the hilltop; Joshua had to be fighting down in the valley. So also, Galatians 5:16 tells believers, "Walk in the Spirit, and ye shall not fulfil the lust of the flesh." God provides, but man must appropriate the victory—he must go out and get it.

It is a principle with God that although He foreordains victory for His own, He requires that they appropriate the victory. For instance, He had promised the Israelites the land of Canaan, but they had to actually go into the land and take it for themselves. God said to Joshua, "Every place that the sole of your foot shall tread upon, that have I given unto you, as I said unto Moses" (Josh. 1:3). God had given the land to the Israelites, but they had to go in and possess it.

This principle of faith is seen in the battle between the Israelites and Amalek and his people. Both elements are stated in Exodus 17:10: "So Joshua did as Moses had said to him, and fought with Amalek: and Moses, Aaron, and Hur went up to the top of the hill." Actual combat along with intercessory prayer brought victory for Israel.

As long as Moses' hands were extended to heaven in intercession, the Israelites experienced victory in the valley. But when his arms became tired and his hands lowered, the battle went against the Israelites. Verse 12 reveals how Moses was helped in this matter: "But Moses' hands were heavy; and they took a stone, and put it under him, and he sat thereon; and Aaron and Hur stayed up his hands, the one on the one side, and the other on the other side; and his hands were steady until the going down of the sun."

Although in this particular instance Moses' hands were extended to heaven, this is not necessarily the posture one should always assume in praying. This was a common posture throughout Bible times, but the important matter in praying is one's heart attitude, not his physical posture. This incident in the life of Israel was for the purpose of teaching them that the victory belonged to God alone. They were not to glory in their own numbers and strength but were to glory in God.

Joshua and Moses illustrate what the believer is to do in spiritual warfare. Joshua is a picture of a Spirit-filled man who fights in the front-line attack. He used the sword just as the believer should use the sword of the Spirit. But fighting alone is not enough; there must be intercessory prayer. Moses is a picture of the Spirit-filled man who is on good praying terms with God.

Satan's Opposition

Satan opposes praying, so he will oppose the praying person first and foremost. Satan realizes that prayer is the key to total victory. The real battle between Israel and Amalek took place on the hilltop as Moses interceded for Israel. His arms became tired, and it's also possible for the believer to grow weary in the battle of intercession. On some days it seems so hard for the believer to spend time in prayer. Satan can do many things to disturb our prayer life, and if he can keep us from praying, he certainly will, since he knows that is how spiritual battles are won.

Although we grow weary in the battle of supplication, Luke 18:1 exhorts us, "Men ought always to pray, and not to faint." We tire so easily in the serious business of intercessory prayer. And remember, it was no different when Jesus was on earth with the disciples. As He was contemplating going to the cross, He left His disciples in one spot while He moved a little distance away from them to talk to His heavenly Father. When He returned to the disciples, Jesus found them asleep. He said to them, "Could ye not watch with me one hour? Watch and pray, that ye enter not into temptation: the spirit indeed is willing, but the flesh is weak" (Matt. 26:40,41).

Notice that it was a battle between the Spirit and the flesh—"the spirit indeed is willing, but the flesh is weak" (v. 41). This is the same battle mentioned in Galatians 5:17: "For the flesh lusteth against the Spirit, and the Spirit against the flesh: and these are contrary the one to the other." Because of the seriousness of the spiritual battle, believers are told, "Pray without ceasing" (I Thess. 5:17). This is the way spiritual battles are won, but we often sadly fail. Our hearts, our bodies and our minds grow weary so easily. Remember, as soon as we forsake our dependency on God, the flesh prevails.

But there is encouraging news concerning weariness in prayer. Moses became weary as he interceded for Israel, but Aaron and Hur willingly and ably helped him. Aaron was later established as the head of Israel's priesthood, so this incident speaks plainly of the high priest and his intercessory responsibilities. We, too, have a High Priest in the heavenlies who is making intercession for us—the Lord Jesus Christ. Hebrews 7:25 says of Him, "Wherefore he is able also to save them to the uttermost that come unto God by him, seeing he ever liveth to make intercession for them." So even while the believer is interceding for others, the Lord Jesus Christ is interceding for him. This gives us the spiritual strength we need as we pray and as we enter spiritual warfare.

Not only is the Lord Jesus Christ interceding for us, but also the Holy Spirit enables us to pray as we should. Hur, at Moses' side and supporting one of his arms, is a good illustration of this fact. Romans 8:26 says, "Likewise the Spirit also helpeth our infirmities: for we know not what we should pray for as we ought: but the Spirit itself maketh intercession for us with groanings which cannot be uttered." This reveals what the Holy Spirit does for us as He strives against the flesh (Gal. 5:17). Romans 8:27 says of the Holy Spirit, "He that searcheth the hearts knoweth what is the mind of the Spirit, because he maketh intercession for the saints according to the will of God." What an encouraging truth this is!

Every believer should be encouraged when he realizes that the Holy Spirit is helping him to pray as he should and that the Lord Jesus Christ is interceding in heaven before the Father. Jesus Christ especially intercedes for us when we sin. First John 2:1 says, "My little children, these things write I unto you, that ye sin not. And if any man sin, we have an advocate with the Father, Jesus Christ the righteous." Because of what the Lord Jesus Christ accomplished for us when He died on the cross, He is able to intercede in our behalf. The shedding of His blood paid the complete penalty for sin.

Prayer and God's Word

Joshua and his activity completes the typical picture of the battle array. Exodus 17:13 says, "Joshua discomfited Amalek and his people with the edge of the sword." This was accomplished because Moses was on the hilltop, assisted by Aaron and Hur as he interceded for Joshua and the Israelites.

We, too, can do battle against the old nature when we use the sword as Joshua did. Whereas Joshua used an actual sword, we are to use "the sword of the Spirit, which is the word of God" (Eph. 6:17). Our battle is primarily against the old nature, because Satan usually approaches us through the desires of our old nature. As we fortify ourselves with the Word of God and use the sword of the Spirit, we will have victory over the old nature.

Hebrews 4:12 reveals how effective the Word of God is: "For the word of God is quick [living], and powerful, and sharper than any twoedged sword, piercing even to the dividing asunder of soul and spirit, and of the joints and marrow, and is a discerner of the thoughts and intents of the heart." Thus, the Word of God is an effective weapon. So as we engage in spiritual warfare, we must remember that it is not by prayer alone and it is not by the use of the sword alone that we win spiritual battles. But by using both of these weapons together, we can experience victory.

It is important to have the Word of God stored in one's heart. The psalmist said, "Thy word have I hid in mine heart, that I might not sin against thee" (Ps. 119:11). The Word of God has a highly significant part in the things accomplished in each believer. Jesus told His followers, "Now ye are clean through the word which I have spoken unto you" (John 15:3). In His prayer to the heavenly Father, Jesus said, "Sanctify them through thy truth: thy word is truth" (17:17). God's Word is now available to us in written form. God reveals Himself to us in the Bible. If anyone wants to know Jesus Christ better, he must know the Bible better.

Through the Bible we learn of our position in Jesus Christ and what He accomplished for us when He died in our place. As we learn what Jesus Christ has done for us, we are then responsible to live accordingly. Proper doctrine determines proper living. Thus, Romans 6:3-6 reveals what we are to know; verse 11 reveals that we are to count on it by an act of faith; verses 12 and 13 reveal that we are to present ourselves to the Lord to carry out His will in us. This presentation of ourselves is a result of what we know and count on. This is all accomplished through the Holy Spirit. Romans 8:13 says, "For if ye live after the flesh, ye shall die: but if ye through the Spirit do mortify the deeds of the body, ye shall live." The Holy Spirit enables the believer to live in victory over sin as he puts the acts of flesh to death by saying no to sin and expecting the Holy Spirit to accomplish the victory.

Potential Victory

Remember that every believer has a sin nature as well as a new nature, so sin dwells in him, but it is not to reign supreme in his life. This is why Romans 6:12 says, "Let not sin therefore reign in your mortal body, that ye should obey it in the lusts thereof." And verse 14 adds, "For sin shall not have dominion over you: for ye are not under the law, but under grace." So while sin still dwells in the believer, it is not to reign in him.

Potential victory has been provided in Jesus Christ, but we must enter into the warfare and claim the victory for ourselves. This is done by an act of faith. The pastor who baptized me reminded me of an especially meaningful verse concerning this matter: "Fight the good fight of faith, lay hold on eternal life, whereunto thou art also called, and hast professed a good profession before many witnesses" (I Tim. 6:12). At the end of his life the Apostle Paul was able to say, "I have fought a good fight, I have finished my course, I have kept the faith" (II Tim. 4:7). Are you able to say that? You can be if you heed the instructions of Ephesians 6:11: "Put on the whole armour of God, that ye may be able to stand against the wiles of the devil."

In realizing the need for us to appropriate the victory Christ has provided, it is encouraging to see what Paul had to say. On the one hand he said, "O wretched man that I am! Who shall deliver me from the body of this death?" (Rom. 7:24). But on the other hand, he was able to triumphantly say, "I thank God through Jesus Christ our Lord" (v. 25). Paul realized that victory came by means of Jesus Christ.

Spiritual victory is possible for a believer as he knows Jesus Christ—the source of victory—and trusts Him. The Bible says, "Whatsoever is born of God overcometh the world: and this is the victory that overcometh the world, even our faith" (I John 5:4). By faith we trust Jesus Christ as personal Saviour, and this relationship with Him becomes the basis of spiritual victory as we believe Him for it. Thus, we can stand fearlessly against the Enemy. Faith is the victory—"Thanks be to God, which giveth us the victory through our Lord Jesus Christ" (I Cor. 15:57).

As Moses interceded for Joshua, who was battling Amalek in the valley, his "hands were heavy; and they took a stone, and put it under him, and he sat thereon; and Aaron and Hur stayed up his hands, the one on the one side, and the other on the other side; and his hands were steady until the going down of the sun" (Ex. 17:12).

Although Moses' arms wavered, we are not to waver in what we ask of the Lord. The Bible says, "If any of you lack wisdom, let him ask of God, that giveth to all men liberally, and upbraideth not; and it shall be given him. Let him ask in faith, nothing wavering. For he that wavereth is like a wave

of the sea driven with the wind and tossed. For let not that
man think that he shall receive any thing of the Lord" (James
1:5-7). In coming to the Lord, we are not to waver, but we
are to "believe that he is, and that he is a rewarder of them
that diligently seek him" (Heb. 11:6).

Whereas unsteady hands receive nothing, the promises of
God never produce unsteadiness. The Bible says, "Hast thou
not known? Hast thou not heard, that the everlasting God,
the Lord, the Creator of the ends of the earth, fainteth not,
neither is weary? There is no searching of his understanding.
He giveth power to the faint; and to them that have no might
he increaseth strength" (Isa. 40:28,29).

As Amalek fought against Joshua and the Israelites, God
made a final decree against him. Exodus 17:13-16 reveals
what was involved in this decree: "And Joshua discomfited
Amalek and his people with the edge of the sword. And the
Lord said unto Moses, Write this for a memorial in a book,
and rehearse it in the ears of Joshua: for I will utterly put out
the remembrance of Amalek from under heaven. And Moses
built an altar, and called the name of it Jehovah-nissi: for he
said: Because the Lord hath sworn that the Lord will have
war with Amalek from generation to generation."

Notice especially verse 16: "The Lord hath sworn that
the Lord will have war with Amalek from generation to
generation." In the Christian warfare, which is a segment of
the battle of the ages, there must be no compromise. We
cannot afford to spare the flesh, the old nature. Paul said, "I
know that in me (that is, in my flesh,) dwelleth no good
thing" (Rom. 7:18). Because there is nothing good in the old
nature, Paul told believers, "Put ye on the Lord Jesus Christ,
and make not provision for the flesh, to fulfil the lusts
thereof" (13:14).

Ultimatum Against the Flesh

God's decree against the flesh is one of death. Colossians
3:5-10 tells believers what God wants them to do concerning
the flesh, or old nature: "Mortify therefore your members
which are upon the earth; fornication, uncleanness,
inordinate affection, evil concupiscence, and covetousness,
which is idolatry: for which things' sake the wrath of God

cometh on the children of disobedience: in the which ye also walked some time, when ye lived in them. But now ye also put off all these; anger, wrath, malice, blasphemy, filthy communication out of your mouth. Lie not one to another, seeing that ye have put off the old man with his deeds; and have put on the new man, which is renewed in knowledge after the image of him that created him."

The old nature cannot be reformed, corrected or altered in any way. It is totally depraved; it can do nothing that pleases God. The Bible says, "The carnal mind is enmity against God: for it is not subject to the law of God, neither indeed can be" (Rom. 8:7).

Although God makes no attempt to change the old nature, He has made a way for the believer to have victory over it. God gives the Holy Spirit to us at the time of salvation, and by relying on Him, we experience victory over the desires of the old nature. Galatians 5:16,17 says, "Walk in the Spirit, and ye shall not fulfil the lust of the flesh. For the flesh lusteth against the Spirit, and the Spirit against the flesh: and these are contrary the one to the other: so that ye cannot do the things that ye would." So there is victory through the Holy Spirit as the believer yields to Him.

The Bible tells of the victory the believer can expect: "Thanks be unto God, which always causeth us to triumph in Christ" (II Cor. 2:14).

If you know Jesus Christ as Saviour, you can expect victory because "greater is he that is in you, than he that is in the world" (I John 4:4). The Holy Spirit is within the believer, and the Devil is in the world. But how wonderful it is to realize that the indwelling Holy Spirit gives us victory over the flesh and the Devil as we respond to His leading and enablement.

Strategy of the Old Nature

It is important that the believer know the strategy of the old nature. The old nature, or flesh, is deceptive, because Satan works through it to defeat the believer. Satan is very wise, and he knows how to work through the desires of the flesh to tantalize and tempt the Christian.

On one occasion Jesus told His disciples, "Watch and pray, that ye enter not into temptation: the spirit indeed is willing, but the flesh is weak" (Matt. 26:41).

There is an excellent analogy between the way the flesh operates and the way Amalek worked as he attacked Israel. Later, in Deuteronomy, Moses told the Israelites, "Remember what Amalek did unto thee by the way, when ye were come forth out of Egypt; how he met thee by the way, and smote the hindmost of thee, even all that were feeble behind thee, when thou wast faint and weary; and he feared not God" (Deut. 25:17,18).

Notice the way Amalek attacked—he attacked from behind when the people were at their weakest. Amalek's method of attacking is also mentioned in I Samuel 15:2: "Thus saith the Lord of hosts, I remember that which Amalek did to Israel, how he laid wait for him in the way, when he came up from Egypt."

Satan works through the flesh to attack the believer in the same way. He sneaks up on the believer and attacks when he is at his weakest point. This is why the Bible says, "Be sober, be vigilant; because your adversary the devil, as a roaring lion, walketh about, seeking whom he may devour: whom resist stedfast in the faith" (I Pet. 5:8,9). These words of warning should alert believers to the deceitfulness of Satan.

But even though we grow weary and occasionally drop our guard, the Bible says, "Hast thou not known? Hast thou not heard, that the everlasting God, the Lord, the Creator of the ends of the earth, fainteth not, neither is weary? There is no searching of his understanding. He giveth power to the faint; and to them that have no might he increaseth strength. Even the youths shall faint and be weary, and the young men shall utterly fall: but they that wait upon the Lord shall renew their strength; they shall mount up with wings as eagles; they shall run, and not be weary; and they shall walk, and not faint" (Isa. 40:28-31). This is the victory God promises each believer. How wonderful it is to realize that God even now gives complete victory over Satan (Heb. 2:14) and will eventually completely destroy Satan and all of his forces.

Final Victory

After Joshua had defeated Amalek and his people by means of Moses' intercessory prayer on the hilltop, the Lord said to Moses, "Write this for a memorial in a book, and rehearse it in the ears of Joshua: for I will utterly put out the remembrance of Amalek from under heaven" (Ex. 17:14). Although Amalek would eventually be blotted out, Israel had to contend with him and his descendants for many, many years. So, too, even though the believer will eventually be delivered from the presence of sin, he must contend with the sin nature as long as he lives in his body of flesh.

Paul referred to his expectation of being delivered from the presence of sin when he said, "We ourselves groan within ourselves, waiting for the adoption, to wit, the redemption of our body" (Rom. 8:23). Philippians 3:21 says that Jesus Christ "shall change our vile body, that it may be fashioned like unto his glorious body, according to the working whereby he is able even to subdue all things unto himself." When our body experiences this change, we will be delivered from the presence of sin.

That every believer will someday receive a glorified body is also mentioned in I Corinthians 15:51-58. Verses 51 and 52 say, "Behold, I shew you a mystery; We shall not all sleep, but we shall all be changed, in a moment, in the twinkling of an eye, at the last trump: for the trumpet shall sound, and the dead shall be raised incorruptible, and we shall be changed." This refers to the time when Jesus Christ will appear in the air and catch away believers from the earth. Believers who have already died by that time will be raised first, then living believers will be caught up to meet the Lord (I Thess. 4:16,17).

Considering this time of victory, the Apostle Paul said, "O death, where is thy sting? O grave, where is thy victory?" (I Cor. 15:55). Because of the blessed hope of the complete triumph over sin, Paul said, "Therefore, my beloved brethren, be ye stedfast, unmoveable, always abounding in the work of the Lord, forasmuch as ye know that your labour is not in vain in the Lord" (v. 58). So remember, we can have victory over sin's dominion now, but we also have the glorious hope of deliverance from its presence at His coming. Can you say hallelujah because of this?

After God instructed Moses to write a memorial in a book concerning Amalek, Moses built an altar and called it "Jehovah-nissi" (Ex. 17:15). This reveals the confident assurance Moses had of God's ultimate victory over Amalek and his people. The name Moses gave the altar literally means "the Lord our banner." Moses was standing firm in the might and power of God over Amalek.

The New Testament tells believers, "Be strong in the Lord, and in the power of his might" (Eph. 6:10). Just like Moses, we are to realize that victory is certain because God is all powerful. Even now we can rejoice and praise God for the ultimate victory over the flesh which will occur when we receive glorified bodies (Phil. 3:20,21).

But as long as we are in this life, we need to be reminded of the tragedy of sparing the flesh. We learn this lesson from the way Saul spared Amalek, as recorded in I Samuel 15. God had told Saul to completely destroy all of the Amalekites and their livestock because of the way they had treated Israel, "but Saul and the people spared Agag, and the best of the sheep, and of the oxen, and of the fatlings, and the lambs, and all that was good, and would not utterly destroy them: but every thing that was vile and refuse, that they destroyed utterly" (v. 9).

When Saul was confronted by Samuel for his disobedience, Saul tried to blame the people. Saul said, "But the people took of the spoil, sheep and oxen, the chief of the things which should have been utterly destroyed, to sacrifice unto the Lord thy God in Gilgal" (v. 21). Think of it! Saul was trying to cover up his disobedience by claiming that his motive was the worship of God. However, Samuel clearly made known to Saul God's attitude about such disobedience: "Hath the Lord as great delight in burnt-offerings and sacrifices, as in obeying the voice of the Lord? Behold, to obey is better than sacrifice, and to hearken than the fat of rams" (v. 22).

Because of Saul's incomplete obedience, the Amalekites troubled him to his dying day. In fact, an Amalekite had a part in Saul's death.

Let us not spare the flesh and the works of the flesh, but rather by the Holy Spirit let us put to death everything that has to do with the old nature. This is the only way of victory for the child of God.

Chapter 14

Delegating Responsibility

God always works through people. When He has a job to do, He calls a person to do it. That is exactly what He did in leading the nation of Israel. For the gigantic task of leading Israel from Egypt to Canaan, God called Moses at the burning bush (Ex. 3).

Advice From Jethro

God prepared and strengthened Moses for this enormous responsibility—God always gives a person the ability he needs to perform the task He calls that individual to do. As Moses led the Israelites through the wilderness, however, he became burdened with the heavy responsibility of leadership. When Moses' father-in-law came to visit him in the wilderness, he observed that Moses spent a whole day deciding small and great matters for the people. "Moses sat to judge the people: and the people stood by Moses from the morning unto the evening" (18:13). When he saw this, Moses' father-in-law asked him why he was doing all of this by himself and why the people were standing from morning until evening (v. 14). Moses explained that they were bringing their problems to him so he could make decisions for them and teach the people God's laws (v. 16).

Moses' father-in-law said to him, "The thing that thou doest is not good. Thou wilt surely wear away, both thou, and this people that is with thee: for this thing is too heavy for thee; thou art not able to perform it thyself alone" (vv. 17,18).

144

Moses' father-in-law then explained what he thought was a much better method of administration: "I will give thee counsel, and God shall be with thee: Be thou for the people to God-ward, that thou mayest bring the causes unto God: and thou shalt teach them ordinances and laws, and shalt shew them the way wherein they must walk, and the work that they must do" (vv. 19,20). The suggestions of Jethro retained for Moses the position of representing God to the people and of teaching the people God's laws and ordinances.

But Jethro had still other suggestions concerning how Moses could relieve himself of the heavy responsibility: "Moreover thou shalt provide out of all the people able men, such as fear God, men of truth, hating covetousness; and place such over them, to be rulers of thousands, and rulers of hundreds, rulers of fifties, and rulers of tens: and let them judge the people at all seasons: and it shall be, that every great matter they shall bring unto thee, but every small matter they shall judge: so shall it be easier for thyself, and they shall bear the burden with thee" (vv. 21,22). Thus, Jethro suggested that Moses delegate responsibility to qualified men who feared God.

Jethro continued, "If thou shalt do this thing, and God command thee so, then thou shalt be able to endure, and all this people shall also go to their place in peace" (v. 23). So the suggestions of Jethro were intended to relieve the heavy burden that was on Moses personally and, at the same time, to make sure that the people had someone to help them make wise, godly decisions.

Some think that the suggestions of Jethro were of the flesh. However, Jethro emphasized that Moses should determine the Lord's will before accepting his suggestions. Jethro said, "I will give thee counsel, and God shall be with thee" (v. 19); "If thou shalt do this thing, and God command thee so" (v. 23). So Jethro was well aware that Moses should not adopt his suggestions unless God directed him to do so. Thus, the advice of Jethro seems to have been given in the right spirit; he was used of God to wisely advise Moses.

Do you wonder what Moses thought when Jethro suggested that he give up some of his responsibility? Most of us have the tendency to hold on to responsibility rather than to delegate it to others. One of the lessons I had to learn in the Back to the Bible ministry was the need to delegate responsibility as the ministry grew beyond what I could do personally. This was not an easy lesson to learn. Over the years God had to use various methods and individuals to help me face this need. I will never forget the day when this lesson was driven home to me in an especially pointed way. Our organization was small at the time, with only eight or ten employees. The work responsibility was very heavy on me personally. At that time a certain person told me, "Mr. Epp, there's just one problem with you; you can't let go of anything."

Inwardly, I reacted against that remark, but as I went to the Lord concerning it, He made clear to me that this person was speaking the truth. God had used this young person to reveal something about myself that I desperately needed to see.

Advice can be misleading, however. So it is the responsibility of every person receiving advice to go to the Lord for guidance and direction. This was Moses' responsibility, and it is what Jethro expected him to do.

Principles of Leadership

As I have studied the Word of God concerning leadership, I have come to certain conclusions about spiritual principles of good leadership. These principles can be applied not only by leaders of organizations but by Sunday school teachers or by anyone with responsibility.

First, God uses people to do His work. When He has a job to do, He calls an individual to do it. We have seen this in our study of Moses, and I am sure you have also seen it in your own experience and observation. Remember, however, that it took Moses a long time to become prepared for his task, and it sometimes takes leaders today a long time to be prepared for their tasks.

Second, when the task becomes too much for the one person God originally called, He calls others to work with the first individual. This principle is illustrated over and over again in the Word of God.

Third, God holds the first individual responsible for the work done by the other individuals. This principle applies

especially to the spiritual aspects of the work. This principle
was particularly evident in Moses' leadership. Even though
responsibility and authority could be delegated to others, he
was still directly responsible before God. Jethro said to him,
"Be thou for the people to God-ward, that thou mayest bring
the causes unto God" (Ex. 18:19). Another translation
renders this verse: "You be the people's representative before
God, and you bring the disputes to God" (NASB). Literally,
this portion reads: "You be for the people in front of God."

Even though Moses could delegate much of his
responsibility and authority, he could not delegate this
primary responsibility of spiritual leadership.

Moses accepted Jethro's advice; he "hearkened to the
voice of his father in law, and did all that he had said. And
Moses chose able men out of all Israel, and made them heads
over the people, rulers of thousands, rulers of hundreds,
rulers of fifties, and rulers of tens. And they judged the
people at all seasons: the hard causes they brought unto
Moses, but every small matter they judged themselves"
(vv. 24-26).

Examples of Delegation

In a parallel passage where Moses revealed to God his
weariness and inability to take care of all of the
responsibilities, he was admonished to delegate responsibility
to 70 men (Num. 11). Verse 25 says, "The Lord came down
in a cloud, and spake unto him, and took of the spirit that
was upon him, and gave it unto the seventy elders: and it
came to pass, that, when the spirit rested upon them, they
prophesied, and did not cease." Some say that there was no
more power than before, just more machinery. But this
viewpoint does not seem to be realistic or even scriptural.

Jesus Himself chose 12 men, and later He chose others,
like Paul, to carry on His work. And even Paul was given the
right to choose others to assist him.

So I cannot agree with those who think that there was a
diminishing of the Spirit that rested on Moses, for it is very
difficult to think of the Spirit's being subdivided. You cannot
draw the Spirit from one man and divide Him among others
as you draw water and divide it among several containers. So

the indication is that Numbers 11:25 refers to taking the same Spirit which was on Moses, and putting Him on the 70 others. Just as a flame of fire increases as it reaches out and engulfs more objects, so the Holy Spirit is made more effective by His extension to other lives.

In the Exodus account Moses accepted the advice of his father-in-law, appointed qualified men for the responsibility, and became an even greater mediator between God and the people. This is evident as we study the rest of Moses' life. Whenever the people murmured or whenever God's judgment fell on the people, Moses interceded mightily. As the mediator, Moses received the Law and communicated it to the people. In his responsibility of spiritual leadership, the Book of Deuteronomy records how he rehearsed for the younger generation the faithfulness of God to their fathers in the wilderness. Moses wanted to make sure that they did not forget God's faithfulness when they entered the Promised Land.

The New Testament also reveals principles for spiritual leadership. When the physical needs of some were neglected, the apostles realized they could not take on this kind of responsibility and still remain faithful to prayer and the study of the Word. So the apostles instructed, "It is not reason [desirable] that we should leave the word of God, and serve tables. Wherefore, brethren, look ye out among you seven men of honest report, full of the Holy Ghost and wisdom, whom we may appoint over this business. But we will give ourselves continually to prayer, and to the ministry of the word" (Acts 6:2-4). No one can do everything, so those who have the responsibility of prayer and the ministry of the Word must delegate the responsibility of other important matters to qualified, Spirit-filled people.

The following is a good motto: "If you cannot learn to delegate, your ministry will never become larger than that which you are able to dominate."

God knows what work He wants accomplished, and He gives individuals responsibilities in order to accomplish that work. The only way that God's work can be done effectively is for individual believers to know what God wants them to do.

Holy Spirit's Sovereignty

In studying the Scriptures concerning God's work, we learn that the primary work being done today has to do with the building of the Church. Jesus Christ said, "I will build my church; and the gates of hell shall not prevail against it" (Matt. 16:18). However, the Holy Spirit has been delegated the responsibility of directing the work of building the Church. Before the Lord Jesus ascended to heaven, He told the disciples that He would send the Holy Spirit (John 14:16; 16:7). The Holy Spirit has been given absolute sovereignty in choosing the individuals and distributing gifts to accomplish God's work.

First Corinthians 12 tells of the spiritual gifts given by the Holy Spirit to believers so that the Body of Christ may fulfill its purpose on earth. Verse 7 indicates that every believer has a spiritual gift: "The manifestation of the Spirit is given to every man to profit withal." Verse 11 reveals that these gifts are given, not as an individual might desire, but as the Holy Spirit desires: "All these worketh that one and the selfsame Spirit, dividing to every man severally as he will." Each believer has a particular work to perform within the Body of Christ. Verse 18 says, "But now hath God set the members every one of them in the body, as it hath pleased him." So we are not to serve our own desires but to discover what God wants us to do. Then we are to use our spiritual gift to benefit the Body of Christ.

Today, there is a great deal of emphasis on methods. When people are concerned about increasing the effectiveness of a given work, they usually look for better methods. However, God uses people. Instead of seeking better methods, He wants individuals who will do His will. The Lord Jesus Christ said, "Ye have not chosen me, but I have chosen you, and ordained you, that ye should go and bring forth fruit" (John 15:16).

Throughout the Scriptures we read of those who were chosen of God to accomplish His purpose. In the Old Testament we learn that He chose such men as Abraham, Isaac and Jacob to perform His distinctive purposes. In the New Testament men like the Apostle Paul were distinctly chosen of God to take the gospel to the Gentiles. But whoever the individual is, the Holy Spirit chooses him and equips him with the spiritual gift necessary to accomplish God's purpose. The gift the individual possesses is the sovereign choice of the Holy Spirit rather than a selection of the individual himself. Thus, we need to see that the Holy Spirit is absolutely sovereign in His administrative work of choosing men, giving gifts and placing individuals where He desires.

Chapter 15

The Giving of the Law

Exodus 19 and 20 record an event that was a great turning point in the life of Israel as well as all mankind. These chapters record the giving of the Law by God through Moses to the nation of Israel.

Time Elements

Exodus 19:1,2 says, "In the third month, when the children of Israel were gone forth out of the land of Egypt, the same day came they into the wilderness of Sinai. For they were departed from Rephidim, and were come to the desert of Sinai, and had pitched in the wilderness; and there Israel camped before the mount."

God fulfilled His promise to Moses. When God had called Moses at the burning bush in the wilderness of Sinai, He said, "I will be with thee; and this shall be a token unto thee, that I have sent thee: When thou hast brought forth the people out of Egypt, ye shall serve God upon this mountain" (3:12). Moses and the Israelites were now at Mount Sinai, thus fulfilling God's promise to him.

Notice three specific time elements mentioned in the Bible concerning Israel at Mount Sinai. Exodus 19:1 says, "In the third month, when the children of Israel were gone forth out of the land of Egypt, the same day came they into the wilderness of Sinai." This was the beginning of the third month; it had taken them two months to reach this spot from the time they left Egypt.

Numbers 1:1 says, "The Lord spake unto Moses in the wilderness of Sinai, in the tabernacle of the congregation, on the first day of the second month, in the second year after they were come out of the land of Egypt." At this time the Lord told Moses to number the people in preparation for leaving Mount Sinai. By comparing the time elements, we find that the Israelites were at Mount Sinai 11 months. During that time God gave the Law, and they built the tabernacle according to His instructions.

But after leaving Mount Sinai and coming to Kadesh-barnea, the people refused to enter the land. They failed God completely. Thus, they wandered in the wilderness for another 38 years. At the end of that time they again found themselves at Mount Sinai with God's giving them instructions to enter the land. "It came to pass in the fortieth year, in the eleventh month, on the first day of the month, that Moses spake unto the children of Israel, according unto all that the Lord had given him in commandment unto them . . . saying, The Lord our God spake unto us in Horeb, saying, Ye have dwelt long enough in this mount: turn you, and take your journey, and go to the mount of the Amorites, and unto all the places nigh thereunto, in the plain, in the hills, and in the vale, and in the south, and by the sea side, to the land of the Canaanites, and unto Lebanon, unto the great river, the river Euphrates" (Deut. 1:3,5-7). These references in Exodus, Numbers and Deuteronomy make it clear that Mount Sinai figured prominently in the life of Israel during the 40 years it took them to go from Egypt to Canaan.

At Mount Sinai the covenant by which God would deal with them for about the next 1500 years was given. In other words, this covenant remained in effect until the Lord Jesus Christ was crucified at Calvary, thus changing the order of God's dealings with mankind.

At Sinai, at the beginning of the third month after the Israelites had left Egypt, God gave the people a wondrous manifestation of Himself as He gave them a new covenant. Think of God's true revelation in comparison with some of the revelations which have been claimed by various religious groups. Claims are often made by those who have nothing tangible to prove their claims, but God made sure that the Israelites knew absolutely that His revelation was true. Those who claim to have found stones and yet have no stones to offer for inspection are highly suspect. Others base their so-called revelation on dreams or visions. But God erased all questions as to the truth of His revelation to Israel.

Contrasting Covenants

Note the contrast between the covenant God made with Abraham and the covenant He made with Israel through Moses. The covenant with Abraham was an unconditional covenant—God promised to fulfill it regardless of the circumstances. It was based on God's eternal purpose and did not depend on man's behavior at all.

Genesis 12:1-3 records the Abrahamic covenant: "Now the Lord had said unto Abram, Get thee out of thy country, and from thy kindred, and from thy father's house, unto a land that I will shew thee: and I will make of thee a great nation, and I will bless thee, and make thy name great; and thou shalt be a blessing: and I will bless them that bless thee, and curse him that curseth thee: and in thee shall all families of the earth be blessed."

The Abrahamic covenant contained seven promises but not one condition. This covenant was confirmed later in Genesis 17:6-8: "I will make thee exceeding fruitful, and I will make nations of thee, and kings shall come out of thee. And I will establish my covenant between me and thee and thy seed after thee in their generations for an everlasting covenant, to be a God unto thee, and to thy seed after thee. And I will give unto thee, and to thy seed after thee, the land wherein thou art a stranger, all the land of Canaan, for an everlasting possession; and I will be their God." The covenant was not only confirmed but was also made everlasting.

God's covenant with Abraham was an unconditional one, but His covenant with Israel through Moses was a conditional one. God promised great benefits if the Israelites met the conditions. Personal and temporal blessings depended entirely on their behavior, based on the covenant of the Law. However, this Mosaic covenant in no way altered the plan and purpose of God as revealed in the Abrahamic covenant. The Abrahamic covenant was unconditional and will remain unchanged until it is completely fulfilled after the Second Coming of Christ. The Mosaic covenant was conditional and was fulfilled by Christ at His first coming.

When Jesus Christ was on earth, He said, "Think not that I am come to destroy the law, or the prophets: I am not come to destroy, but to fulfil. For verily I say unto you, Till heaven and earth pass, one jot or one tittle shall in no wise pass from the law, till all be fulfilled" (Matt. 5:17,18). Galatians 3:19 reveals how long the Mosaic covenant would be in force: "Wherefore then serveth the law? It was added because of transgressions, till the seed should come to whom the promise was made; and it was ordained by angels in the hand of a mediator." Note that "it was added because of transgressions, till the seed should come to whom the promise was made." This was fulfilled at the first coming of Christ.

At Sinai God's dealings with the Israelites changed completely. Up until this time, God had led the people from Egypt to Sinai on the basis of His unconditional covenant with Abraham. At Sinai God told the people, "Ye have seen what I did unto the Egyptians, and how I bare you on eagles' wings, and brought you unto myself" (Ex. 19:4).

As God led the people on the basis of the Abrahamic covenant during the first two months after they left Egypt, He did not in any way judge them because of their murmurings. They had witnessed the plagues in Egypt, they had seen God's display of power at the Red Sea, they had experienced the guidance of the pillar of cloud and the pillar of fire, they had witnessed God's grace in providing manna and water, and they had won victory over Amalek and his people. Certainly God had borne them on eagles' wings, for He had taken care of all their needs even though they were grumbling and complaining much of the time. Even though the people were unfaithful, God was faithful to His promises; He never denies Himself (II Tim. 2:13). God was faithful to the promises He made to Abraham and to his seed.

That God was being faithful to His promise to Abraham is clear from what the Bible says concerning His attitude toward Israel while they were still in Egypt. Exodus 2:24 says, "God heard their groaning, and God remembered his covenant with Abraham, with Isaac, and with Jacob." In response to this covenant, God intervened to deliver the Israelites from Egypt—not because of any actions of the Israelites but because He was faithful to His unconditional covenant with Abraham. Psalm 105 tells of the many things God did for Israel in delivering them from Egypt, and the basis of all of these provisions is stated in verse 42: "For he remembered his holy promise, and Abraham his servant."

But at Sinai God began to deal with the Israelites on a different basis. The conditions involved in God's dealings with the Israelites are seen in Exodus 19:5,6: "Now therefore, if ye will obey my voice indeed, and keep my covenant, then ye shall be a peculiar treasure unto me above all people: for all the earth is mine: and ye shall be unto me a kingdom of priests, and an holy nation." This is what God instructed Moses to communicate to the Israelites. The conditions of the covenant are expressed in the words, "if ye will obey my voice indeed, and keep my covenant" (v. 5).

This reference was not to the Abrahamic covenant because there were no conditions attached to it. In fact, on the basis of the Abrahamic covenant God is fulfilling and will continue to fulfill His sovereign plan to eventually regather the nation of Israel in Palestine and fully establish them as a nation that will inherit the land. But at Sinai God added another covenant between Himself and Israel which involved conditions. Israel was required to meet the conditions if they were to expect the blessings connected with that covenant.

Unanimous Acceptance

At Sinai Israel overwhelmingly accepted God's proposal to enter into the legal covenant. The people were in unanimous agreement and said, "All that the Lord hath spoken we will do" (v. 8). After God had revealed His high standards to the Israelites through the Law, they said again, "All that the Lord hath said will we do, and be obedient" (24:7). This covenant was then confirmed and ratified by blood.

Later, when the Israelites entered Canaan, they were under the Mosaic covenant. But from Mount Sinai onward, because the people were bound by a conditional covenant, God dealt with them by chastening them whenever they failed, as they did at Kadesh-barnea. Also, after the people had entered the land of Canaan, God dealt with them there on the basis of the Mosaic covenant. He allowed persecution,

and later He even permitted the people to be expelled from
the land for disobedience.

Grace and Good Works

Just as there were two covenants for Israel, there are two
different aspects of God's relationship with the believer.
Concerning salvation, God's relationship with the believer is
one entirely of grace. An unregenerate person can do absolutely nothing that merits standing before God. Salvation is
totally of grace. Ephesians 2:8,9 says, "For by grace are ye
saved through faith; and that not of yourselves: it is the gift
of God: not of works, lest any man should boast." But one
should not stop reading at verse 9, because verse 10 gives the
second aspect of God's relationship with a believer. This
aspect involves the works produced after salvation. Verse 10
says, "For we are his workmanship, created in Christ Jesus
unto good works, which God hath before ordained that we
should walk in them."

Although a person receives salvation entirely by grace
through faith in Jesus Christ, it is God's purpose that he
produce good works after salvation, which He rewards
accordingly.

These two aspects of God's relationship to the believer
are also seen in Romans 5. Salvation by grace through faith is
seen in verses 8 and 9: "But God commendeth his love
toward us, in that, while we were yet sinners, Christ died for
us. Much more then, being now justified by his blood, we
shall be saved from wrath through him." We did not deserve
God's love—we were still sinners when He died for us.

The aspects of grace extended for salvation and the
intention of God that a believer's life produce good works is
seen in verse 10: "For if, when we were enemies, we were
reconciled to God by the death of his Son, much more, being
reconciled, we shall be saved by his life." Concerning salvation, we can do nothing except believe in what Jesus Christ
has done for us. But after receiving Christ as Saviour, we are
to produce good works by allowing Christ to live in us.

The two aspects of grace for salvation and the producing
of works after salvation are also seen in I Corinthians 3.
Salvation is seen in the foundation referred to in verse 11:

"For other foundation can no man lay than that is laid, which is Jesus Christ." The producing of works after salvation and the rewarding of such works are emphasized in verses 12-15: "Now if any man build upon this foundation gold, silver, precious stones, wood, hay, stubble; every man's work shall be made manifest: for the day shall declare it, because it shall be revealed by fire; and the fire shall try every man's work of what sort it is. If any man's work shall be burned, he shall suffer loss: but he himself shall be saved; yet so as by fire."

Why is such a person saved even though he produces no good work to be rewarded? It is because a person's salvation does not depend on good works but on the grace of God. Any person who realizes his need and trusts Jesus Christ as personal Saviour is a child of God, regardless of the amount of good works he produces later. However, where there are no good works, God chastens the believer so that he will produce those things which honor Him.

Philippians 2 tells how good works are to be produced in the life of a believer. Verses 12,13 say, "Wherefore, my beloved, as ye have always obeyed, not as in my presence only, but now much more in my absence, work out your own salvation with fear and trembling. For it is God which worketh in you both to will and to do of his good pleasure." Notice that this passage does not say an individual is to work for his salvation, but he is to work out his salvation. Before a person can work out his salvation, he must already have salvation. The one who has trusted Jesus Christ as personal Saviour has salvation; therefore, he has the Lord Jesus Christ living within him. The believer produces good works as he allows the Lord Jesus Christ to work out His life through him.

Transition Periods

It is commonly taught that a new dispensation began at Mount Sinai. However, the distinctiveness of Israel as a nation actually began on the Passover night in Egypt. In most of the dispensations there is an overlapping from one to the other—a transition period. This is true in this case also. Although the Law was given to the Israelites at Mount Sinai, the people had actually become a nation two months earlier in Egypt. Up until that time they had been a multitude of disorganized slaves, but they became an organized nation led by God Himself through His servant Moses.

On the Passover night for the first time the people were called an "assembly" (Ex. 12:6), and their calendar was dated from that time forward by divine order (v. 2).

Before the Law was actually given on Mount Sinai, the people were not without a covenant; they still had the unconditional covenant made with Abraham. But, as recorded in Exodus 19 and 20, the Mosaic covenant came into operation and specifically concerned Israel. So there was a transition period of about two months from the time they became a nation in Egypt until they actually received the Law at Mount Sinai.

The Dispensation of Grace, the present dispensation, was also marked by a transition period. When Jesus Christ died on the cross, He made it possible for every person to have immediate access to God. At His crucifixion, the veil of the temple was torn from top to bottom, and the Book of Hebrews says, "Having therefore, brethren, boldness to enter into the holiest by the blood of Jesus, by a new and living way, which he hath consecrated for us, through the veil, that is to say, his flesh" (10:19,20). But even though Jesus Christ ended the Dispensation of the Law when He died on the cross, it was not until 50 days later, on the Day of Pentecost, that the Holy Spirit came to indwell every believer, thereby marking the official opening of the new dispensation. So there was a transition period of at least 50 days between those two dispensations.

The Mediator and the Message

At Mount Sinai Moses was established by God as the mediator of a new revelation from Him. Because God is holy, He could not enter into direct communication with the sinful nation of Israel, but He worked through a mediator. Moses was God's special vessel whom He used for this occasion. Therefore, Moses needed to receive special credentials to establish confidence with the people that he was indeed God's spokesman to them.

Many false religions have arisen with claims about dreams revealed to certain people or concerning tablets and other objects that have been found. Yet, when these claims are investigated, no hard evidence can be found to indicate that God revealed Himself in such a way to them.

God saw to it that the Israelites would know for sure that what He was revealing to them through Moses was really of Him. Thus, God spoke audibly with Moses, and the people heard God speaking on the mountain. This established Moses' credentials, proving that he was indeed the mediator between God and the people. God said to Moses, "I come unto thee in a thick cloud, that the people may hear when I speak with thee, and believe thee for ever" (Ex. 19:9).

We see from the Bible that God provided credentials concerning Himself through Jesus Christ. John 1:14 says of Christ, "The Word was made flesh, and dwelt among us, (and we beheld his glory, the glory as of the only begotten of the Father,) full of grace and truth." God saw to it that Jesus Christ was seen in person. What tremendous credentials for God Himself. God became flesh in the Person of Jesus Christ. Thus, Jesus was able to say, "He that hath seen me hath seen the Father" (14:9).

As God gave the Law to Israel, He spoke audibly from the mountaintop. The Bible says, "So Moses went down unto the people, and spake unto them" (Ex. 19:25). But notice that the following verse says, "And God spake all these words" (20:1). The audible voice of God was proof that Moses was the leader of Israel and that the Law had come directly from God.

Later, when Moses reviewed the history of Israel for the people, he said, "Ye came near and stood under the mountain; and the mountain burned with fire unto the midst of heaven, with darkness, clouds, and thick darkness. And the Lord spake unto you out of the midst of the fire: ye heard the voice of the words, but saw no similitude; only ye heard a voice. And he declared unto you his covenant, which he commanded you to perform, even ten commandments; and he wrote them upon two tables of stone" (Deut. 4:11-13).

Moses also told the people, "The Lord our God made a covenant with us in Horeb. . . . The Lord talked with you face to face in the mount out of the midst of the fire"

(5:2,4). But what was the peoples' reaction when they heard
the voice of God at Mount Sinai? Exodus 20:18 says, "And
all the people saw the thunderings, and the lightnings, and
the noise of the trumpet, and the mountain smoking: and
when the people saw it, they removed, and stood afar off."
These people were frightened because of all that was taking
place. They said to Moses, "Speak thou with us, and we will
hear: but let not God speak with us, lest we die" (v. 19).

Moses told the people, "Fear not: for God is come to
prove you, and that his fear may be before your faces, that
ye sin not" (v. 20). As the people stood a long way off,
Moses "drew near unto the thick darkness where God was"
(v. 21).

The Lord said to Moses, "Thus thou shalt say unto the
children of Israel, Ye have seen that I have talked with you
from heaven" (v. 22). Notice that the people heard God
speak from heaven. Their reaction was one of fear, and they
begged Moses to speak with them instead of God. Thus,
Moses was established before the people as the official
mediator between God and them. This is what God desired,
because He eventually spoke all of the Law through Moses.
However, God wanted the people to realize that the Law was
not some concoction of Moses himself, so He gave credentials
to establish Moses and the message before their eyes. As a
result, the people never doubted the true origin of the Law.

The purpose of God in all of this was alluded to earlier:
"The Lord said unto Moses, Lo, I come unto thee in a thick
cloud, that the people may hear when I speak with thee, and
believe thee for ever" (19:9). God wanted the people to hear
Him speaking audibly so they would not doubt the authority
of Moses as the mediator or the validity of the message.

A Way to Meet God

By giving the Law, God did not cease to deal with Israel
on the basis of grace and mercy, because He did provide a
way through which Israel could always meet Him—the
ceremonial law. So whereas God provided the Ten Commandments, which the people could not keep—although they said
that they would keep them—God also provided the ceremonial law by which they could approach Him. The people

were intensely aware of their inability to stand in the presence of God; thus, they "stood afar off" (Ex. 20:21). But in His mercy God provided an altar on which the Israelites could offer sacrifices so that they would be able to enter His presence (vv. 24-26).

Concerning the Law, the Scofield Reference Bible notes, "There is a threefold giving of the law. First, orally, in Ex. 20. 1-17. This was pure law, with no provision of priesthood and sacrifice for failure, and was accompanied by the 'judgments' (Ex. 21. 1-23. 13) relating to the relations of Hebrew with Hebrew; to which were added (Ex. 23. 14-19) directions for keeping three annual feasts, and (Ex. 23. 20-33) instructions for the conquest of Canaan. These *words* Moses communicated to the people (Ex. 24. 3-8). Immediately, in the persons of their elders, they were admitted to the fellowship of God (Ex. 24. 9-11). Second, Moses was then called up to receive the *tables* of stone (Ex. 24. 12-18). The story then divides. Moses, in the mount, receives the gracious instructions concerning the tabernacle, priesthood, and sacrifice (Ex. 25.-31.). Meantime (Ex. 32.), the people, led by Aaron, break the first commandment. Moses, returning, breaks the tables 'written with the finger of God' (Ex. 31. 18; 32. 16-19). Third, the *second* tables were made by Moses, and the law again written by the hand of Jehovah (Ex. 34. 1,28,29; Deut. 10. 4)" (p. 95).

Chapter 16

God Meets His People

In considering all that took place on Mount Sinai, we need to retrace some of the events and highlight some of the important details.

Requirements for Meeting God

As the people were being prepared to meet Him, God said to Moses, "Go unto the people, and sanctify them to day and to morrow, and let them wash their clothes, and be ready against the third day: for the third day the Lord will come down in the sight of all the people upon mount Sinai" (Ex. 19:10,11).

In addition to going through the process of cleansing before they could meet God, the people also had definite bounds set for them. God told Moses, "Thou shalt set bounds unto the people round about, saying, Take heed to yourselves, that ye go not up into the mount, or touch the border of it: whosoever toucheth the mount shall be surely put to death: there shall not an hand touch it, but he shall surely be stoned, or shot through; whether it be beast or man, it shall not live: when the trumpet soundeth long, they shall come up to the mount" (vv. 12,13).

All of this emphasized the contrast between the holiness of God and the sinfulness of man. God was unable to allow sinful men to come directly into His presence without a process of cleansing and the setting of definite limitations. But in the meeting He had with the people, God gave them the way of access to Himself.

Just as God revealed the way through which the Israelites could approach Him, so He has revealed a way by which we can approach Him. When Jesus Christ died on the cross in our place, this way was opened. Hebrews 10:19,20 says, "Having therefore, brethren, boldness to enter into the holiest by the blood of Jesus, by a new and living way, which he hath consecrated for us, through the veil, that is to say, his flesh." Through what Jesus Christ accomplished in His physical body on the cross, the way of access to God has been opened to all believers. Previously, the veil of the temple had kept the people away from the presence of God, but through His death Jesus Christ made access available to all.

In the case of the Israelites, death would come to anyone who even touched the mountain on which God revealed Himself. Such instructions emphasized the holiness of God to the people. Then they were really awed on the third day, for "there were thunders and lightnings, and a thick cloud upon the mount, and the voice of the trumpet exceeding loud; so that all the people that was in the camp trembled. And Moses brought forth the people out of the camp to meet with God; and they stood at the nether part of the mount. And mount Sinai was altogether on a smoke, because the Lord descended upon it in fire: and the smoke thereof ascended as the smoke of a furnace, and the whole mount quaked greatly. And when the voice of the trumpet sounded long, and waxed louder and louder, Moses spake, and God answered him by a voice" (Ex. 19:16-19).

The people were not to approach God until He revealed the way, and then they had to come in precisely that way. The people trembled, and it is certainly easy to understand why they were afraid of God, who is absolutely holy and who was giving instructions to them through Moses.

But notice God's purpose in all of this. Moses told the people, "Fear not: for God is come to prove you, and that his fear may be before your faces, that ye sin not" (20:20). In the light of all that happened at Mount Sinai, it is strange that some people today think they can come to God in any way they want. The way into God's presence has been made possible through the shedding of the blood of the Lord Jesus Christ. But some deny the effectiveness of Christ's shed blood and yet think that they can come into the presence of

God. Were it not for the shed blood of the Lord Jesus Christ, we would all remain in sin, for Hebrews 9:22 says, "Almost all things are by the law purged with blood; and without shedding of blood is no remission [forgiveness]." That more people do not die at the hands of God because of their blasphemous ideas is only because of the longsuffering and mercy of God.

Those today who think they have access to God without coming on the basis of the shed blood of Christ are not really entering into the presence of God, or they would be struck dead, just as God threatened to destroy any Israelite who came in a way not prescribed. God is holy; He is absolutely righteous. He cannot be approached except through Jesus Christ, who is the Mediator between God and man (I Tim. 2:5). Jesus Christ became man in order that He might open the way to God for all mankind. God wanted to impress on the Israelites, and He wants to impress on us, that no one can come into His presence unless He comes by the prescribed way. Jesus said in John 14:6, "I am the way, the truth, and the life: no man cometh unto the Father, but by me."

The Majesty of God

God's appearance to the Israelites was accompanied by thunder and lightening, a reminder that His judgments are sure and that His voice is fearful. No wonder the Israelites trembled as they "saw the thunderings, and the lightnings, and the noise of the trumpet, and the mountain smoking" (Ex. 20:18).

In considering the glory, majesty and power of God and the trembling that is caused by His presence, notice what Psalm 114 says: "When Israel went out of Egypt, the house of Jacob from a people of strange language; Judah was his sanctuary, and Israel his dominion. The sea saw it, and fled: Jordan was driven back. The mountains skipped like rams, and the little hills like lambs. What ailed thee, O thou sea, that thou fleddest? Thou Jordan, that thou wast driven back? Ye mountains, that ye skipped like rams; and ye little hills, like lambs? Tremble, thou earth, at the presence of the Lord, at the presence of the God of Jacob; which turned the rock into a standing water, the flint into a fountain of waters" (vv. 1-8).

Fire is referred to in the Bible as a symbol of God. It is awesome and causes people to fear because of its power to consume. The Book of Hebrews warns, "See that ye refuse not him that speaketh. For if they escaped not who refused him that spake on earth, much more shall not we escape, if we turn away from him that speaketh from heaven. . . . For our God is a consuming fire" (12:25,29). No wonder Hebrews 10:31 says, "It is a fearful thing to fall into the hands of the living God."

It is my personal desire, and it should be the desire of every Christian, to have a new and greater understanding of the holiness of God. It is only because of His grace that any of us are allowed to stand in His presence. No one is able to stand before Him on the basis of his own merits. But how terrible it would be to be totally beyond the benefits of God's presence. That is why hell will be so horrible; none of the benefits of His presence will be there. And remember, the ones who go to hell are those who try to enter God's presence on their own merits rather than on the merits of the shed blood of the Lord Jesus Christ.

God instructed the Israelites not to touch the mountain for the purpose of causing them to respect His holiness and to tremble before Him. Note that believers are told to work out their salvation "with fear and trembling" (Phil. 2:12). Remember, this verse does not apply to gaining salvation, because one must already have salvation before it can be worked out through his life. This verse is instructing believers how to live out the salvation which they have. Because of salvation, Jesus Christ lives within the believer, and He wants to express this salvation through the believer's life. The believer should fear and tremble lest he miss God's will in his daily walk.

The Israelites did not see the face of God or any likeness of Him on Mount Sinai. But the audible voice they heard provided evidence that He was there. So, too, we do not worship a God who is seen by the naked eye. True, Christ lived among men for a period of time, but He has gone to be with the Father.

That we walk by faith and not by sight is evident from II Corinthians 5:16: "Wherefore henceforth know we no man after the flesh: yea, though we have known Christ after the flesh, yet now henceforth know we him no more [after the flesh]." And Jesus told the woman at the well, "The hour cometh, and now is, when the true worshippers shall worship the Father in spirit and in truth: for the Father seeketh such to worship him. God is a Spirit: and they that worship him must worship him in spirit and in truth" (John 4:23,24).

As God was about to ratify the Mosaic covenant, He presented Himself to the people and demonstrated His holiness so that they would be aware of the absolute righteousness of the One with whom they were making the covenant. God wanted the people to fear and tremble so that they would understand that they could never stand in His presence on the basis of their own merits.

God wanted the people to be impressed with His holiness to the extent that they would not sin. This is evident from what Moses told the people: "God is come to prove you, and that his fear may be before your faces, that ye sin not" (Ex. 20:20). Moses later reminded the Israelites, "Ye said, Behold, the Lord our God hath shewed us his glory and his greatness, and we have heard his voice out of the midst of the fire: we have seen this day that God doth talk with man, and he liveth" (Deut. 5:24).

A view of God's majesty such as Israel saw at Sinai is the crying need of our day. The eye of faith needs to see Him not only as a loving Father but also as "the high and lofty One that inhabiteth eternity, whose name is Holy" (Isa. 57:15). We also need to think of God as did Daniel, who spoke of Him as "the great and dreadful God" (Dan. 9:4).

Concerning this matter, I would encourage you to meditate on Isaiah 40. Notice especially verses 15, 17 and 18: "Behold, the nations are as a drop of a bucket, and are counted as the small dust of the balance: behold, he taketh up the isles as a very little thing. . . . All the nations before him are as nothing; and they are counted to him less than nothing, and vanity. To whom then will ye liken God? Or what likeness will ye compare unto him?"

This God of the Old Testament is also the God of the New Testament. And be sure to note that He is also our God.

Therefore, we should reverence Him, obey Him, worship Him and serve Him with fear and trembling.

God's Absolute Monarchy

From their time in Egypt until they arrived at Mount Sinai, God dealt with the Israelites in marvelous grace. He had borne with them in tender patience and had supplied their every need. On the shores of the Red Sea the people declared that Jehovah was indeed their God and that He should reign forever.

Exodus 15 records the great song they sang as they worshiped and praised God. The people declared, "The Lord is my strength and song, and he is become my salvation: he is my God, and I will prepare him an habitation; my father's God, and I will exalt him. The Lord is a man of war: the Lord is his name" (vv. 2,3). As they marveled at God's majesty, they said, "Who is like unto thee, O Lord, among the gods? Who is like thee, glorious in holiness, fearful in praises, doing wonders? . . . Thou in thy mercy hast led forth the people which thou hast redeemed: thou hast guided them in thy strength unto thy holy habitation" (vv. 11,13).

As they reached the climax of their song, they said, "The Lord shall reign for ever and ever" (v. 18). There was no doubt at that time concerning the devotion of the people to God; they had seen Him work in their behalf, and they rejoiced in His majesty and power.

However, the Israelites were to learn another basic lesson—that God was to reign as their absolute monarch. They had not yet seen that they were destined to be a kingdom and that God was to be their king.

The reality of God's government was at that time unrealistic to the Israelites. They didn't realize that God wanted them as His nation and that He wanted to be the absolute monarch over them. With their lips the Israelites acknowledged God as their ruler, yet primarily they saw only Moses as their leader, not God. They had not made Him their personal God.

So also, it is one thing for the believer today to exalt God in his soul and heart, but it is quite another thing for the believer to recognize God as the absolute monarch in his life.

Perhaps we can sing praises to the majesty of God when we are with a crowd of believers, and perhaps we can say amen when a great sermon is preached, but do we really recognize God as the absolute monarch in our lives? Are we looking to human leaders, or are we looking to *the* leader?

The Israelites needed to see God, not Moses, as their real leader, legislator, lawgiver and king. After all, Moses was only a mouthpiece for God, an intermediary to communicate God's decrees to the people.

Israel had reached the point where the people needed to be taught that God had righteous claims on them. They needed to see that God was a personal God to them. They needed to recognize that His throne had to be established over them in reality and that His authority had to be acknowledged personally. They needed to recognize that His will was supreme and that it must always regulate their lives. They needed to recognize themselves as a redeemed people whom God had bought for Himself. They were under the deepest possible obligation to fear, obey and serve God.

But remember that I Corinthians 10:11 says, "All these things happened unto them for ensamples: and they are written for our admonition, upon whom the ends of the world are come." We are to learn from the example of the Israelites. We, too, need to recognize that this God—the God of Abraham, Isaac, Jacob, Moses and Israel—is also our God.

While in divine love God provided the Law, the main purpose for His giving it was to maintain His authority. Israel had to see that they were under His government. God continued to reveal grace and mercy to the people—He prescribed in the ceremonial law how they could enter His presence. Through sacrifices the people were able to obtain forgiveness of sin.

Until the Law was given through Moses, God had worked with the Israelites on the basis of the Abrahamic covenant. Although the Abrahamic covenant still remained in force, God began to work with the people on the basis of their behavior. If they obeyed, He blessed; if they disobeyed, He withheld blessing and even permitted severe chastening. However, the national blessings involving a land, descendants and spiritual blessings still depended on the Abrahamic covenant (Gen. 12:1-3). Today, many Jews—descendants of

Abraham—are returning to the land. Although most are returning in unbelief, a national conversion will eventually take place (Rom. 11:26).

A reading of the account of God's revealing Himself to the people at Mount Sinai seems to reveal that the people evidenced a haughty attitude. They immediately responded, "All that the Lord hath spoken we will do" (Ex. 19:8). Yet, they had been guilty of grumbling and complaining against Moses (actually against God), and after making this promise, they were frequently guilty of the same thing. They were quick to say they would obey God, but they were slow to practice it. They were much like those referred to in the New Testament: "For if any be a hearer of the word, and not a doer, he is like unto a man beholding his natural face in a glass: for he beholdeth himself, and goeth his way, and straightway forgetteth what manner of man he was" (James 1:23,24).

May those of us who know Jesus Christ as Saviour not be guilty of the same thing. Let us be like those mentioned in verse 25: "But whoso looketh into the perfect law of liberty, and continueth therein, he being not a forgetful hearer, but a doer of the work, this man shall be blessed in his deed."

Chapter 17

The Law's Time and Purpose

Much confusion exists today concerning the time the Law spanned and what its actual purpose was. Some say that the Law was to be in effect from the time it was given until the end of time. Others say the Law was binding only until the time of Christ. Some say the purpose of the Law is to provide salvation to those who keep it; others say no one can be saved by keeping the Law. These are tremendously important subjects, and the crucial question that needs answering is, What does the Bible indicate about the Law's time and purpose?

Galatians 3:19 is a key verse concerning this matter: "Wherefore then serveth the law? It was added because of transgressions, till the seed should come to whom the promise was made; and it was ordained by angels in the hand of a mediator." Notice three important elements in this verse: the Law had a beginning—"it was added"; the Law had a reason for being given—"because of transgressions"; the Law was destined to have an end—"till the seed should come."

The Law's Beginning

Let us now consider these three elements in more detail. First, the Law had a beginning. The Law given through Moses had not always existed; it began at a point in time. Romans 5:13,14 says, "(For until the law sin was in the world: but sin is not imputed when there is no law. Nevertheless death reigned from Adam to Moses, even over them that had not sinned after the similitude of Adam's transgression, who is

the figure of him that was to come." We see from these verses
that the Law, as given through Moses, has not always existed;
there was no such Law between the time of Adam and Moses.

Galatians 3:19 says that the Law was added. But the
question might be asked, To what was the Law added? The
clue to the answer is found in the three preceding verses
where we read about God's earlier covenant of grace made
with Abraham: "Now to Abraham and his seed were the
promises made. He saith not, And to seeds, as of many; but
as of one, And to thy seed, which is Christ. And this I say,
that the covenant, that was confirmed before of God in
Christ, the law, which was four hundred and thirty years
after, cannot disannul, that it should make the promise of
none effect. For if the inheritance be of the law, it is no more
of promise: but God gave it to Abraham by promise"
(vv. 16-18).

It is important to realize that God has always dealt in
grace. This was true before the Law was given, while the Law
was in effect and after the Law had served its purpose. The
Law did not take the place of grace, and it was not mixed
with grace.

The Law was added as one railroad track is added alongside of another. Law and grace existed and worked side by
side. Thus, when the Law had done its work of convicting
and condemning, a person could flee to grace. It is important
to remember that even during the time of the Law, salvation
was by means of grace only. So it was not Law *and* grace, but
Law was added to grace, or placed alongside of it.

The Law's End

Second, the Law had an end. This is actually the third
element mentioned in Galatians 3:19, but we want to
consider it before discussing the purpose of the Law. Galatians 3:19 says the Law was added "till the seed should come
to whom the promise was made." From these words we see
that there was an end to the judicial function of the Mosaic
Law.

Notice the words "seed" and "promise" in the phrase
"till the seed should come to whom the promise was made."
What seed is being referred to? What promise is referred to?

The seed mentioned in Galatians 3:19 is specifically stated in verse 16 to be Christ—"He saith not, And to seeds, as of many; but as of one, And to thy seed, which is Christ." So we see that the Law's judicial function ended with Christ.

Another translation renders Galatians 3:19 in this way: "What then was the purpose of the Law? It was added—later on, after the promise, to disclose and expose to men their guilt—because of transgressions and [to make men more conscious of the sinfulness] of sin; and it was intended to be in effect until the Seed (the Descendant, the Heir) should come, to and concerning Whom the promise had been made" (Amplified).

In considering that the Law was in effect only until the time of Christ, notice what Galatians 4:4,5 says, "But when the fulness of the time was come, God sent forth his Son, made of a woman, made under the law, to redeem them that were under the law, that we might receive the adoption of sons."

So Jesus Christ came at the appointed time in order to fulfill the Law. Many people do not realize that the Law has been fulfilled by Jesus Christ. While He was on earth, the Lord said, "Think not that I am come to destroy the law, or the prophets: I am not come to destroy, but to fulfil. For verily I say unto you, Till heaven and earth pass, one jot or one tittle shall in no wise pass from the law, till all be fulfilled" (Matt. 5:17,18).

Jesus Christ came to earth while the Law was still in effect and lived under its jurisdiction until His death. He fulfilled the Law and thereby brought an end to its judicial function.

Another passage showing that the Law was in effect only until the time of Christ is Galatians 3:23-25: "Now before the faith came we were perpetually guarded under the Law, kept in custody in preparation for the faith that was destined to be revealed (unveiled, disclosed). So that the Law served [to us Jews] as our trainer—our guardian, our guide to Christ, to lead us—until Christ [came], that we might be justified (declared righteous, put in right standing with God) by and through faith. But now that the faith has come, we are no longer under a trainer—the guardian of our childhood" (Amplified). The Law served its purpose until Christ came, and then mankind was no longer under the judicial system of the Law.

A parallel to the change that took place after Christ came can be found in the changes made in the laws of a particular government. During special times, such as a time of war, special laws are enacted. Once the situation changes, however, people are no longer bound by those laws; they have served their purpose. Nothing is wrong with the laws themselves; they simply are no longer needed because of a new situation.

So also, nothing was wrong with the Law that God gave through Moses, but after Jesus Christ came, it was no longer necessary. Jesus Christ Himself fulfilled the Law in two ways—by keeping every jot and tittle of it and by becoming the sacrificial Lamb, slain in behalf of us who could not keep the Law.

Because Christ fulfilled the Law and brought an end to it, the Apostle Paul asked the Galatian believers, "Wherefore then serveth the law?" (3:19).

The Law's Purpose

Third, the Law had a purpose. Galatians 3:19 says the Law was added "because of transgressions." The Law was given so that sin would be revealed as a transgression. The Law showed the awfulness of sin.

Even though there was no Law from Adam to Moses, everyone had a sin nature and was guilty of sin. But something was needed to show that sin was a transgression against God. Romans 5:12,13 says, "Wherefore, as by one man sin entered into the world, and death by sin; and so death passed upon all men, for that all have sinned: (for until the law sin was in the world: but sin is not imputed when there is no law.'' The word "imputed" means "placed on one's account." From Adam to Moses, individual sins were not charged against a person's account because no specific law existed which showed those sins to be a transgression against God. For instance, if there were no speed limit on the highway, one could drive at any speed and not be in transgression of a specific law. But once a speed limit is set, exceeding that limit is definitely a transgression of the law.

As we consider the Old Testament times before the Mosaic Law, it is interesting to notice the situation involving Cain and Abel. Genesis 4 reveals that Cain was jealous of his brother Abel because Abel had brought a sacrifice which met the Lord's requirements. However, Cain's sacrifice was rejected (vv. 3-5). One day out in the field, Cain killed his brother (v. 8). No one apprehended Cain because at that time, there was no law against murder. This law was not enacted until Noah and his family came out of the ark after the worldwide flood (9:6).

The purpose of the Mosaic Law was to reveal to mankind in general, but to Israel in particular, the awfulness of sin in the human heart. Just as a thermometer measures temperature but does not control it, so the Law revealed sin but it did not remedy it. Or, to use another parallel, the Law served as a mirror to show man his sinful heart, but it had no ability to wash his heart clean.

The Law revealed sin and death. The Apostle Paul wrote: "For the law of the Spirit of life in Christ Jesus hath made me free from the law of sin and death. For what the law could not do, in that it was weak through the flesh, God sending his own Son in the likeness of sinful flesh, and for sin, condemned sin in the flesh" (Rom. 8:2,3).

Whereas the Law revealed sin and death, Jesus Christ revealed life. Romans 3:21,22 says, "But now the righteousness of God without the law is manifested, being witnessed by the law and the prophets; even the righteousness of God which is by faith of Jesus Christ unto all and upon all them that believe: for there is no difference."

So the Law was added, or placed alongside of, grace to reveal the sinful condition of man and to make sin a transgression against God. In addition, it allowed grace to become even more evident. "Where sin abounded, grace did much more abound" (5:20).

Sin had always been morally wrong, but under the Law it became legally wrong. Sin was made a transgression. The Law did not produce sin or make sin worse, but it was given to make sin exceedingly sinful; that is, to show the awfulness of sin. The Law revealed the true nature of sin and drove man to seek grace.

Sin has always been morally wrong, but it was not legally wrong until the Law was given. This is an important distinction, even concerning some laws today. And the opposite is also true—something may be legally right but morally wrong. For instance, gambling has been legalized in some states, but this does not make gambling right. Gambling is a moral sin. It always has been and always will be, even though it is accepted from a legal standpoint.

Also, the consumption of liquor was illegal during the prohibition period. It is now legal to drink, but this does not make it morally right. Other examples, such as abortion and divorce, could be given to support this principle. But the purpose of the Law given through Moses was to make legally wrong what was also morally wrong.

Another purpose of the Law was to convince people of sin. Romans 3:19,20 says, "Now we know that what things soever the law saith, it saith to them who are under the law: that every mouth may be stopped, and all the world may become guilty before God. Therefore by the deeds of the law there shall no flesh be justified in his sight: for by the law is the knowledge of sin."

Fallen man often thinks that he can keep the holy standards of God in his own strength. In fact, when the Law was given to the Israelites, they responded, "All that the Lord hath spoken we will do" (Ex. 19:8). They really thought they could meet God's righteous demands. But the Law demonstrated the inability of man to make himself acceptable to God. Man could not, under the moral law or any kind of law, make himself acceptable to God. This is why God provided the ceremonial law whereby man could make sacrifices for his sin.

In one sense, Israel was more blessed and pampered of God than any other nation ever has been. But even in this they provide a valuable lesson for us. God gave them the Law to prove that the best people under the most advantageous circumstances are a complete failure when it comes to keeping His holy demands.

Preparation for Christ's Coming

All of this served to prepare for the coming of the Son of God, who was proven sinless by the fact that He kept the Law perfectly and fulfilled God's righteous demands. In addition, the Lord Jesus Christ also served as God's Lamb who was slain for mankind, who had so miserably failed Him. In other words, the Lord Jesus Christ not only fulfilled the moral law, but He also completely fulfilled the ceremonial law which God had given to Israel so that they might have a way to God.

The Law did not cause sin, it only revealed sin. And the Law was in force only until Jesus Christ came and completely fulfilled it. Matthew 5:17 reveals that one of the purposes of Christ's coming was to fulfill the Law. He did not destroy it; rather, He set it aside as having any legal jurisdiction over the Church, which is His Body.

After the Lord Jesus Christ had perfectly fulfilled the Law, He ascended to the Father and sent the Holy Spirit to "reprove [convict] the world of sin, and of righteousness, and of judgment" (John 16:8). What the Law did in revealing sin is much more effectively done by the convicting power of the Holy Spirit. The Holy Spirit came on the Day of Pentecost, 50 days after the resurrection of Jesus Christ, and began His convicting work. Notice what happened. During the time of the Law, relatively few were deeply convicted of their sin, as indicated by the fact that there was only a handful of believers when Jesus Christ died, rose from the dead and went to be with the Father. But on the very first day that the Holy Spirit came, about 3000 were convicted of sin, received the message of salvation and were added to the Church (Acts 2:41,47).

It is highly significant to recognize that the Law was given specifically to Israel for a precise time—from Moses to Christ. Unless one is aware of this truth, he will not understand the present-day believer's relationship to the Law.

The Scriptures abound in passages which show that the Law was given specifically to Israel. Exodus 19:3-5 says, "And Moses went up unto God, and the Lord called unto him out of the mountain, saying, Thus shalt thou say to the house of Jacob, and tell the children of Israel; ye have seen what I did unto the Egyptians, and how I bare you on eagles' wings, and brought you unto myself. Now therefore, if ye will obey my voice indeed, and keep my covenant, then ye shall be a peculiar treasure unto me above all people: for all the earth is mine." Notice that these words were spoken to those known as "the house of Jacob" and "the children of Israel" (v. 3). The Gentile nations were not included in this special promise of blessing.

That God's agreement, or covenant, was only with the nation of Israel is also seen in Exodus 34:27: "The Lord said unto Moses, Write thou these words: for after the tenor of these words I have made a covenant with thee and with Israel." So it is clear from these references that the Law was given specifically and only to Israel.

By means of the Law, special blessings were promised to Israel and depended on Israel's obedience. This conditional element is seen in Exodus 19:5: "Now therefore, if ye will obey my voice indeed, and keep my covenant, then ye shall be a peculiar treasure unto me above all people: for all the earth is mine." However, Psalm 78 reveals how the Israelites failed to keep the Law as they wandered in the wilderness soon after they had received it. The psalmist said, "They kept not the covenant of God, and refused to walk in his law; and forgat his works, and his wonders that he had shewed them" (vv. 10,11). After telling of some of the wonderful things God had done for the people, the psalmist added, "They sinned yet more against him by provoking the most High in the wilderness. And they tempted God in their heart by asking meat for their lust. Yea, they spake against God; they said, Can God furnish a table in the wilderness?" (vv. 17-19).

Although the Mosaic covenant was conditional and the people miserably failed under it, the Abrahamic covenant was unconditional, and God will yet bless the nation in spite of individual disobedience. God will remain faithful to His promises given in the Abrahamic covenant even though the Israelites failed miserably in their responsibility under the Mosaic covenant. Even in this we see the wonderful grace of God.

Chapter 18

The Christian and the Law

Some say, "We are under the moral law but not under the ceremonial law." Others say, "We are under the moral law as a rule of life, but we are not under the Law as to salvation." That is, they are saying that we are under the Law for sanctification but not for justification. What does the Bible teach about the Christian's relationship to the Mosaic Law?

Source of Righteousness

The New Testament Books of Romans and Galatians have a great deal to say about a Christian's relationship to the Law. Romans 6:14,15 says, "For sin shall not have dominion over you: for ye are not under the law, but under grace. What then? Shall we sin, because we are not under the law, but under grace? God forbid." Galatians 5:18 says, "But if ye be led of the Spirit, ye are not under the law."

It is clear from these scriptures that the Law, as law, has absolutely nothing to contribute in accomplishing sanctification. On the contrary, being free from the bondage of the Law makes it possible for the Holy Spirit to operate effectively in the believer. A comparison of Romans 6:14,15 with Galatians 5:18 reveals that the believer is not under the Law and that he should walk in the Spirit so that he will not become entangled in the bondage of the Law. The Holy Spirit leads us on to righteousness.

Notice other scriptures that comment about the Christian's relationship to the Law. Romans 7:4 says that believers are "dead to the law." Verse 6 says they are "delivered from the law."

178

The Lord Jesus Christ not only fulfilled the Law, but He was also the end of the Law. Romans 10:3,4 says concerning Israel, "For they [Israel] being ignorant of God's righteousness, and going about to establish their own righteousness, have not submitted themselves unto the righteousness of God. For Christ is the end of the law for righteousness to every one that believeth."

Because Jesus Christ led a perfect, righteous life, He was able to fulfill the demands of the Law completely, and His righteousness was placed on our account—counted as our righteousness—when we trusted Him as personal Saviour. What glorious news! We do not become righteous by keeping the Law; we become righteous by trusting Christ as Saviour and having His righteousness placed on our account. Thus, the Apostle Paul, a Jew by birth, said that his desire was to "be found in him [Christ], not having mine own righteousness, which is of the law, but that which is through the faith of Christ, the righteousness which is of God by faith" (Phil. 3:9). The righteousness any person has in the presence of God is not that which he has produced on his own, but it is the righteousness of God that was produced in him when he trusted Jesus Christ as Saviour.

That this righteousness does not come through keeping the Law but by receiving Christ as Saviour is evident from Romans 10:10: "For with the heart man believeth unto righteousness; and with the mouth confession is made unto salvation." So the person who believes in Jesus Christ as personal Saviour is the one who becomes righteous. Every believer has this righteous standing before God. How tremendous it is to realize that the very righteousness of God is placed on our account the moment we believe Christ as Saviour. No believer can boast of such righteousness; all he can say is, "Thank You, Lord, that my standing with You is complete because of what Christ has accomplished for me."

As the believer studies the Scriptures, he learns that the Holy Spirit indwells him in order to work out His righteousness through the believer's life. This is the point of Romans 8:4: "That the righteousness of the law might be fulfilled in us, who walk not after the flesh, but after the Spirit." The indwelling Holy Spirit focuses attention on the indwelling Christ. Thus, Colossians 1:27 says, "Christ in you, the hope of glory." That Christ lives within the believer is also seen in Galatians 2:20: "I am crucified with Christ: nevertheless I live; yet not I, but Christ liveth in me: and the life which I now live in the flesh I live by the faith of the Son of God, who loved me, and gave himself for me."

So the evidence from the Scriptures is that the Christian is not under the Mosaic Law. Second Corinthians 3:11 refers to the Mosaic Law as being "done away," and verse 13 refers to it as having been "abolished." Revealing what Christ has done to the Law, Ephesians 2:15 says, "Having abolished in his flesh the enmity, even the law of commandments contained in ordinances." Colossians 2:14 refers to the "blotting out" of the "handwriting of ordinances that was against us." All this has been accomplished because Christ fulfilled every demand of both the moral and ceremonial law.

The Law Reveals Grace

The Mosaic Law was not given to produce salvation. The purpose of the Law was to help people see how far short they had fallen of God's righteous demands so they would cast themselves on the grace of God. Even during the time of the Law grace was made available through the specified sacrifices for sin. These pointed forward to the Lord Jesus Christ who was the sacrifice for sin. But because Jesus Christ came and offered Himself as the sacrifice for sin, the Law is no longer needed.

According to Romans 5:20, the Law was given so that God could reveal more of His grace: "Moreover the law entered, that the offence might abound. But where sin abounded, grace did much more abound."

When the people gathered at Mount Sinai and heard God speak, they became frightened and "stood afar off" (Ex. 20:18). This is also the result of today's preaching of the Law apart from the context of the grace of God.

Exodus 20:24 reveals the grace aspect of the Law, for God instructed that an altar be made so that sacrifices, which would bring the people into harmony with God, could be offered.

Today, there is too much preaching of the moral law (the Ten Commandments) without the element of grace that was revealed in the ceremonial law. We must recognize that Jesus Christ was the sacrifice for sin and has made the grace of God available to all who will receive Him as personal Saviour.

The Christian is not under the Mosaic Law in any sense. But the whole Law is an essential part of the Scriptures, and as such it is profitable to believers of all ages. The profit of any part of the Scriptures is emphasized in II Timothy 3:16,17: "All scripture is given by inspiration of God, and is profitable for doctrine, for reproof, for correction, for instruction in righteousness: that the man of God may be perfect, throughly furnished unto all good works."

But although we are to profit from all the scriptures in that we learn valuable lessons from them, not all Scripture passages were written to us specifically. This is evident from the fact that we no longer bring sacrifices to the altar as God instructed Israel to do. Christ was our sacrifice once for all. The Bible says, "Every priest standeth daily ministering and offering oftentimes the same sacrifices, which can never take away sins: but this man, after he had offered one sacrifice for sins for ever, sat down on the right hand of God. . . . For by one offering he hath perfected for ever them that are sanctified" (Heb. 10:11,12,14). Thus, we learn from seeing the Law, in type, presenting God's righteous demands and from seeing His loving grace in the fulfillment of the Law through Christ.

Law set forth what man ought to be; grace sets forth what God is. We behold the face of Christ in the Holy Scriptures, and we see who God is by beholding Christ, "for in him dwelleth all the fulness of the Godhead bodily" (Col. 2:9). We know and understand what Christ has done for us as we study the Scriptures and see Him revealed in even the Mosaic Law. Even though the Mosaic Law is not in force for the believer today, it is important to consider what place—if any—the Law has in relationship to molding Christian character.

The Christian's Standard of Living

If the Christian is not under the Law, what is his standard of living? Basically, the standard for a Christian is to do the

will of God by the enabling grace that is supplied in Christ
Jesus our Lord through the Holy Spirit.

The key in this matter is knowing Christ. This is emphasized in II Peter 1:3: "According as his divine power hath
given unto us all things that pertain unto life and godliness,
through the knowledge of him that hath called us to glory
and virtue."

We are to have "knowledge of him," but what are we to
know about the Lord Jesus? One of the important factors we
need to know is His indwelling presence. Verse 4 says,
"Whereby are given unto us exceeding great and precious
promises: that by these ye might be partakers of the divine
nature, having escaped the corruption that is in the world
through lust." That Christ indwells the believer is also evident
from the clear statement of Colossians 1:27: "Christ in you,
the hope of glory."

Knowing about the death, burial and resurrection of
Jesus Christ is very important because these things comprise
the gospel, and unless one believes the gospel, there is no
salvation. But the Christian also needs to know that Christ
indwells him, and he needs to have an intimate relationship
with Him.

The proper formula for getting to know Christ as a
believer is presented in Romans 8:1-4: "There is therefore
now no condemnation to them which are in Christ Jesus,
who walk not after the flesh, but after the Spirit. For the law
of the Spirit of life in Christ Jesus hath made me free from
the law of sin and death. For what the law could not do, in
that it was weak through the flesh, God sending his own Son
in the likeness of sinful flesh, and for sin, condemned sin in
the flesh: that the righteousness of the law might be fulfilled
in us, who walk not after the flesh, but after the Spirit."

What a glorious truth it is to realize that "there is therefore now no condemnation to them which are in Christ
Jesus"! (v. 1). The believer's standing with God is secure.
And how wonderful it is to know that "the law of the Spirit
of life in Christ Jesus hath made me free from the law of sin
and death" (v. 2). But what is "the law of sin and death"?
This is a reference to the Law of Moses which revealed the
awfulness of sin, made sin a transgression and pronounced
death as the penalty for sin. That which has made us free

from the law of sin and death is "the law of the Spirit of life in Christ Jesus." The word "law" in this phrase is used in the sense of "principle." In other words, now that we have Jesus Christ as Saviour, we have a new life principle—"the law of the Spirit of life in Christ Jesus." Because God has set a new principle into operation within the believer, the believer is enabled to live a life of victory. Therefore, even though the believer is delivered from the Mosaic Law, the righteousness of that Law is really fulfilled in him through Christ (v. 4).

Knowing Christ Through Scripture

In order that we might know Christ, the whole body of scripture has been given to us, and, as II Timothy 3:16 indicates, it is profitable for every basic sphere of life. It is not enough to know about Christ; we must know Christ Himself.

After His resurrection the Lord Jesus appeared to two people on the way to Emmaus, and "beginning at Moses and all the prophets, he expounded unto them in all the scriptures the things concerning himself" (Luke 24:27). Later, when Jesus appeared to ten of the disciples, He told them, "These are the words which I spake unto you, while I was yet with you, that all things must be fulfilled, which were written in the law of Moses, and in the prophets, and in the psalms, concerning me" (v. 44). In this verse the Lord Jesus referred to the three major divisions of the Old Testament scriptures and emphasized that they specifically spoke of Him. So no matter what portion of the Bible we study, some aspect of the Lord Jesus Christ is being revealed to us.

Only the Scriptures "are able to make thee wise unto salvation through faith which is in Christ Jesus" (II Tim. 3:15). Only in the Holy Scriptures do we learn that Jesus Christ has paid the complete penalty for sin and that anyone who recognizes that he is a sinner and trusts Christ as personal Saviour has forgiveness of sin and eternal life. Having received Jesus Christ as Saviour, the believer is not to neglect any portion of the Scripture, because "all scripture is given by inspiration of God, and is profitable for doctrine, for reproof, for correction, for instruction in righteousness" (v. 16).

What the Scripture accomplishes in a believer's life is seen
in verse 17: "That the man of God may be perfect, throughly
furnished unto all good works." The Greek word translated
"perfect" in this verse means "complete, capable, efficient."
It is derived from a word meaning "to fit" or "to be especially adapted." The Greek word translated "throughly
furnished" has the sense of "altogether fit" or "fully fitted."
From this we see that the Scriptures lack nothing in prepar-
ing the believer to do "all good works."

The Law's Usefulness Today

In relation to the Christian, the Law has been completely
fulfilled and satisfied in Christ. It has been brought to an end
and has been done away with as a system which condemns.
However, because the Mosaic Law is part of the inspired
Scripture, it remains for all time to teach believers profitable
lessons. For instance, the moral law serves even now as a
mirror, revealing what a Christian ought to be but is not.
However, the Law cannot condemn the believer, because
Christ took the believer's condemnation when He died on the
cross. The ceremonial law serves as a type of all that Christ
has accomplished for us in that He kept the moral law
perfectly and became the sacrificial Lamb. His death in our
place made it possible for us to be free from the Law.

It is important to recognize, however, that Christ fulfilled
all aspects of the Law, and now His righteousness is imputed
to, or placed on the account of, those who receive Him as
personal Saviour. With the exception of Christ, no one has
ever been able to keep the entire Law. His ability to keep the
entire Law revealed that He was absolutely righteous; that is,
that He was God incarnate. Because He had no sin of His
own, He was able to die on the cross for our sin so that His
righteousness could be made available to all who believe.

The great mystery not known before the time of Christ
was that the perfect Christ, reflected in the entire Scriptures,
would indwell Church-Age believers. Thus, by the power of
the Holy Spirit, Jesus Christ lives His life in us.

The same person who once lived on earth and perfectly
kept the Law now lives in believers, enabling them to live the
life of victory. This is why the Scriptures make statements

such as "Christ in you, the hope of glory" (Col. 1:27) and
"For ye are dead, and your life is hid with Christ in God.
When Christ, who is our life, shall appear, then shall ye also
appear with him in glory" (3:3,4).

Concerning what the believer has in Jesus Christ,
Ephesians 4:24 says, "Put on the new man, which after God
is created in righteousness and true holiness." The new man
formed in every believer is Jesus Christ. Since Christ has been
formed in us who have believed in Him as personal Saviour,
we are to put on those things which characterize a life of
righteousness and holiness. And we are to put off those
things that are not honoring to Christ (v. 22). We are to say
no to sin and yes to Christ. How wonderful it is to realize
that the indwelling Christ gives us all the power necessary to
enable us to walk as He walked. And I John 2:6 tells the
believer, "He that saith he abideth in him ought himself also
so to walk, even as he walked."

The Christian, because he has Christ indwelling him, has
the mind of Christ available to him. Thus, the believer is to
think like Christ thinks. Christians are told, "We have the
mind of Christ" (I Cor. 2:16). The Bible also tells the
believer, "Let this mind be in you, which was also in Christ
Jesus" (Phil. 2:5). As we spend time in the whole Word of
God, learning about Jesus Christ, we will think as He
thinks—we will love what He loves and hate what He hates.
Has the truth of the indwelling Christ really gripped your
own heart? Do you recognize that He lives within you and
that He is there to live out His life in you?

The Law of Christ

Believers are commanded to "fulfil the law of Christ"
(Gal. 6:2). The first phrase of this verse indicates the nature
of this law of Christ: "Bear ye one another's burdens." The
law of Christ is really the law of love.

Jesus told His disciples, "A new commandment I give
unto you, That ye love one another; as I have loved you, that
ye also love one another. By this shall all men know that ye
are my disciples, if ye have love one to another" (John
13:34,35). Jesus also said, "This is my commandment, That
ye love one another, as I have loved you" (15:12).

Later, the Apostle John wrote: "This is his commandment, That we should believe on the name of his Son Jesus Christ, and love one another, as he gave us commandment" (I John 3:23). So even though a person in this age is not bound by the Mosaic Law, there are definite commandments of God that are in force today—"that we should believe on the name of his Son Jesus Christ, and love one another."

The law of love is not a new law in itself because it was at the heart of the Old Testament Law system, but to love as Christ loved is a new law, or principle. The only reason it is possible for a believer to love as Christ loved is that the believer has Christ within him to express this love. Thus, the Apostle Paul said, "I am crucified with Christ: nevertheless I live; yet not I, but Christ liveth in me" (Gal. 2:20).

It is the distinct ministry of the Holy Spirit, who also indwells the believer, to reveal the love of God through the believer. Romans 5:5 says, "The love of God is shed abroad in our hearts by the Holy Ghost which is given unto us." And this love fulfills the Law. Romans 13:8,10 says, "Owe no man any thing, but to love one another: for he that loveth another hath fulfilled the law. . . . Love worketh no ill to his neighbour: therefore love is the fulfilling of the law."

On the surface it may seem extremely difficult for the believer to express this kind of love, even though the Holy Spirit is working within him to produce this love through his life. But the believer can have victory in this area if he will obey the injunction of Galatians 5:16: "Walk in the Spirit, and ye shall not fulfil the lust of the flesh." Keep in mind that the word "walk" refers to every step we take in life. Verse 18 assures the believer, "If ye be led of the Spirit, ye are not under the law." As we depend on the Holy Spirit to accomplish His ministry in us, He will give us victory over sin and produce the love of Christ in and through our lives.

Although it is not a person's normal characteristic to love with the kind of love Christ had, when a person receives Christ as Saviour, He indwells his life and enables him to express this kind of love. No wonder the Apostle Paul said, "I can do all things through Christ which strengtheneth me" (Phil. 4:13). Our wonderful God not only has provided salvation for all who believe but also has provided victory and a loving spirit for all who will rely on Him for it.

Chapter 19

The Broken Law

After Moses was used of God to lead the children of Israel out of Egypt, they came to Mount Sinai. There they were to receive the great revelation of God, commonly known as the "Law" or the "Mosaic Law."

The Israelites gathered at the foot of Mount Sinai, although they were instructed by God not to touch the mountain, or they would die (Ex. 19:12,13). The Lord called Moses to the top of Mount Sinai and then instructed him to return to the people and warn them again not to touch the mountain (vv. 20-24).

God then spoke what are commonly referred to as the "Ten Commandments" (20:1-17). "All the people saw the thunderings, and the lightnings, and the noise of the trumpet, and the mountain smoking: and when the people saw it, they removed, and stood afar off. And they said unto Moses, Speak thou with us, and we will hear: but let not God speak with us, lest we die" (vv. 18,19). The people were filled with awe and fear at this mighty revelation of God.

Three Aspects of Giving the Law

There were three aspects to the giving of the Law. First, there was the oral giving of the Law when God Himself spoke directly to the people as they stood at the foot of the mountain (Ex. 20:1-17). God had a very important purpose for speaking directly to the people. No such direct communication was made concerning laws of the priesthood or the various sacrifices; only the Ten Commandments were given in this way. Such an unusual communication, as well as

187

the phenomena that accompanied it, let the people know for
sure that the message was of God. It also clearly established
Moses in their eyes as God's mediator between them and
Him. No one had ever seen such an awesome display; there
was no mistaking that God was giving Moses the Law.

A second aspect of the giving of the Law involved Moses'
being called to the mountaintop to receive the tables of
stone, which were engraved by God Himself (24:12-18).
These contained the Ten Commandments, and it was these
tables of stone that Moses broke when he came down from
the mountain and discovered the people worshiping an idol.

The third aspect of the giving of the Law included the
producing of a second set of stone tables after the first had
been broken (34:1,28,29). These, too, were engraved by God
Himself.

In connection with the oral giving of the Law, God also
gave Moses some regulations and judgments concerning
personal relationships—Hebrew to Hebrew. God did not give
only ten commandments; many others were included in the
Law. Later, the ceremonial law associated with the tabernacle
was given on the mountaintop.

A Warning and a Covenant

Following God's oral communication of the Ten
Commandments to Israel, He warned the people not to make
any gods of silver or gold. Within the Ten Commandments
God had specifically said, "Thou shalt not make unto thee
any graven image, or any likeness of any thing that is in
heaven above, or that is in the earth beneath, or that is in the
water under the earth" (20:4). Then after the people
responded in fear and trembling, God again said, "Ye shall
not make with me gods of silver, neither shall ye make unto
you gods of gold" (v. 23). From this time on others were told
not to make gods of silver and gold, but only Israel had the
specific privilege of hearing God orally communicate this
prohibition. More than anyone else, Israel had conclusive
proof that this command was directly from God.

Before Moses went up on the mountaintop to spend 40
days and 40 nights there, he communicated to the people the
words and judgments of the Lord. The people responded by

saying, "All the words which the Lord hath said will we do" (24:3). The people were quick to obligate themselves to the commands of God, and they even repeated their willingness to do anything the Lord said: "All that the Lord hath said will we do, and be obedient" (v. 7).

This covenant, or agreement, was ratified by blood from offerings: "Moses took the blood, and sprinkled it on the people, and said, Behold the blood of the covenant, which the Lord hath made with you concerning all these words" (v. 8).

Moses on the Mountain

After Moses had done this, the Lord told him, "Come up to me into the mount, and be there: and I will give thee tables of stone, and a law, and commandments which I have written; that thou mayest teach them" (24:12).

Joshua, who is well known because of the book which bears his name, went partway up the mountain with Moses: "Moses rose up, and his minister Joshua: and Moses went up into the mount of God" (v. 13). As Moses left the people, he delegated the authority to take care of any problems that arose while he was away to Aaron and Hur (v. 14).

While on the mountaintop, Moses waited for six days while a cloud covered the mountain. Then on the seventh day God "called unto Moses out of the midst of the cloud" (v. 16). As Moses later recorded this incident, he wrote: "The sight of the glory of the Lord was like devouring fire on the top of the mount in the eyes of the children of Israel" (v. 17). What a display of the glory of God! Israel was given the opportunity to observe the awesome sight of the presence of God as He revealed Himself to Moses. Moses was on the mountaintop communicating with God for 40 days and nights (v. 18).

Exodus 25—31 records the various instructions and regulations God gave to Moses concerning the tabernacle. God then interrupted His communication with Moses to tell him of the hideous sin the Israelites were committing at the foot of the mountain. Exodus 32—34 tells of this awful sin, but these chapters also reveal in depth the character of Moses. They reveal his holy anger against sin, his firmness in judging sin and his greatest moments of love and intercession for the people of Israel. That time of intercession in behalf of his people was possibly the finest moment of Moses' life. These three chapters of Exodus (32—34) center around Israel's great sin as Aaron led them in worshiping false gods while Moses was on the mountaintop with God.

What a contrast the Book of Exodus presents! On the one hand we read of God's grace as He revealed to Moses His plan of love, grace and mercy toward Israel (chs. 25—31). On the other hand we read of that which exhibits the awful depravity of fallen man—the worship of false gods (ch. 32). On the one hand we see unveiled the manifold glories of Christ, but on the other hand we see exposed the awful abominations which Satan produces. On the one hand God revealed for His people the provision for godly worship; on the other hand we see the Israelites bowing down to worship the idolatrous golden calf.

The majestic awesomeness of God's presence was made known to the people. In fact, they could see it even while they were sinning. They feared God only until He was a little farther away.

At first He came down to the people. Then He moved to the mountaintop where He and Moses could be alone. When the people were left alone with Aaron as their leader, they revealed the true attitude of their hearts. This attitude had come to the surface numerous times before as they traveled from Egypt to Sinai, but in the absence of Moses, they threw away all restraint. Having convinced themselves that something had happened to their chosen leader, the people turned for leadership to something that had just been expressly forbidden by God—false gods.

After the Lord had communicated with Moses, He gave him "two tables of testimony, tables of stone, written with the finger of God" (31:18). But at the foot of the mountain the people gave up hope of Moses' ever returning because he had been gone from them for 40 days and 40 nights. In seeking for leadership, they told Aaron, "Up, make us gods, which shall go before us; for as for this Moses, the man that brought us up out the land of Egypt, we wot [know] not what is become of him" (32:1).

Forgetfulness and Impatience

The New Testament Book of the Acts refers to Israel's attitude at this point. When Stephen defended his preaching after the resurrection of Christ, he reminded the Jewish leaders, "In their hearts [they] turned back again into Egypt, saying unto Aaron, Make us gods to go before us: for as for this Moses, which brought us out of the land of Egypt, we wot not what is become of him" (7:39,40). This is the key—within their hearts they turned back to Egypt.

The people of Israel were not angry with Moses because he lingered on the mountaintop for 40 days. Rather, they were impatient and were quick to forget God's dealings with them. It had only been three months since they had come out of Egypt. They had experienced the miracle of the Passover, in which God spared the firstborn of the Israelites and destroyed those of the Egyptians, and they had experienced the miracle at the Red Sea, which allowed the Israelites to pass through on dry ground whereas the pursuing Egyptians were drowned. Then God had provided water, manna and meat for them by His miracle-working power. Yet they were quick to forget all that God had done for them. At Mount Sinai, while Moses was actually receiving the Law, they cast off their allegiance to Jehovah, the ever-present One.

But even while the Israelites were doing this, God knew all that was going on. When God had spoken to the people, it had terrified them. Then the cloud enveloped the mountaintop for six days before God began communing alone with Moses. God had not moved away from them; He had only moved to the mountaintop, and the cloud was within their sight.

Moses had been on the mountaintop 40 days and nights, or about six weeks. Although the people couldn't see God or Moses, who was with Him, the cloud was still a visible evidence of His presence. But the people grew cynical and impatient, and then their hearts turned to false gods.

How easily we forget when God has spoken to us. Maybe He has spoken to us through an accident in the family or among our close acquaintances. Perhaps there has been a death, and we have been awed at such a tragedy. But soon it is forgotten again, and our hearts are no longer tender toward God. It's possible that God allowed whatever took place to happen so that He could get our attention and cause us to see our spiritual need. But how quickly the human heart turns from God, and we refuse to let Him deal with our soul's need.

The Israelites somehow forgot that God had been leading them so gloriously and wonderfully during the three months since they had come out of Egypt. Nevertheless, they did not forget the idols of Egypt. Even much later Joshua had to remind them to put away the gods which their fathers had served in Egypt (Josh. 24:14).

From the Israelites we see what a terrible thing the fretfulness of impatience is. From the time they left Egypt they had shown their impatience. They were impatient at the Red Sea when they were hemmed in. At the waters of Marah and at Rephidim when they needed water to drink, they were impatient not only with their leader, Moses, but also with God Himself. They did not realize that God was using these exact circumstances to teach them patience.

How much the Israelites were like believers today! It is so easy to forget all that God has done for us in the past, and we fail so often to see that He is trying to teach us valuable lessons as we pass through trials. Someone has described impatience as an attempt to do for oneself what God has not done or has delayed to do. As such, impatience is the enemy of faith.

The Results of Impatience

Abraham is a good illustration of one who became impatient with the promises of God and could no longer wait for God to act. Genesis 16 tells the sad story. Abraham could no longer wait for God to fulfill His promise to provide a son. As a result of his impatience, Ishmael was born to Abraham and Hagar, but Abraham was later to experience great anxiety because of this lack of patience.

At Mount Sinai, Israel's impatience resulted in idolatry. They refused to wait on the Lord. And even today, waiting on the Lord is a lost art. Believers today don't seem to have time to wait on the Lord. They rush here and there, involved in all kinds of activities, but don't give enough attention to getting the direction of the Lord before they rush off. Waiting does not mean sitting in a rocking chair, twiddling your thumbs, expecting God to do something sensational; rather, waiting on the Lord is simply putting your confidence in Him and waiting for God to act at His chosen time.

God didn't really need 40 days to reveal to Moses all that He had or to produce the two tables of stone with the Law on them. This length of time that Moses was on the mountaintop was just another test for the people of Israel. They were quick to say that they would obey the Lord (Ex. 24:3,7), but when Moses was gone from them for only six weeks, they turned to false gods.

Faith must be tried, not to prove to God that it is genuine, because He knows what is in the heart, but to show the person involved whether or not he has genuine faith. The New Testament says, "That the trial of your faith, being much more precious than of gold that perisheth, though it be tried with fire, might be found unto praise and honour and glory at the appearing of Jesus Christ" (I Pet. 1:7).

Much time had gone into God's dealing with Moses so God could show him the true character of his faith. It took 80 years of patient training for Moses to be what God wanted him to be.

Aaron Makes an Image

Because of impatience the Israelites called on Aaron to make them some gods to follow, since they did not know what had happened to Moses. This would have been an opportune time for Aaron to have taken a strong position and to have admonished the Israelites for their lack of faith and patience. But instead, notice what Aaron told them: "Break off the golden earrings, which are in the ears of your wives, of your sons, and of your daughters, and bring them unto me" (Ex. 32:2). Perhaps Aaron chose this particular means because he knew what they requested was wrong, and he wanted to make it hard for them. Perhaps he thought they would change their minds if they realized what it would cost them. But regardless of what he thought, they did not change their minds. "All the people brake off the golden earrings

which were in their ears, and brought them unto Aaron"
(v. 3).

Aaron still did not rebuke them for turning away from
God; instead, "he received them at their hand, and fashioned
it with a graving tool, after he had made it a molten calf: and
they said, These be thy gods, O Israel, which brought thee up
out of the land of Egypt" (v. 4).

It is incredible to think that Aaron would do something
like this after he had been so closely related to Moses in his
dealings with God. But notice what else Aaron did: "When
Aaron saw it, he built an altar before it; and Aaron made
proclamation, and said, To morrow is a feast to the Lord"
(v. 5).

Aaron and Hur had been left to look after the affairs of
Israel while Moses was absent. Joshua, Moses' servant, had
gone partway up the mountain with Moses, so he was not
with the people at the time of this sin. But while Moses was
on the mountaintop speaking to God face to face, the people
wanted some likeness to worship as a substitute. The people
were never allowed to see God face to face, but they knew
He was on the mountaintop because of all the evidences they
saw. But they wanted something they could feel with their
hands, something they could see.

The religion of the natural man demands something he
can perceive with his eyes. That is why so many people
today—even Christians—go after things that are earthly. They
need the security that is provided only by what they are able
to touch and see.

The Israelites were no different; they wanted a god they
could see. Moses was gone, and because their eyes had been
on him rather than on God, they wanted an image. Perhaps
this is why God took Moses away from them for a time. God
not only wanted to talk to Moses face to face, but He also
wanted to reveal to the Israelites that they were not really
trusting God as they thought they were. What a lesson this is
for believers today! Our trust should be in God, not in man.

A Prophet and a Priest

In order for us to better understand the situation Aaron
faced, it is necessary to examine more closely the difference

between the ministries of Moses and Aaron. Moses was a prophet; Aaron was a priest. There is a vast difference in these two offices. A prophet went before God to receive a divine message and then went before the people to speak on behalf of God. Thus, he represented God before man.

In one sense, preachers today are prophets since they deliver the message from God's Word to the people, but they are not prophets in the technical sense such as Moses was.

Moses was on the mountaintop receiving new revelation from God, but the people at the foot of the mountain were impatient. They just could not wait any longer for God's word. We frequently act in the same way; we do not take time to study the Word of God as we should. This is why the Word of God never seems to affect the lives of many believers even though they hear fine messages.

Moses was a prophet, but Aaron was a priest. The roles of a prophet and a priest were completely opposite. A prophet represented a holy God before sinful man; a priest represented sinful man before a holy God.

A prophet and a priest were equally important even though they had distinctively different functions. Another contrast of the two ministries is that a prophet declared doctrine—he gave God's teaching to the people. On the other hand, a priest declared experience—he presented the experiences of people to God. Doctrine and experience are related, but experience must come out of doctrine. Doctrine must not come out of experience.

Some people have an experience and then go to the Scriptures in an attempt to substantiate what they have experienced. They are really trying to build a doctrine on the basis of experience rather than making sure their experience is based on proper doctrine. We face many problems in evangelicalism today that are related to this matter of wanting to determine doctrine by experience. The believer should always move from doctrine to experience, never from experience to doctrine.

Christ as Prophet, Priest and King

Three great offices known in the Old Testament were prophet, priest and king. The Lord Jesus Christ is qualified to

fill each of these positions. When He came to earth, He filled
the position of prophet, for He declared God's message of
love, grace and mercy to mankind. Having shed His blood for
the forgiveness of sins and having ascended to heaven, Christ
is now the priest of all those who call on Him. He represents
their needs to the Heavenly Father. The Apostle John
reminded his readers of this when he said, "My little children,
these things write I unto you, that ye sin not. And if any man
sin, we have an advocate with the Father, Jesus Christ the
righteous" (I John 2:1). The Lord Jesus Christ is at the
Father's side interceding in behalf of believers.

Referring to the Lord Jesus Christ, Hebrews 7:25 says,
"Wherefore he is able also to save them to the uttermost that
come unto God by him, seeing he ever liveth to make
intercession for them." He is able to intercede for believers
because He understands their needs. "Seeing then that we
have a great high priest, that is passed into the heavens, Jesus
the Son of God, let us hold fast our profession. For we have
not an high priest which cannot be touched with the feeling
of our infirmities; but was in all points tempted like as we
are, yet without sin. Let us therefore come boldly unto the
throne of grace, that we may obtain mercy, and find grace to
help in time of need" (4:14-16).

Someday, Jesus Christ will return as king. The Bible
refers to Him as "King of Kings, and Lord of Lords" (Rev.
19:16). The Lord Jesus Christ will rule personally on earth
during the thousand-year kingdom (20:1-6).

Aaron's Weak Leadership

It was normal for the Israelites to approach Aaron with
their request, because he was their priest to represent them
before God. They thought Moses would never return, and
they wanted divine guidance for the future, so they came to
Aaron with their proposal.

But how could Aaron, who had witnessed and had
assisted in the performance of the miracles in Egypt, be so
forgetful and so blind that he yielded to Israel's whims and
wishes? Aaron had personally seen that the gods of Egypt
had no power, yet when he was asked to produce a god, he
went along with the request. Without question, Aaron knew

that God's presence was on the mountain with Moses, yet knowing this, he still gave in to the wishes of the Israelites.

God calls for and needs true and fearless leadership. Moses had been prepared by God for a period of 80 years, but Aaron had only one year of preparation in Egypt. Aaron was a weak leader from the beginning. The perils of weak leadership are exemplified in Aaron.

In the first crisis he faced after having been put in the position of responsibility, Aaron totally failed. He became a compromiser, a situation adapter, a servant of the people. His weakness was also seen later in the excuses he gave to Moses and in his outright lying about the golden calf. He sought only to justify himself.

While God was communicating with Moses on the mountaintop, He confronted Moses with what was taking place below. He said to Moses, "Go, get thee down; for thy people, which thou broughtest out of the land of Egypt, have corrupted themselves: they have turned aside quickly out of the way which I commanded them: they have made them a molten calf, and have worshipped it, and have sacrificed thereunto, and said, These be thy gods, O Israel, which have brought thee up out of the land of Egypt" (Ex. 32:7,8).

Earlier, when God spoke before all the people, He had specifically told them: "Thou shalt not make unto thee any graven image, or any likeness of any thing that is in heaven above, or that is in the earth beneath, or that is in the waters under the earth. Thou shalt not bow down thyself to them, nor serve them: for I the Lord thy God am a jealous God, visiting the iniquity of the fathers upon the children unto the third and fourth generation of them that hate me" (20:4,5).

To what God had spoken, the people had answered, "All the words which the Lord hath said will we do" (24:3). But they had done precisely what God had forbidden them to do. While Moses was on the mountaintop with God, the Israelites broke the first two commandments. And, according to James 2:10, when a person breaks one of the commandments, he is guilty of all. They had promised to keep the Law, but before they had received it in written form they had broken it.

Notice the words God used when He told Moses about the terrible sin of the people. God referred to the Israelites as "thy" people which "thou" (Moses) brought out of the land

of Egypt (32:7). At this point, God was actually disclaiming
the people of Israel. They had, by their sin, forfeited the
right to all of His blessings. After they had made such a
strong statement about being willing to do all that God said,
they had utterly failed. And if God had treated them
according to the Law which He had just spoken to them,
they would have been lost beyond recovery and would have
perished because of their own willful sin and apostasy.

Chapter 20

Moses Intercedes for Israel

In righteousness, God was ready to consume the Israelites. He said to Moses, "I have seen this people, and, behold, it is a stiffnecked people: now therefore let me alone, that my wrath may wax hot against them, and that I may consume them: and I will make of thee a great nation" (vv. 9,10).

The greatness of Moses is revealed here because he completely ignored God's offer to make of him a great nation. Moses began immediately to intercede for his people. Verses 11-13 record his intercession for them: "Lord, why doth thy wrath wax hot against thy people, which thou hast brought forth out of the land of Egypt with great power, and with a mighty hand?" (v. 11).

Whereas God had referred to the Israelites as "thy people" (v. 7) when talking to Moses, Moses referred to them as "thy people" (v. 11) when he talked with God. Moses refused to accept God's statement that they were his people, for he knew they belonged to the Lord. And Moses was absolutely right. All that had been done for the people had been done by God.

Moses was possibly the greatest intercessor who has ever lived, apart from the Lord Jesus Christ Himself. Moses' powerful intercession came at the time of his greatest test, for God was willing to make of him a great nation if Moses would let Him alone so He could wipe out the Israelites. God was willing to start all over again with one man. He had done this at the time of the flood when only Noah and his family had been spared. And now God was willing to destroy Israel and start all over with Moses.

On the surface, it is difficult to understand this passage, for it seems so unlike God to want to destroy the Israelites after bringing them into existence as a nation. I think the key to the passage, however, is that God was pleased with Moses' intercession and was really testing him to show us the type of man he was.

As Moses pleaded with God, he did not use his own close relationship to God as the basis of his appeal. Moses' thoughts were only of God and the Israelites, which indicated his genuine love for God and the people. Moses did not plead for that which would further his own cause temporarily, but he pleaded with eternal values in view. Moses had already made the decision to follow God by faith. Hebrews 11:24-26 says, "By faith Moses, when he was come to years, refused to be called the son of Pharaoh's daughter; choosing rather to suffer affliction with the people of God, than to enjoy the pleasures of sin for a season; esteeming the reproach of Christ greater riches than the treasures in Egypt: for he had respect unto the recompence of the reward."

Earlier Moses had refused to be called the son of Pharaoh's daughter; here he declined the offer to be made the head of a nation. He chose rather to be identified with the stiffnecked and disobedient Israelites. More than 40 years previously, he had chosen to go with them, and here he reaffirmed his choice.

In Moses we see a Christlike spirit. He did not seek his own glory, but he sought the best for others. Philippians 2:5-8 reveals that the Lord Jesus Christ laid aside personal glory to come to earth and shed His blood for the sin of mankind. This was unselfishness at its greatest!

Although Moses is not to be placed on the same level as the Lord Jesus Christ, he was selfless in his appeal to God not to destroy the Israelites and make of him a nation. The appeals of Moses had three bases: God's grace and mercy, God's glory and God's faithfulness.

Appeal to God's Grace and Mercy

Moses' appeal to God's grace and mercy is seen in Exodus 32:11: "Moses besought the Lord his God, and said, Lord, why doth thy wrath wax hot against thy people, which thou hast brought forth out of the land of Egypt with great power, and with a mighty hand?"

God had brought the Israelites out of Egypt by His grace, purely and simply. Everything God had done for the people, both in Egypt and after they left Egypt, was because of His grace. He had delivered them from Egypt by the Passover, He had brought them through the Red Sea, He had given them manna and meat to eat and water to drink in the wilderness, and He had fought for them against Amalek. All of this was simply because of His grace.

God had also extended much mercy to the Israelites. There is a distinction between grace and mercy. Grace is that which God gives to people because of who He is and what He is. He does not give to people because they are deserving but only because of His own person and character. Mercy is also given by God to people, but it is given when man deserves to be judged by God for sin. In His mercy, God makes provision for the sinfulness of man, although He does not overlook sin.

Moses made no effort to deny or to excuse Israel's sin. He knew God's grace had delivered Israel from bondage in Egypt, and he also seemed to be aware that where sin abounds, grace abounds much more (see Rom. 5:20). Moses knew that grace and mercy were part of God's character, so he pleaded on this basis.

Appeal to God's Glory

Moses also appealed on the basis of God's glory. Moses said, "Wherefore should the Egyptians speak, and say, For mischief did he bring them out, to slay them in the mountains, and to consume them from the face of the earth? Turn from thy fierce wrath, and repent of this evil against thy people" (Ex. 32:12).

Dealing with Israel's sin involved the character of God. If He spared the people, would they not think of Him as weak and consider His warnings and also His promises as nothing to be taken seriously? On the other hand, His glory was at stake if He destroyed them. To destroy the Israelites would bring great reproach on His name, especially from the Egyptians who knew He had taken them out of their land by miraculous power. If God destroyed the Israelites in the

wilderness, it would give the enemy an occasion to boast over
their destruction and to bring reproach on the name of God.

Just as at a later time God will gather the Israelites from
among all nations for His name's sake (Ezek. 36:21-24), so
He had brought the Israelites out of Egypt; and it was important that He preserve them for His name's sake.

This reveals to us two of the prime secrets in prevailing
prayer. The first secret is bowing the heart to God's will, and
the second secret is doing all to the glory of God. These two
elements should always be found together in our lives.
Whenever we accept something as God's will, we should also
honor Him in all that we do. The Bible tells believers,
"Whether therefore ye eat, or drink, or whatsoever ye do, do
all to the glory of God" (I Cor. 10:31). This "do all" includes
prayer.

Appeal to God's Faithfulness

Moses not only appealed on the basis of God's grace and
mercy and on the basis of His glory but also on the basis of
God's faithfulness. Moses said, "Remember Abraham, Isaac,
and Israel, thy servants, to whom thou swarest by thine own
self, and saidst unto them, I will multiply your seed as the
stars of heaven, and all this land that I have spoken of will I
give unto your seed, and they shall inherit it for ever" (Ex.
32:13).

God had made binding, unconditional promises, and
Moses was reminding God of those promises. Notice that
Moses used nothing in the lives of the Israelites as a basis for
his pleading, for they had committed sin worthy of His
wrath. Moses' plea was based on the character of God,
particularly His faithfulness.

When God promised the land to Abraham, Isaac and
Jacob, He had made unconditional agreements, or covenants,
with them. God promised to do certain things whether
individual descendants of Abraham responded favorably or
not. So the fact that God told Moses He wanted to destroy
the Israelites and make of Moses a new nation indicates that
it was only a test of Moses.

Concerning God's promise to Abraham, the Book of
Hebrews says, "For when God made promise to Abraham,

because he could swear by no greater, he sware by himself.... Wherein God, willing more abundantly to shew unto the heirs of promise the immutability of his counsel, confirmed it by an oath: that by two immutable things, in which it was impossible for God to lie, we might have a strong consolation, who have fled for refuge to lay hold upon the hope set before us" (6:13,17,18).

Since God had bound Himself by His own Word, there was no greater basis for Moses' plea than the faithfulness of God. It would have been hopeless for Moses to have pleaded on the basis of what Israel was, because all that they were and did only exposed them to the righteous indignation of a holy God. Moses pleaded on the basis of God's faithfulness, because he knew that "God is not a man, that he should lie; neither the son of man, that he should repent: hath he said, and shall he not do it? Or hath he spoken, and shall he not make it good?" (Num. 23:19).

These considerations weighed so heavily on Moses that he refused to even think about the divine offer to make him the only survivor and the progenitor of a great nation. Speaking of this time in Israel's history, the psalmist wrote: "Therefore he said that he would destroy them, had not Moses his chosen stood before him in the breach, to turn away his wrath, lest he should destroy them" (Ps. 106:23). Remember, God had told Moses, "Let me alone, that my wrath may wax hot against them, and that I may consume them" (Ex. 32:10).

After Moses' great intercession for the people of Israel, "the Lord repented of the evil which he thought to do unto his people" (v. 14). These words do not mean that God changed His mind or altered His purpose, because with Him there is "no variableness, neither shadow of turning" (James 1:17). God never deviates even slightly from His eternal purpose.

When the Scriptures speak of God's "repenting," they are employing a figure of speech in language we can understand. As far as Moses was concerned, God seemingly changed His mind. The statement of Exodus 32:14 simply expresses in human terms the fact that God had answered Moses' prayer.

Moses' faith rose above all difficulties. He claimed God's help and—inasmuch as God cannot deny Himself—Moses'

prayer was answered. It was answered because his
intercession was based on the grace and mercy of God for His
people, on the glory of God which was at stake, and on the
faithfulness of God to His own Word.

The Mediator Becomes the Judge

The scene changed suddenly as Moses finished interceding
for his people and received God's affirmative answer. "Moses
turned, and went down from the mount, and the two tables
of the testimony were in his hand: the tables were written on
both their sides; on the one side and on the other were they
written. And the tables were the work of God, and the
writing was the writing of God, graven upon the tables" (Ex.
32:15,16).

As Moses and Joshua were on their way down the
mountain, they heard the people shouting, and Joshua said,
"There is a noise of war in the camp" (v. 17). But Moses and
Joshua soon decided that the noise was not that of war but
that the people were singing. "And it came to pass, as soon as
he came nigh unto the camp, that he saw the calf, and the
dancing: and Moses' anger waxed hot, and he cast the tables
out of his hands, and brake them beneath the mount"
(v. 19).

After his magnificent intercession before God, Moses
came down the mountain and saw Israel's idolatry. He
immediately agreed with God about the awfulness of the
peoples' sin and began at once to pronounce judgment on
them.

On the mountain, Moses was the typical mediator,
pleading effectually before the Lord to turn away His wrath
from His stiffnecked people. But at the foot of the mountain,
as Moses viewed the idolatrous Israelites breaking the first
two commandments, he threw down the tables of the Law in
holy indignation. This was the same holy indignation which
Moses had seen in God. He had been with God long enough
that he expressed the very characteristics of God. Moses'
wrath was not so much against the people as it was against
their horrible sin of idolatry, which God had specifically
forbidden.

After Moses threw down the tables of stone and broke them, "he took the calf which they had made, and burnt it in the fire, and ground it to powder, and strawed [scattered] it upon the water, and made the children of Israel drink of it" (v. 20). Then he publicly rebuked Aaron as the one responsible and, therefore, guilty of this most shameful act of idolatry. Moses asked Aaron, "What did this people unto thee, that thou hast brought so great a sin upon them?" (v. 21).

After rebuking Aaron for his part in this hideous sin, "Moses stood in the gate of the camp, and said, Who is on the Lord's side? Let him come unto me. And all the sons of Levi gathered themselves together unto him. And he said unto them, Thus saith the Lord God of Israel, Put every man his sword by his side, and go in and out from gate to gate throughout the camp, and slay every man his brother, and every man his companion, and every man his neighbor. And the children of Levi did according to the word of Moses: and there fell of the people that day about three thousand men" (vv. 26-28).

Notice the extreme contrast between the intercession and the judging. The contrast is so radical that many have been perplexed by it and have suggested many absurd explanations which are out of harmony with the overall incident as it is presented by the Scriptures. Sin against the person of God, as in all cases of idolatrous worship and practices, requires drastic measures. Judgment had to take place before the call to consecration.

So we learn that Moses, who so effectively interceded in behalf of the people and stopped the destroying hand of God, suddenly judged the people himself because of their sin.

Christ as Judge

The question that arises here is, Was Moses, in his judging, no longer the foreshadowing of Christ as our intercessor? The answer is yes—an emphatic yes.

On the mountain, he is seen as a type of Christ making intercession in behalf of his people. When God wanted to destroy the Israelites, Moses brought forth a threefold argument against such action. He appealed to the grace and

mercy of God, to the glory of God and to the faithfulness of
God. But when he came down from the mountain and saw
firsthand how the people had sinned against the person of
God, Moses acted as judge. Awful sin had been committed,
and judgment had to fall on it.

In his hands Moses carried the tables of stone which
declared that the righteous requirements of the Law cannot
be set aside in any way. Sin had to be judged. Galatians 6:7
states the timeless principle: "Whatsoever a man soweth, that
shall he also reap."

Notice what the Apostle John saw in his vision of the
Lord Jesus Christ while on the Isle of Patmos: "I turned to
see the voice that spake with me. And being turned, I saw
seven golden candlesticks; and in the midst of the seven
candlesticks one like unto the Son of man, clothed with a
garment down to the foot, and girt about the paps [chest]
with a golden girdle" (Rev. 1:12,13).

This is the way John saw the Lord Jesus Christ's
appearing to the seven churches, because the seven
candlesticks symbolized the seven churches (see v. 20). But
the aspect of judgment could also be seen in the appearance
of Christ: "His head and his hairs were white like wool, as
white as snow; and his eyes were as a flame of fire; and his
feet like unto fine brass, as if they burned in a furnace; and
his voice as the sound of many waters. And he had in his
right hand seven stars: and out of his mouth went a sharp
twoedged sword: and his countenance was as the sun shineth
in his strength" (vv. 14-16). So in these verses we see aspects
of the character of Christ which judged—"eyes . . . as a flame
of fire"; "feet like unto fine brass, as if they burned in a
furnace"; and "out of his mouth went a sharp twoedged
sword."

A true picture of Christ not only includes characteristics
that reflect His love but also characteristics that reflect His
judgment. He is both Saviour and intercessor, and He is a
judge who cannot overlook sin. He Himself has borne the
penalty for sin for the entire world (I John 2:2), and any
person who wants to be delivered from condemnation must
personally receive Jesus Christ as Saviour.

So as we consider Moses' actions, we see that he
foreshadowed Jesus Christ even in the judging of sin. Just as

Moses, in holy indignation, threw down the tables of stone and shattered them (Ex. 32:19), so Jesus "went into the temple, and began to cast out them that sold and bought in the temple, and overthrew the tables of the moneychangers, and the seats of them that sold doves" (Mark 11:15). He said to the people, "Is it not written, My house shall be called of all nations the house of prayer? But ye have made it a den of thieves" (v. 17).

Prior to worshiping the golden calf, the Israelites had seen the great majesty and awesomeness of God when He spoke to them from the mountain. Six weeks later, while they could still see the evidence of God's awesome presence on the mountaintop as He spoke to Moses, they repudiated God and called for a substitute god. There was no other choice—judgment had to be exercised.

Moses Rebukes Aaron

What a contrast we see between Moses and Aaron! Aaron responded to Moses, "Let not the anger of my lord wax hot: thou knowest the people, that they are set on mischief. For they said unto me, Make us gods, which shall go before us: for as for this Moses, the man that brought us up out of the land of Egypt, we wot not what is become of him. And I said unto them, Whosoever hath any gold, let them break it off. So they gave it me: then I cast it into the fire, and there came out this calf" (Ex. 32:22-24).

Aaron had no sense of the terribleness of the sin he had just committed; there was no indication of repentance at this time. He accepted no blame himself but endeavored to place all the blame on others. How ridiculous of him to expect Moses to believe that he had just thrown the jewelry into the fire and the calf came out! He was like Adam and Eve in the Garden of Eden, who refused to accept personal responsibility for what had taken place.

Leaders in Christian circles so often claim they must make concessions because the people demand it. The life of Saul provides a good lesson concerning this matter. God told Saul to completely wipe out the remembrance of Amalek by destroying everyone and everything, but Saul was disobedient (see I Sam. 15:2-9). When Samuel faced him with this disobedience, Saul said, "The people spared the best of the sheep and of the oxen, to sacrifice unto the Lord thy God; and the rest we have utterly destroyed" (v. 15). This was Saul's excuse—he had made concessions because the people demanded it. But Samuel told him, "To obey is better than sacrifice" (v. 22).

Aaron was afraid of the people more than he was afraid of God. We all have this tendency; we seem to be more concerned about what people say than about what God's Word says on a given subject. It is important for every believer to fix his eyes on God and to obey Him, regardless of what people say.

Aaron could not stand up against a few people, but Moses feared God and walked so close to Him that he did not fear an army of over 600,000 Israelites (see Num. 1:46). Moses boldly proclaimed the execution of judgment on those who led in this sin.

The contrast between Aaron and Moses reveals the contrast between a servant of men and a servant of God. Each Christian should ask himself, Am I serving God, or am I only serving people? When a person acts with God, he always acts with power. The person who acts with men or because of fear of men, acts with weakness.

Not only did Aaron blame the others, but he also refused to take any personal responsibility. Not only that, he told an outright lie. He had fashioned the golden calf with a graving tool (Ex. 32:4), but he told Moses he had just thrown the jewelry in the fire, and the calf came out (v. 24).

If it had not been for the intercession of Moses, God would have destroyed Aaron for his responsibility in this terrible sin. In telling the people of this incident later, Moses said, "The Lord was very angry with Aaron to have destroyed him: and I prayed for Aaron also the same time" (Deut. 9:20).

No Neutrality

The Exodus account refers to the nakedness of the people: "When Moses saw that the people were naked; (for Aaron had made them naked unto their shame among their

enemies:) then Moses stood in the gate of the camp, and said,
Who is on the Lord's side?" (Ex. 32:25,26).

The people were naked because they had indulged in
idolatrous sensualism, which accompanies idol worship. This
called for drastic action. Thus, Moses asked the people who
had not bowed their knee to the golden calf to take a stand
as to whether they were on the Lord's side or not. Where
there is open apostasy, there can be no neutrality. The Bible
says, "What agreement hath the temple of God with idols?
For ye are the temple of the living God; as God hath said, I
will dwell in them, and walk in them; and I will be their God,
and they shall be my people. Wherefore come out from
among them, and be ye separate, saith the Lord, and touch
not the unclean thing; and I will receive you" (II Cor.
6:16,17).

Hebrews 10 clearly reveals that there can be no neutrality
where there is open apostasy. Verse 26 says, "For if we sin
wilfully after that we have received the knowledge of the
truth, there remaineth no more sacrifice for sins." Israel had
sinned willfully; they knew the truth. God had mercifully
and graciously delivered them from Egypt and had sustained
them in the wilderness. They had seen God's miracle-working
power on several occasions. But at the foot of Mount Sinai
they sinned against all this knowledge.

To those who sin against knowledge, the Book of
Hebrews says, "There remaineth no more sacrifice for sins,
but a certain fearful looking for of judgment and fiery
indignation, which shall devour the adversaries" (vv. 26,27).
The writer of Hebrews was not referring to eternal
condemnation but to physical judgment.

He went on to say, "He that despised Moses' law died
without mercy under two or three witnesses" (v. 28). This is
precisely what happened to the Israelites after they made the
golden calf; Moses brought judgment on them.

Hebrews 10:30 says, "For we know him that hath said,
Vengeance belongeth unto me, I will recompense, saith the
Lord. And again, The Lord shall judge his people." And as a
summary statement concerning any who would rebel against
God, verse 31 says, "It is a fearful thing to fall into the hands
of the living God."

Because there was open apostasy among the Israelites, Moses was concerned that there be no neutrality lest the vengeance of God come on them. Earlier, God had told Moses, "Let me alone, . . . that I may consume them" (Ex. 32:10). The judgment of God was suspended because of Moses' great intercession for the people. But as Moses saw the hideous sin with his own eyes, he was concerned that his judgment be exercised immediately, or else God might have still judged.

Physical Judgment

The judgment involved was not an eternal condemnation in hell; rather, it was a physical judgment for the sin they had committed. Sin cannot be overlooked, and those who had sinned suffered physical consequences because of it.

Moses wanted every person to take a definite stand for or against God; thus, he commanded, "Who is on the Lord's side? Let him come unto me" (v. 26).

Today, as we take our stand with the Lord, it is important to realize that we are not to fight people, we are to fight sin. Ephesians 6:12 tells believers, "For we wrestle not against flesh and blood, but against principalities, against powers, against the rulers of the darkness of this world, against spiritual wickedness in high places." Because our battle is not against flesh and blood, we are not to fight people. Our battle is against spiritual wickedness, so our real fight is against sin wherever it is found. The greatest means of fighting is by prayer against the evil forces that promote sin. What a shame it is when believers fight believers. Christians should be able to live in such harmony that the unsaved will be attracted to Christ as a result. Jesus said, "That they all may be one; as thou, Father, art in me, and I in thee, that they also may be one in us: that the world may believe that thou hast sent me" (John 17:21). The unity of believers is a convincing proof that God has sent Jesus Christ into the world to take care of the sin issue.

When Moses commanded the Israelites to take their stand for the Lord, "all the sons of Levi gathered themselves together unto him" (Ex. 32:26). To this group, Moses presented what must have amounted to the most severe test they had ever faced. He instructed them to kill those who had been guilty of worshiping the golden calf, most likely referring to the leaders in the sin. Apparently, there was no other remedy for cleansing Israel of this atrocious sin.

Hebrews 10:29 says, "Of how much sorer punishment, suppose ye, shall he be thought worthy, who hath trodden under foot the Son of God, and hath counted the blood of the covenant, wherewith he was sanctified, an unholy thing, and hath done despite unto the Spirit of grace?" This New Testament passage reveals what took place when the Israelites worshiped the golden calf. The Israelites had trodden under foot God Himself, who was even then on the mountaintop in the cloud. They could see the cloud of His glory, but they completely disregarded Him and even trod under foot the blood which had emancipated them from Egypt.

Aaron had told the people, "These be thy gods, O Israel, which brought thee up out of the land of Egypt" (Ex. 32:4). What a total disregard for the blood that had redeemed them! There was no alternative but to bring the severest of judgments on the people.

This may perplex some people, because it does not seem to harmonize with the love of God that the Bible speaks of. God is love (I John 4:8), yet that love demands righteous judgment. In addition to preaching the love of God, there also needs to be the preaching of the wrath of a holy God on all those who disown Him as Saviour and Lord.

Everyone will someday be forced to acknowledge Jesus Christ as Saviour and Lord. Philippians 2 says that Jesus Christ was willing to leave the glory He had with the Father and come to earth to die on the cross for the sin of the world (see vv. 5-8). "Wherefore God also hath highly exalted him, and given him a name which is above every name: that at the name of Jesus every knee should bow, of things in heaven, and things in earth, and things under the earth; and that every tongue should confess that Jesus Christ is Lord, to the glory of God the Father" (vv. 9-11).

During the coming Great Tribulation, people will endeavor to escape the wrath of God but will be unable to do so. "The kings of the earth, and the great men, and the rich men, and the chief captains, and the mighty men, and every bondman, and every free man, hid themselves in the dens and in the rocks of the mountains; and said to the mountains and rocks, Fall on us, and hide us from the face of him that sitteth on the throne, and from the wrath of the Lamb: for the great day of his wrath is come; and who shall be able to stand?" (Rev. 6:15-17). No wonder Hebrews 10:31 says, "It is a fearful thing to fall into the hands of the living God."

God cannot lower His standards for even one minute. Open repudiation of God, as seen in the worship of the golden calf, calls for open judgment of sin. The judgment resulted in the death of about 3000 men (Ex. 32:28).

Moses' Power and Authority

The people were terror-stricken and awed by the irrefutable power exercised by Moses. He stood, one man against more than 600,000 soldiers (Num. 1:46), and commanded that those who were guilty of this sin be put to death. Moses had just been in the very presence of God, and no one was able to resist his authority and power.

As the people viewed the threatening cloud on the mountaintop above them, revealing God's presence, they could offer no resistance, and 3000 were slain because they had repudiated God. Every person must have been weighed down—some with remorse for their sin, others with dread that the wrath of God would destroy even more of them. No doubt they were vividly reminded at this time of the great numbers of Egyptians who had been destroyed at the time of the Passover and in the Red Sea. Perhaps they wondered if they would suffer a similar fate in the desert. They undoubtedly remembered the awful voice of God which they had heard about six weeks earlier, specifically prohibiting them from making any graven images. They had been quick at that time to say they would do everything God commanded, but they had committed a terrible sin. They had not feared God as they should have.

Regrettably, we are living in similar days. Relatively few people fear God. People speak mockingly of an almighty God, and He may have to lash out in fury again to show them the seriousness of such sin. We who know the Lord Jesus Christ as Saviour possess the sword of the Spirit, and with it we must engage in spiritual warfare and smite the Enemy whenever he lifts his head against Christ. As has been indicated previously, we do this, not by attacking people, but by attacking sin wherever it is found. Ephesians 6:10-18 instructs believers concerning spiritual warfare. Because we live in days of apostasy, it is extremely important that we take this passage seriously and obey its instructions.

Some speak of Jesus Christ, but they actually deny the effectiveness of the blood of Christ which has provided salvation for mankind. Many, even in religious circles, deny the inerrancy of the Scriptures, the virgin birth of Christ, His substitutionary death, His resurrection from the dead and His personal return. These are the fundamentals of the faith, and anyone who denies them actually denies the foundational truths of Christianity.

There is also a sense, however, in which those who know Jesus Christ as Saviour can deny Him. By their actions, they can deny that they belong totally to God. The tendency today is for believers to become consumed with the materialistic philosophy of the age. Those who do so are guilty of worshiping the idol of materialism.

May those of us who know Jesus Christ as Saviour determine within our hearts to fix our eyes on Christ and to serve and honor Him, regardless of the apostasy that is everywhere about us. Remember Moses' searching question: "Who is on the Lord's side?" (Ex. 32:26).

Chapter 21

Moses' Greatest Moment

After the judgment of God had fallen on the leaders of those responsible for the golden-calf incident, Moses told the people, "Consecrate yourselves to day to the Lord, even every man upon his son, and upon his brother; that he may bestow upon you a blessing this day" (Ex. 32:29). Moses was concerned that the people separate themselves from all the contamination of sin so that God might bless them.

Moses' Intercession

The following day, Moses said to the people, "Ye have sinned a great sin: and now I will go up unto the Lord; peradventure I shall make an atonement for your sin" (v. 30). This gives us the background for what was probably Moses' greatest moment. At this time Moses made his unparalleled intercession for the people.

Notice that Moses was not absolutely sure he would be able to gain atonement for the people's sin. Moses said, "Peradventure [perhaps] I shall make an atonement for your sin" (v. 30). Moses put himself into the breach—between God and His people—in an endeavor to achieve atonement for the sin of the Israelites.

Scripture records no other intercession that parallels Moses' intercession for Israel. Of course, the Lord Jesus Christ—because He is God—intercedes on a higher level than any human being. But Moses' intercession superceded that of any other human being recorded in the Bible. The Apostle Paul's intercession for his fellow Israelites came near in

214

greatness to Moses' great intercessory prayer, but I do not believe it was quite as great in its nature (see Rom. 9:1-5).

Moses' intercession was a beautiful foreshadowing of the atonement God has provided for the human race. Although mankind has been separated from God because of sin, God Himself made reconciliation possible by sending His only Son to pay the penalty for sin (John 3:16; Rom. 3:25). Because Moses loved the Israelites, he gave himself in interceding for them; because God loved mankind, He gave His only-begotten Son. Love and giving are inseparably linked—when one loves, he gives.

Through Moses, those who had led the people into the sin of idolatry had been punished, and the loyalty of the people had been reclaimed. There is, however, no record which indicates that the Israelites truly repented of their sin at that time. But they bent under the load of the terrible judgment, and Moses went before God to seek atonement for them.

In so doing, Moses was exercising his office of prophet—one who received a message from God and delivered it to the people. As their leader, Moses had a special relationship with the people, but he also had a special relationship to God. He spoke face to face with God concerning the people. What a relationship! It was as if Moses could feel the pulse of God's own heart.

I have often prayed that God would somehow break my own heart as His was broken for our sin. I want to feel the heartbeat of our great God who loved us so much He gave His only-begotten Son to die for our sins.

God's Righteousness and Mercy

As Moses was telling the people to wait while he went to meet God, God was on the mountaintop, as evidenced by the cloud. I can imagine God looking down and watching His servant Moses execute judgment on the people. Moses knew that God still waited in wrath on the mountain. This caused Moses to execute judgment with even greater urgency.

Remember, only part of the Law had been given at this time. But enough had been given that Moses knew a great deal about the horror of this terrible sin. He also knew about the uncompromising righteousness of an almighty God.

In the people's hearing, God had clearly stated, "Thou shalt have no other gods before me. Thou shalt not make unto thee any graven image, or any likeness of any thing that is in heaven above, or that is in the earth beneath, or that is in the water under the earth. Thou shalt not bow down thyself to them, nor serve them: for I the Lord thy God am a jealous God, visiting the iniquity of the fathers upon the children unto the third and fourth generation of them that hate me" (Ex. 20:3-5).

Although these verses list the prohibitions and judgment that would fall on those who disobeyed, verse 6 reveals God's mercy: "Shewing mercy unto thousands of them that love me, and keep my commandments." Even though many of God's people of Israel are still outside the fold of Jesus Christ, God is still showing mercy to them because of the love, compassion and faithfulness of Abraham. What a wonderful God He is!

But since God had said that He would visit the iniquity of the fathers to the third and fourth generations (v. 5), how could Moses' judgment suffice for the awful sin of idolatry? As severe as the judgment of Moses was, it was mild in comparison to the horrible sin that had been committed.

From experience, Moses knew that God had a way of atonement. In Egypt God had spared the life of the firstborn of all who had applied the blood of the substitute lamb. But what animal sacrifice would be sufficient to atone for the great sin of idolatry that the people had just committed? This sin was especially great because they had specific revelation indicating that they should not do it. They had sinned against their own knowledge.

Moses Offers Himself

When God had wanted to destroy the people for their sin, Moses had interceded for them. Moses pleaded on the basis of God's grace and mercy, His glory and His faithfulness. But now, Moses was entering into another aspect of intercession for the people. This intercession involved him specifically, and it involved a reinstatement of the Israelites as God's true people. God had told Moses, "Thy people, which thou broughtest out of the land of Egypt, have corrupted

themselves" (32:7). God was not even claiming the people as
His own at this point. Moses knew that the Israelites needed
to be brought back into a relationship with God whereby He
would claim them as His own and deal with them as His own.
For this reason, on the day after the leaders in the
idolatry had been judged, "Moses said unto the people, Ye
have sinned a great sin: and now I will go up unto the Lord;
peradventure I shall make an atonement for your sin" (v. 30).
One can imagine the mourning that took place among the
Israelites because of the newly made graves—3000 of them.
The awfulness of the sin of idolatry must have begun to
pierce the hearts of the remaining Israelites. Surely they
began to see the awesomeness of God on the mountain. The
people must have been afraid of what judgment of God might
fall on them next.

Think of all that Moses must have gone through between
the day of judgment and the following day when he went to
meet God. It was probably a sleepless night for him. His holy
anger against this vile sin was probably followed by deep
sorrow and pity for the people. No doubt his tears flowed
freely during the night. His deepest compassions had been
aroused. What love Moses had for his people!

By accepting previous sacrifices, God had indicated that
He would accept an innocent substitute in the place of a just
death for sin. He had also given part of the ceremonial law, so
Moses would have had this underscored in his thinking.

But then came the great moment. Would God accept
him—Moses—as the substitute for the sin of the people?
Moses did not yet have the deep understanding of these
matters as did the Apostle Paul, who wrote many centuries
later. That is why I believe the intercession of Moses
superceded that of Paul. Moses apparently did not clearly
realize that man could not possibly make atonement for man.
This is why he said, "Peradventure [perhaps] I shall make an
atonement for your sin" (v. 30).

As Moses spoke to the people, he did not gloss over their
gross wickedness; he did not attempt to minimize the
awfulness of their sin. As he had earlier charged Aaron, he
now—in deep love for God and for his people—charged them
with the horribleness of their sin. He dealt with them

faithfully about their sin, but he also referred to possible atonement.

Moses' hesitancy about whether or not atonement could be made for the people was undoubtedly a result of his concern over the enormity of their sin. Also, the people had given no indication that they had truly repented of their sin. Moses would have known that forgiveness could not be obtained without repentance for the sin.

In his announcement that he would go before the Lord in an endeavor to make atonement, Moses did not tell the people the price he was personally willing to pay—that of sacrificing himself as a substitute for their sin. But deeply locked in his own heart was that agony of love for them which caused him to be prepared to offer himself to God as a sacrifice for their sin.

It is evident that Moses intended to offer himself as a personal sacrifice for Israel's sin, because when he returned to God, he said, "Oh, this people have sinned a great sin, and have made them gods of gold. Yet now, if thou wilt forgive their sin—; and if not, blot me, I pray thee, out of thy book which thou hast written" (vv. 31,32). Moses was willing to be sent to hell for the people's sake if that could atone for their sin. What an offer!

Earlier, God had wanted Moses to step aside so He could consume the people for their sin, and Moses had pleaded with God not to do so. Now, Moses offered himself as a possible substitute sacrifice in behalf of the people. In effect, he said, "Let me die, if that will mean life for them. But if not, then destroy me too."

No doubt this secret was locked in Moses' heart as he climbed the mountain alone that day into the thick, foreboding cloud that was hiding God's presence. As he started up the mountain, probably with his head bowed, the people could see and begin to realize how much this man loved them. Imagine how the people felt as they stood watching and wondering what God would do. Would Moses be able to make atonement for them or not?

Notice the expression Moses used when he confessed his people's sin to God and asked for forgiveness: "If thou wilt forgive their sin—; and if not, blot me, I pray thee, out of thy book which thou hast written" (v. 32). As Moses thought of the alternative if God did not forgive the people of their sin, he could not even finish the sentence. The heart of God must have been moved toward His faithful servant, for this proposal would have reminded Him of another scene that would occur approximately 1500 years later when His own Son would die on the cross for mankind.

Moses' Offer Rejected

Moses soon discovered that his offer could not be accepted by God. No one who has a sin nature can atone for the sins of another. Psalm 49:7 says, "None of them can by any means redeem his brother, nor give to God a ransom for him." Moses himself was a sinner; he had even murdered someone years before. He needed atonement for his own sins, so he was in no position to atone for the sins of others.

God's answer to Moses was clear: "Whosoever hath sinned against me, him will I blot out of my book" (Ex. 32:33). There is no indication that God said this in a harsh way; rather, God must have looked on Moses with love and compassion. But God made it clear to Moses that he could not atone for the sin of the people; rather, whoever sinned would pay the consequences.

Many centuries later another person made a similar request. Concerning his fellow Israelites, the Apostle Paul said, "I say the truth in Christ, I lie not, my conscience also bearing me witness in the Holy Ghost, that I have great heaviness and continual sorrow in my heart. For I could wish that myself were accursed from Christ for my brethren, my kinsmen according to the flesh" (Rom. 9:1-3). But this was not possible for Paul, just as it was not possible for Moses.

As Moses received further revelation from God about sin and laws concerning sacrifice, he would clearly understand why it was not possible for him to make atonement for the Israelites. The blood sacrifices of the Old Testament pointed to the time when the Lord Jesus Christ would enter the human race and become *the* sacrifice for sin. This is why John the Baptist exclaimed concerning Christ: "Behold the Lamb of God, which taketh away the sin of the world" (John 1:29).

The sin of the entire human race was placed on Christ as He hung on the cross; thus II Corinthians 5:21 says, "For he hath made him to be sin for us, who knew no sin; that we might be made the righteousness of God in him." Because He was God as well as man, the Lord Jesus Christ was able to pay the penalty for the sin of the entire human race. No other person could have done this, because all except Christ were born with a sin nature. This is why Acts 4:12 says, "Neither is there salvation in any other: for there is none other name under heaven given among men, whereby we must be saved."

The provision for the payment of the penalty of sin was made entirely because of the grace and mercy of God. The great question since the fall of man had revolved around how God would be propitiated, or satisfied, for the sin of man. God Himself solved the problem by sending His own Son to be that satisfaction for sin.

Romans 3:25 refers to this act of God's grace and mercy when it says concerning the Lord Jesus Christ, "Whom God hath set forth to be a propitiation through faith in his blood, to declare his righteousness for the remission of sins that are past, through the forbearance of God." First John 2:2 also refers to Christ's satisfying the demands of the Heavenly Father for the sins of mankind: "He is the propitiation for our sins: and not for our's only, but also for the sins of the whole world."

Because the Lord Jesus Christ has satisfied the Heavenly Father concerning sin, He alone was able to say, "I am the way, the truth, and the life: no man cometh unto the Father, but by me" (John 14:6).

The seriousness of rejecting this one way of salvation is seen in what Peter told the Israelites on the Day of Pentecost: "For Moses truly said unto the fathers, A prophet shall the Lord your God raise up unto you of your brethren, like unto me; him shall ye hear in all things whatsoever he shall say unto you. And it shall come to pass, that every soul, which will not hear that prophet, shall be destroyed from among the people" (Acts 3:22,23). How significant that Peter quoted Moses, who had offered himself as an atonement for the sin of Israel.

Even though no human could atone for the sin of others,
"when the fulness of the time was come, God sent forth his
Son, made of a woman, made under the law, to redeem them
that were under the law, that we might receive the adoption
of sons" (Gal. 4:4,5).

The Prophet Isaiah predicted the coming of the Lord
Jesus Christ and all that He would endure for mankind. Isaiah
prophesied: "Surely he hath borne our griefs, and carried our
sorrows: yet we did esteem him stricken, smitten of God, and
afflicted. But he was wounded for our transgressions, he was
bruised for our iniquities: the chastisement of our peace was
upon him; and with his stripes we are healed. All we like
sheep have gone astray; we have turned every one to his own
way; and the Lord hath laid on him the iniquity of us all.

"He was oppressed, and he was afflicted, yet he opened
not his mouth: he is brought as a lamb to the slaughter, and
as a sheep before her shearers is dumb, so he openeth not his
mouth.

"Yet it pleased the Lord to bruise him; he hath put him
to grief: when thou shalt make his soul an offering for sin, he
shall see his seed, he shall prolong his days, and the pleasure
of the Lord shall prosper in his hand. He shall see of the
travail of his soul, and shall be satisfied: by his knowledge
shall my righteous servant justify many; for he shall bear
their iniquities" (Isa. 53:4-7,10,11). God was satisfied. God
accepted the offering of the Lord Jesus Christ!

As Moses pleaded with God after the incident of the
golden calf, he did not have all of this revelation concerning
redemption and the Person of Christ. Without a doubt this is
why this intercession was Moses' greatest moment. What
tremendous love Moses had for his fellow Israelites—none
greater was found until Christ Himself came to reveal God's
love to a world of sinners.

God Sends an Angel

Although at first the Israelites were threatened with the
loss of the divine presence, God offered to send His angel
before them to lead them into the land of promise. God told
Moses, "Therefore now go, lead the people unto the place of
which I have spoken unto thee: behold, mine Angel shall go

before thee" (Ex. 32:34). Although those responsible for sin
would suffer for their sin, God conceded to send His angel to
lead them on their way.

The reason God chose to send an angel rather than
leading the Israelites by His own presence is indicated in
Exodus 33:1-3: "And the Lord said unto Moses, Depart, and
go up hence, thou and the people which thou hast brought
up out of the land of Egypt, unto the land which I sware
unto Abraham, to Isaac, and to Jacob, saying, Unto thy seed
will I give it: and I will send an angel before thee; and I will
drive out the Canaanite, the Amorite, and the Hittite, and the
Perizzite, the Hivite, and the Jebusite: unto a land flowing
with milk and honey: for I will not go up in the midst of
thee; for thou art a stiffnecked people: lest I consume thee in
the way."

Moses had secured the Israelites' immediate safety as well
as a promise of angelic guidance and protection. But these
words of God make it clear that further chastisement was
destined for the people because of their sin. No doubt this
was because the offenders had shown no evidence of genuine
repentance.

Although Moses had wanted to be a substitute for the
people's sin, God had told him, "Whosoever hath sinned
against me, him will I blot out of my book" (32:33). Even
after promising an angel to guide them, God said,
"Nevertheless in the day when I visit I will visit their sin upon
them" (v. 34). Then God told them, "For I will not go up in
the midst of thee; for thou art a stiffnecked people: lest I
consume thee in the way" (33:3). Since there had been no
evidence of repentance on the people's part, they had not yet
been restored to fellowship in their covenant relationship
with God. God's righteousness could not allow Him to
personally guide the people because of their sin.

God's Chastening and Israel's Contrition

Moses' intercession had averted the penal wrath of God,
but because of the lack of repentance and confession, the
governmental consequences of their sin had not yet been
removed. The people still needed to appropriate God's
restoring mercy and grace. Because there had been no

repentance, "the Lord plagued the people, because they made the calf, which Aaron made" (Ex. 32:35).

This incident should remind those of us living in the 20th century that if it were not for the mercy of God, we would be consumed. His standards are much higher than we are ever able to attain on our own. If He so chose, He could destroy us because of our sin. Jeremiah realized this also, and he wrote: "But this I recall, therefore have I hope and expectation: it is of the Lord's mercies and loving-kindnesses that we are not consumed, because His (tender) compassions fail not. They are new every morning; great and abundant is Your stability and faithfulness. . . . For the Lord will not cast off for ever! But, though He causes grief, yet will He be moved to compassion according to the multitude of His lovingkindnesses and tender mercies. For He does not willingly and from His heart afflict or grieve the children of men" (Lam. 3:21-23, 31-33, Amplified).

God does not afflict people because He delights to do so; He afflicts because of a special purpose. Hebrews 12:10 clearly reveals that God afflicts us "for our profit, that we might be partakers of his holiness." The afflicting, or chastening, is not enjoyable at the time, but it produces that which is for our best and for God's glory. Verse 11 says, "Now no chastening for the present seemeth to be joyous, but grievous: nevertheless afterward it yieldeth the peaceable fruit of righteousness unto them which are exercised thereby."

Moses had been directed by the Lord to return to the camp with God's message for the people. Moses told them that God would not go up with them Himself, or He would consume them in the way because they were stiffnecked. "When the people heard these evil tidings, they mourned: and no man did put on him his ornaments" (Ex. 33:4).

Even the leaving off of their ornaments was because of the instruction of God: "For the Lord had said unto Moses, Say unto the children of Israel, Ye are a stiffnecked people: I will come up into the midst of thee in a moment, and consume thee: therefore now put off thy ornaments from thee, that I may know what to do unto thee. And the children of Israel stripped themselves of their ornaments by the mount Horeb" (vv. 5,6).

God's word, as delivered through Moses, brought a determined effect on the people. They were made to see the awfulness of their sin. They were brought low, into a state of contrition; repentance and worship were soon to follow. And because repentance was anticipated, the personal, divine presence of God was to be restored to them once they were fully brought into proper relationship with God. But only the fervent intercession of Moses for the people spared them from the righteous anger of God.

Had it not been for Moses' intercession, the people would have been exterminated. This is a beautiful foreshadowing of the Lord Jesus Christ, who now appears in the presence of the Father to intercede in behalf of all believers. Not only does He intercede, but "he is able also to save them to the uttermost that come unto God by him, seeing he ever liveth to make intercession for them" (Heb. 7:25). Because the Lord Jesus Christ is eternal and does not die as the Old Testament priests did, He is able to make intercession for believers forever.

Apart from the intercessory work of the Lord Jesus Christ, we would not be able to survive the holy wrath of God. Jesus Christ pleads our case before God on the merits of His own atoning sacrifice in our behalf. This intercessory ministry of Jesus sustains us in our pilgrim journey on the earth. Hebrews 9:24 says, "For Christ is not entered into the holy places made with hands, which are the figures of the true; but into heaven itself, now to appear in the presence of God for us."

Thus we see that Israel was not consumed, but they were plagued because of their lack of repentance. Unfortunately, there is little emphasis on repentance today. The Lord Jesus Christ said, "Except ye repent, ye shall all likewise perish" (Luke 13:3). The Lord Jesus also told the Church of Ephesus, "Remember therefore from whence thou art fallen, and repent, and do the first works; or else I will come unto thee quickly, and will remove thy candlestick out of his place, except thou repent" (Rev. 2:5).

God pronounced Israel a stiffnecked people, and this required that they be humbled. The first hopeful sign of their repentance is recorded in Exodus 33:4. After they heard God's message, "they mourned: and no man did put on him his ornaments." To "mourn" means to "sorrow" or to "lament." This was the first sign of their repentance. But true repentance is more than sorrow; it is a change of mind about one's sin and about God. Those who recognize their sinful condition and believe in Jesus Christ as Saviour have repented and receive forgiveness of sin and eternal life.

When the Israelites learned that Jehovah Himself would not accompany them to the Promised Land, they were moved to deep contrition. How could they go on without Him? Their eyes were opened, and they saw the seriousness of their sin.

Their situation was so different from that of the Church of Laodicea, to whom the Lord Jesus Christ said, "I know thy works, that thou art neither cold nor hot: I would thou wert cold or hot. So then because thou art lukewarm, and neither cold nor hot, I will spue thee out of my mouth" (Rev. 3:15,16).

This church, which had a nature similar to conditions that will exist at the end of the Church Age, prided itself in its own possessions and accomplishments. However, Christ told this church that it did not realize that it was "wretched, and miserable, and poor, and blind, and naked" (v. 17).

Jesus invited this church to come to Him to have its needs fulfilled. He said, "Behold, I stand at the door, and knock: if any man hear my voice, and open the door, I will come in to him, and will sup with him, and he with me" (v. 20). This verse is commonly used in talking with unsaved people, but these words were spoken by Christ to a church that had put Him on the outside. He was willing to come in to them and have fellowship with them if only they would invite Him to do so.

What is it like in your church? Has Christ been put on the outside? If so, He wants to come inside to have fellowship with believers. How sad that Christians can be so busy in the "work of the Lord" that they actually keep Christ on the outside as far as fellowship with Him is concerned. We have fellowship with Him as we study His Word, meditate on it and talk to Him in prayer. If we are too busy to do these things, we are obviously busier than the Lord ever intended us to be.

As you endeavor to commune with God, does it
sometimes seem that He is far away? Does it seem as if you
cannot contact Him—as if your prayers get no farther than
the ceiling? No doubt every believer experiences this feeling
at times. But we can learn a valuable lesson about this matter
from God's relationship to Israel.

A Special Tent

After the indication of repentance by the Israelites,
"Moses took the tabernacle, and pitched it without the camp,
afar off from the camp, and called it the Tabernacle of the
congregation. And it came to pass, that every one which
sought the Lord went out unto the tabernacle of the
congregation, which was without the camp" (Ex. 33:7).

Although God had pronounced judgment on the people
because of their sin, He also provided a way of escape. God
had refused to come into the midst of the people lest He
destroy them because of their sin, but He made it possible for
them to go outside of the camp to meet Him. Where sin
abounded, grace abounded much more (Rom. 5:20). As
Romans 5:21 says, "That as sin hath reigned unto death,
even so might grace reign through righteousness unto eternal
life by Jesus Christ our Lord."

The "tabernacle" mentioned in Exodus 33 was a special
tent, not the tabernacle mentioned in Exodus 25—31. This
special tent was placed far outside the camp where those who
wished to commune with God could do so. God had been
openly repudiated by the people when they committed the
gross sin of idolatry. Because of His holiness, He could not
enter their midst without destroying them, but they could
approach Him outside the camp. The tent represented God's
abiding presence, and the people were able to meet Him
there. This was an extension of God's grace. Before He
punished them for sin, He furnished them with another
opportunity for repentance. He waited outside the camp to
see how they would respond.

The people availed themselves of God's forbearance.
They were humbled by their sin and awed by the
pronouncement of imminent destruction. In Egypt the
Israelites were delivered from losing their firstborn by being

sheltered beneath the blood; at Mount Sinai they were
invited by God to come outside the camp to meet Him and
thereby escape destruction.

Why was God's action so extreme at this time in
comparison to the other times when the Israelites sinned?
Although the people were guilty of sinning by murmuring
against the leadership of Moses and the goodness of God,
they had never before replaced God and disowned Him as
they had by building and worshiping the golden calf. In fact,
they even praised the golden calf as the one that had led
them out of Egypt (32:4). Although God had delivered them,
they rejected Him.

What a vivid reminder this is of the Lord Jesus Christ who
"came unto his own, and his own received him not" (John
1:11). The Lord Jesus Christ was rejected by the very people
He came to save. Just as God moved outside the camp of the
Israelites, so also Jesus, "that he might sanctify the people
with his own blood, suffered without the gate" (Heb. 13:12).

Jesus was crucified outside the gate of Jerusalem, but by
shedding His blood on the cross, He provided salvation for all
who would believe in His finished work of redemption.
Because of what He has done for us, "let us go forth
therefore unto him without the camp, bearing his reproach"
(v. 13).

God calls for believers to separate themselves from those
who deny Him if they are to have fellowship with Him. We
must be willing to leave others and go outside the camp to
Him. This is not a separation from other believers who may
think differently than we do; it is a separation from those
who deny the Lord. We are not to separate ourselves from
other believers: "Not forsaking the assembling of ourselves
together, as the manner of some is; but exhorting one
another: and so much the more, as ye see the day
approaching" (10:25).

The Bible makes it clear that believers are not to be under
the control of unbelievers. "Be ye not unequally yoked
together with unbelievers: for what fellowship hath
righteousness with unrighteousness? And what communion
hath light with darkness? And what concord hath Christ with
Belial? Or what part hath he that believeth with an infidel?
And what agreement hath the temple of God with idols? For

ye are the temple of the living God; as God hath said, I will dwell in them, and walk in them; and I will be their God, and they shall be my people. Wherefore come out from among them, and be ye separate, saith the Lord, and touch not the unclean thing; and I will receive you" (II Cor. 6:14-17).

God Meets Moses

Notice what happened after Moses moved the tent outside the camp. "It came to pass, when Moses went out unto the tabernacle, that all the people rose up, and stood every man at his tent door, and looked after Moses, until he was gone into the tabernacle" (Ex. 33:8). Why were the people watching so intently? Apparently they were wondering whether they had sinned away their last opportunity or whether God would actually meet Moses, which would be an indication that He would meet with them.

"It came to pass, as Moses entered into the tabernacle, the cloudy pillar descended, and stood at the door of the tabernacle, and the Lord talked with Moses" (v. 9). The Lord met Moses! There was still hope for them! Even this gracious manifestation of God encouraged the people to repent.

Romans 2:4 states the timeless principle that "the goodness of God leadeth thee to repentance."

The Bible reveals that all who come to the Lord will not be cast out (John 6:37), but they must come to Him. This is why it was necessary for the Israelites to go outside of the camp individually to meet the Lord. "He that covereth his sins shall not prosper: but whoso confesseth and forsaketh them shall have mercy" (Prov. 28:13). Wholehearted repentance had to occur before there could be true worship of God.

The Bible clearly reveals that God extends grace and mercy to those who call on Him. God has said, "If my people, which are called by my name, shall humble themselves, and pray, and seek my face, and turn from their wicked ways; then will I hear from heaven, and will forgive their sin" (II Chron. 7:14).

Notice the response of the Israelites after they realized that God had met Moses in the tabernacle: "All the people saw the cloudy pillar stand at the tabernacle door: and all the

people rose up and worshipped, every man in his tent door"
(Ex. 33:10). The worship of the true God was reinstated,
which indicated that the worship of the false god had been
repudiated.

Chapter 22

Moses' Spiritual Excellence

Moses had attained the highest pinnacle in his prayer life and in his fellowship with God. God could completely trust His servant. Because of Moses' intercession, God had even spared the lives of about three million people. Judgment had been meted out, but God spared the lives of the people of Israel, and they were restored to fellowship with Him.

All of this stirred up Moses' inner heart so that he desired an even more intimate relationship with God. Perhaps you wonder how he could desire more since he already had so much. Yet, as long as the believer lives he should continue to grow in his personal relationship with the Lord. However, many believers seem to be content with only salvation. They have been delivered from condemnation by trusting Jesus Christ as Saviour, and they seem to spend the rest of their time enjoying themselves and the things of this world. This is shallow Christianity. We are to enjoy ourselves, but we are to find our enjoyment in God, not in the things of this world.

Moses' Relationship With God

The special relationship Moses had with God is recorded in Exodus 33:11: "The Lord spake unto Moses face to face, as a man speaketh unto his friend." This relationship was different from that enjoyed by any other person in the Old Testament. Rather than revealing Himself to Moses by visions, in dreams or through an angel, God revealed Himself directly to Moses.

The relationship which Moses had with God has been surpassed only by the Lord Jesus when He was on earth, but,

of course, He was the God-Man. No other mere human being
had a relationship with God such as Moses had.

The closeness that Moses had with God was not attained
by special merits or because God was partial to him. Rather,
it was a matter of spiritual growth over many years. In fact,
Moses was well over 80 years of age, and he had been growing
spiritually since he was 40. At that time he had made the
decision mentioned in Hebrews 11:24-26: "By faith Moses,
when he was come to years, refused to be called the son of
Pharaoh's daughter; choosing rather to suffer affliction with
the people of God, than to enjoy the pleasures of sin for a
season; esteeming the reproach of Christ greater riches than
the treasures in Egypt: for he had respect unto the
recompence of the reward."

During the next 40 years Moses was on the backside of
the desert, learning in the "school" of God. This brought him
into a closer relationship with God, because they had contact
on a daily and personal basis. Moses must have climbed
Mount Sinai many times to be alone with God. After God
had trained Moses during these years and had strengthened
his faith through experience for at least a year in Egypt,
Moses took over the leadership of this great people, the
nation of Israel.

It was to Moses' credit that he did not compromise as he
led the Israelites. He also had a holy boldness in the matter of
prayer as he led the people. Meeting God alone made Moses
the leader he was. His frequent meetings alone with God were
the key to his life.

As we spend time alone with God, He will be able to
entrust us with greater things also. But in order for God to
trust us with significant responsibilities, we must become
trustworthy. As we develop a greater reliance on God and
spend more time with Him, He can trust us with more
because we then know Him better.

As Moses spent time alone with God, he not only
interceded for the Israelites but also came to have such a
deep spiritual sense of concern that he was even willing to
give himself to atone for their sin. This reveals a heart that
was near to God's own heart. At one time God had asked
Moses to leave Him alone so He could destroy the people, but
Moses had continued to intercede, and the people were

spared. Moses understood the heart of God because he had
spent much time alone with Him.

Numbers 12 also reveals the type of relationship Moses
had with God. Moses' sister and brother—Miriam and
Aaron—complained because of the position of leadership
Moses had over them. The Bible says, "(Now the man Moses
was very meek, above all the men which were upon the face
of the earth)" (v. 3). The word "meek" does not mean that
Moses had a weak character; rather, it refers to strength
under control.

The close relationship of Moses and the Lord is evidenced
by what the Lord said at this time: "The Lord spake
suddenly unto Moses, and unto Aaron, and unto Miriam,
Come out ye three unto the tabernacle of the congregation.
And they three came out. . . . And he said, Hear now my
words: If there be a prophet among you, I the Lord will
make myself known unto him in a vision, and will speak unto
him in a dream. My servant Moses is not so, who is faithful in
all mine house. With him will I speak mouth to mouth, even
apparently, and not in dark speeches; and the similitude of
the Lord shall he behold: wherefore then were ye not afraid
to speak against my servant Moses?" (vv. 4,6-8).

Moses Seeks God's Glory

A study of Moses' life shows that he sought the glory of
God. As he prayed concerning the people, God granted his
request in various stages. As Moses received one thing from
the Lord, he asked for more and received more. God was not
reluctant to answer Moses' prayer, because Moses' prayers
were not motivated by self. Moses' whole concern was that
God might be glorified.

The prayers of Moses became bolder as he grew to know
the Lord better and had an even closer relationship with Him.
God was not giving in grudgingly to Moses' prayers; He really
wanted to do these things for His people, and Moses dared to
believe Him for what He could do. Moses dared to ask God to
work mightily in behalf of the people.

God is also looking today for people who will dare to
believe Him for mighty things. It is not necessary to be well
known by others or to know everything in the Bible, but it is

important to believe God for what He wants to do. God is looking for those He can trust as He did Moses. God has promised to work through those who call on Him for their strength. Jeremiah 33:3 says, "Call unto me, and I will answer thee, and shew thee great and mighty things, which thou knowest not." The Apostle Paul said that God "is able to do exceeding abundantly above all that we ask or think, according to the power that worketh in us" (Eph. 3:20).

Moses truly became God's man to the people. He was a prophet who gave them the message of God. In delivering God's message, Moses also executed judgment on those guilty of sin. Moses did not compromise God's standards or his own standards. On the other hand, Moses was quick in moving to secure God's mercy for the people.

After the leaders in the sin of idolatry had been killed, Moses pitched a tent outside the camp so the people could go there to meet God. Moses wanted the people to know that God would meet them if they responded and went outside the camp to meet Him. If God had gone within the camp, He would have destroyed the people for their wickedness. But His mercy allowed Him to meet the Israelites outside the camp.

God granted Moses' requests in various stages. First, God agreed to spare the people after Moses' intercession for them. "The Lord repented of the evil which he thought to do unto his people" (Ex. 32:14). God refused to personally lead the people to the Promised Land, but after Moses prayed again, God agreed to send an angel to lead them (v. 34).

But Moses was still not satisfied. After he had pitched the tent outside the camp so the people could meet God there, Moses went before the Lord with another petition. Moses said to Him, "See, thou sayest unto me, Bring up this people: and thou hast not let me know whom thou wilt send with me. Yet thou hast said, I know thee by name, and thou hast also found grace in my sight. Now therefore, I pray thee, if I have found grace in thy sight, shew me now thy way, that I may know thee, that I may find grace in thy sight: and consider that this nation is thy people" (33:12,13). Notice that Moses told God that the Israelites were "thy people."

As Moses talked with God, God gave him a wonderful promise: "My presence shall go with thee, and I will give thee rest" (v. 14). God agreed to spare the people and to personally lead them to the Promised Land.

The Lord also told Moses, "I will do this thing also that thou hast spoken: for thou hast found grace in my sight, and I know thee by name" (v. 17). The Lord's agreement to "do this thing also" was His agreement to personally lead the Israelites as Moses requested. What an answer to prayer! As a result of Moses' prayer, God Himself agreed to lead the Israelites to the Promised Land.

Moses' Bold Request

Having succeeded in receiving several answers to his prayers, Moses then evidenced his greatest boldness in what he requested of God. Moses said, "I beseech thee, shew me thy glory" (v. 18). Moses had been so encouraged by God's answers to his prayers that he sought for the ultimate. The one desire that burned within Moses was to know God better. There is a tremendous need for each believer to have this same desire.

Paul expressed his desire in these words: "That I may know him, and the power of his resurrection, and the fellowship of his sufferings, being made conformable unto his death" (Phil. 3:10). Peter said, "According as his divine power hath given unto us all things that pertaineth unto life and godliness, through the knowledge of him that hath called us to glory and virtue" (II Pet. 1:3).

In Paul's letter to the Ephesians, he recorded his prayers that apply to all believers: "That the God of our Lord Jesus Christ, the Father of glory, may give unto you the spirit of wisdom and revelation in the knowledge of him: the eyes of your understanding being enlightened; that ye may know what is the hope of his calling, and what the riches of the glory of his inheritance in the saints, and what is the exceeding greatness of his power to us-ward who believe, according to the working of his mighty power" (Eph. 1:17-19).

Paul also prayed, "That Christ may dwell in your hearts by faith; that ye, being rooted and grounded in love, may be able to comprehend with all saints what is the breadth, and length, and depth, and height; and to know the love of

Christ, which passeth knowledge, that ye might be filled with all the fulness of God" (3:17-19).

As the believer walks in close communion with God, there is always the desire to know Him better. If this is not the desire of the believer, something is seriously lacking in his spiritual life.

To Moses' request, "Shew me thy glory" (Ex. 33:18), God said, "I will make all my goodness pass before thee, and I will proclaim the name of the Lord before thee; and will be gracious to whom I will be gracious, and will shew mercy on whom I will shew mercy" (v. 19).

God's Glory

Verse 19 reveals that God's glory is seen in His goodness, or it could also be said that His glory is His goodness. Have you ever really considered what is involved in the goodness of the Lord? Someone has said, "His goodness is what He is in Himself." The sum total of His personal excellency is what He is and what He does. The only way we can really know Him and His glory today is to know what He does.

God also indicated to Moses that His glory is seen in His name: "I will proclaim the name of the Lord before thee" (v. 19). The Hebrew word translated "Lord" in this verse is the one from which "Jehovah" is derived. The word is related to what God told Moses earlier when He revealed Himself as "I Am That I Am" (3:14). This expression, as well as the name "Jehovah," reveals God as the ever-present One.

This was the God that Moses learned to know at the burning bush after he had spent 40 years in His wilderness school. There Moses learned much about the character of God.

Knowing the glory of God is seeing what God does because of His goodness. Exodus 34:6,7 says, "The Lord passed by before him, and proclaimed, The Lord, The Lord God, merciful and gracious, longsuffering, and abundant in goodness and truth, keeping mercy for thousands, forgiving iniquity and transgression and sin, and that will by no means clear the guilty; visiting the iniquity of the fathers upon the children, and upon the children's children, unto the third and to the fourth generation." These verses correspond with

Exodus 33:19—the same Hebrew word for "Lord" is used in
both references.

Having told Moses that He would make His goodness pass
before him, God said, "Thou canst not see my face: for there
shall no man see me, and live. And the Lord said, Behold,
there is a place by me, and thou shalt stand upon a rock: and
it shall come to pass, while my glory passeth by, that I will
put thee in a clift of the rock, and will cover thee with my
hand while I pass by: and I will take away mine hand, and
thou shalt see my back parts: but my face shall not be seen"
(33:20-23).

God is spirit, so no one is actually able to see Him. If a
person could see God, he would be unable to stand the
awesomeness of His glory. Thus, even Moses was able to see
God only by what He is and by what He does. In effect, God
was telling Moses, "I can't show you My face, because if I
did, you would not live. But I will show you my goodness,
which reveals who I am and what I do." God was going to
reveal Himself to Moses by showing His grace and mercy to
him.

Grace and Mercy

Notice that God said, "I . . . will be gracious to whom I
will be gracious, and will shew mercy on whom I will shew
mercy" (Ex. 33:19). As discussed previously, the words
"grace" and "mercy" are not synonymous; they are not used
interchangeably. Grace is God's unmerited favor—favor which
He bestows on mankind in spite of the fact that man deserves
condemnation. Mercy follows grace, and it emphasizes God's
seeing man in his pitiful condition and doing something to
deliver him. Mercy always follows grace.

All the way from Egypt to Sinai, God had dealt with the
Israelites on the basis of grace. They did not deserve any
favors from God. In fact, they deserved exactly the opposite.
Even though God had shown them so many favors, they
murmured and complained again and again. Finally, they
even repudiated God's leadership and asked Aaron to make
gods to lead them. The Israelites certainly deserved the
condemnation of God for repudiating His grace.

But then mercy was added to grace. God had pity on them in their miserable situation and did not destroy all of them, even though the leaders in the sin were destroyed.

In this incident, God made known something of His nature which had never been revealed to the people in depth—He made known His mercy. Mercy is one of His attributes, and when He extended mercy, He acted from Himself and of Himself. He extends mercy to whomever He chooses (v. 19). Mercy is the wonderful provision of God to meet the desperate need of the person who has failed to respond to His grace.

Since God is just, He must mete out a penalty on sin. Thus, justice and mercy met at Calvary. On the cross, the Lord Jesus Christ bore the sin of the world so that the penalty was paid. This, in turn, allowed God to extend mercy to all.

An interesting study of grace and mercy is found in Psalm 105 and 106. Psalm 105 gives the history of grace, and mercy is not once mentioned. But Psalm 106 tells the history of God's mercy, and the sin of Israel is frequently mentioned. Notice especially Psalm 106:4,5: "Remember me, O Lord, with the favor that thou bearest unto thy people: O visit me with thy salvation; that I may see the good of thy chosen, that I may rejoice in the gladness of thy nation, that I may glory with thine inheritance." Mercy is that wonderful quality of God's nature which meets the deep and desperate need of those who have sinned against His grace.

God's grace extends to us because we are worthless, empty and without hope in this world. But He extends His mercy to us because we are sinful and wicked. He can extend His mercy only because of the sacrifice of His Son, who shed His blood to pay the penalty for our sin. Thus, we are to come to the throne of grace to obtain mercy (Heb. 4:16).

Exodus 33:19 reveals that a person should not presume upon the mercy of God. God said, "I . . . will shew mercy on whom I will shew mercy." No one can claim mercy as a right. If that were the case, it would no longer be mercy. Moses prayed as no other man has prayed for his people and their needs. He obtained mercy for those he loved, and in so doing, he was able to behold the glory of God. Moses saw the wonderful grace of God extended to Israel in their

experiences from Egypt to Sinai. Then, when Israel
repudiated God, Moses was able to obtain mercy for them
from God. God did not have to extend His mercy, but in
Moses' greatest hour of intercession he obtained it for them
from God. This, then, is the manner in which Moses beheld
the glory of God. "And he [God] said, I will make all my
goodness pass before thee, and I will proclaim the name of
the Lord before thee" (v. 19).

Dealing With Sin

Today people have many different opinions about what it
means to see the glory of God. Some think this means having
a vision, and some talk about seeing Christ in the clouds or
standing by their bedside. But when Moses asked to see the
glory of the Lord, he was shown God's goodness. It was as if
God were saying, "My glory is my goodness—what I've done
for you in the past and what I will do for you in the future."

God had done so many things for Moses and the Israelites
that His glory should never have been questioned. But at this
time of intercession, Moses especially longed to know God
even better. That is why he wanted the glory of God to be
revealed to him in a special way.

As we consider that God's glory is revealed in His
goodness, we have much to be thankful for, just as the
Israelites did. God had done so many things for them out of
His grace, in spite of the fact that they deserved exactly the
opposite. This is also the way He has dealt with us. Because
we are sinners, we all justly deserve condemnation. But
because of His love and grace, the Lord Jesus Christ came in a
human body and shed His blood on the cross to pay the
penalty for our sin. "While we were yet sinners, Christ died
for us" (Rom. 5:8). God cannot overlook sin—it has to be
dealt with. This was true in Israel's case, and it is true in our
case. Because of His character, God must always deal
righteously and justly, and the penalty of sin had to be paid
before anyone could enter heaven.

We are usually quick to categorize sin into gross sins and
small sins, but as far as God is concerned, any sin is deserving
of eternal condemnation. Of course, individual sins are the

results of the sin nature which every person has. The Bible says, "As by one man sin entered into the world, and death by sin; and so death passed upon all men, for that all have sinned" (v. 12).

So sin has to be dealt with if any person is to be delivered from condemnation and enabled to enter the presence of God. The Old Testament sacrifices were a picture of *the* sacrifice—the Lord Jesus Christ—which would take away sin by paying its penalty. When Jesus Christ died on the cross, He paid the penalty for all sin—past, present and future.

No one benefits from Christ's finished work on the cross, however, unless he believes in Christ as his personal Saviour. A person has to change his mind about his own condition by admitting that he is a sinner. He also has to change his mind about Christ by admitting that Christ's shed blood paid the penalty for sin. When a person believes in Christ as Saviour, he indicates that he has changed his mind about these matters. Have you seen the awfulness of your sinful condition and trusted Jesus Christ as your personal Saviour? If so, you have received the forgiveness of sin, and you have eternal life. If not, you need to make this decision before it is eternally too late.

Commandments Given Again

Because Moses desired to see the glory of God in a special way, God placed Moses in a cleft of a rock and passed by him. But Moses was not allowed to look directly at God (see Ex. 33:22,23). Although it is difficult to understand all that took place when God revealed His glory to Moses at this time, it seemed to have satisfied Moses.

Then the grace of God was again manifested in that Moses was called back into His presence. We have no way of knowing how many times Moses ascended the mountain during this time of receiving the Law and interceding for the people. No doubt he went up and down the mountain several times as he communicated with God and then passed on this communication to the people.

The Lord told Moses, "Hew thee two tables of stone like unto the first: and I will write upon these tables the words that were in the first tables, which thou brakest. And be ready in the morning, and come up in the morning unto mount Sinai, and present thyself there to me in the top of the mount" (34:1,2). Although the people had committed a gross sin, God welcomed Moses again after he had interceded for the people.

At this time God did not want any other person on the mountain, and the animals were not to be in front of the mountain. God said to Moses, "No man shall come up with thee, neither let any man be seen throughout all the mount; neither let the flocks nor herds feed before that mount" (v. 3).

Moses did as the Lord told him: "He hewed two tables of stone like unto the first; and Moses rose up early in the morning, and went up unto mount Sinai, as the Lord had commanded him, and took in his hand the two tables of stone" (v. 4).

Israel, once again in full fellowship with God, was about to receive the whole Law from the hand of God. God was going to engrave another set of tablets containing the Ten Commandments. But the whole Law included many more commands. In fact, it is generally considered that, in all, there were over 600 laws. This law system was entirely binding on the people. The Bible says, "Whosoever shall keep the whole law, and yet offend in one point, he is guilty of all" (James 2:10). This verse refers not only to the Ten Commandments but also to the other commands.

The Law given to Moses included moral, ceremonial and civil regulations. In addition, God gave specific instructions about the construction of the tabernacle and its use.

The moral law reflected the character of God; the ceremonial law revealed God's justice and mercy; the civil law dealt with relationships within the nation.

Moses had spent agonizing days—and maybe weeks—on the mountain interceding for the sin of the people and had won abundant mercies from God. Later, he saw the glory of God in a special way. After that he was alone with God for fellowship and to receive special revelation.

On the mountain, "the Lord said unto Moses, Write thou these words: for after the tenor of these words I have made a covenant with thee and with Israel. And he was there with the Lord forty days and forty nights; he did neither eat bread, nor drink water. And he [God] wrote upon the tables the words of the covenant, the ten commandments" (Ex. 34:27,28).

Notice the miracle that occurred—Moses neither ate nor drank for 40 days. This is humanly impossible and reveals that God performed a miracle to sustain Moses during this time.

Moses Reflects God's Glory

Moses was changed when he came down from the mountain. Earlier, he had asked to see the glory of the Lord, but when he came down from the mountain with the two tablets of stone, he did not know "that the skin of his face shone while he talked with him" (v. 29). Moses did not realize that his face reflected the glory of God. This was proof of the closeness between Moses and God, and it revealed to those who saw him that he had truly been in the presence of God's glory.

"When Aaron and all the children of Israel saw Moses, behold, the skin of his face shone; and they were afraid to come nigh him" (v. 30). Moses still did not realize the extent to which his face reflected the glory of God. He was not glorious in his own eyes, but he was in the eyes of others.

True Christian excellence is not conscious of its beauty. Such glory is not seen by those who possess it; rather, it is seen by those who behold the one who possesses it. Beware of the person who talks about his own greatness. It is even possible for a person to boast about his humility by emphasizing his nothingness. Although he talks of his nothingness, he may be inwardly proud of the way he behaves and of the way God is using him.

Consider the contrasts between the two times Moses descended from the mountain with the tablets of stone. The first time, his face was distorted with anger because of the Israelites' sin, and he threw down the tablets and shattered them. The second time he descended with the tablets, his face radiated the glory of God. Earlier he found the people engaged in idolatry, but he later returned to a people humbled by the mercies of God. The first time he descended the mountain, Moses threw the tablets of stone to the ground. The second time, he prepared to deposit them in the ark of the covenant, where they were to be kept.

The glory that was evidenced on Moses' face is a reminder of what the leaders in Jerusalem saw in the lives of Peter and John when they had been called before the Sanhedrin—the highest ruling court of the Jews. Peter and John had been preaching the gospel of the Lord Jesus Christ, and they were asked, "By what power, or by what name, have ye done this?" (Acts 4:7). Peter boldly answered the Sanhedrin and told the Jewish leaders, "Neither is there salvation in any other: for there is none other name under heaven given among men, whereby we must be saved" (v. 12). The Bible says, "When they saw the boldness of Peter and John, and perceived that they were unlearned and ignorant [untrained] men, they marvelled; and they took knowledge of them, that they had been with Jesus" (v. 13). Peter and John radiated the glory of the Lord Jesus Christ.

One cannot fellowship with the Lord Jesus Christ for very long without His glory being reflected in his life. Such a person does not need to wear a badge proclaiming his virtues or his victorious life—these will be evident to others.

When Aaron and the other Israelites saw the glory of God reflected in the face of Moses, "they were afraid to come nigh him" (Ex. 34:30). Perhaps they were afraid because God's reflected glory searched out their hearts and consciences, making them intensely aware that they could not, in themselves, meet even the smallest requirement of God's holiness. No doubt the reflected glory in Moses' face also emphasized their unworthiness—they knew they could not stand in God's presence as Moses had.

Can the glory of Christ be seen in those of us who have received Christ as Saviour? No one should ever attempt to minister God's message without first spending time in God's presence. God's glory must shine, not ours.

Every day before you go out to meet the world, spend some time with God by reading His Word and talking to Him in prayer. Spending time in His presence will bring the sunshine of heaven to your face, and others will observe this in you throughout the day.

Chapter 23

Israel Leaves Sinai

The Israelites had spent 11 months at Mount Sinai. They had come into the wilderness of Sinai in the third month after they were delivered from Egypt (Ex. 19:1,2). Numbers 10:11,12 records their leaving Sinai: "And it came to pass on the twentieth day of the second month, in the second year, that the cloud was taken up from off the tabernacle of the testimony. And the children of Israel took their journeys out of the wilderness of Sinai."

Wasted Time

The Israelites spent more time at Mount Sinai than should have been necessary because their sin had to be dealt with. They did receive the Law from God, along with specific instructions about the tabernacle and worship related to it. But most of the 11 months spent at Mount Sinai were apparently due to the sin of the people and the judgment and restitution that were necessary.

A principle seen throughout the Word of God is that time out of fellowship with the Lord is wasted time. Time spent in sin and in dealing with sin's results obviously shortens the time spent in effective fellowship and service.

Abraham is an example of one who lost time because of refusing to act immediately on the word of the Lord. He was instructed to leave his home and relatives and to go to a land that the Lord would show him (see Gen. 11:31; 12:1-3). As Abraham journeyed from his home in Ur of the Chaldees, however, he was with his relatives and remained with them when they reached Haran. Abraham wasted 15 years at

Haran, for it was not until his father died that he journeyed
on to the land of Canaan as God had instructed.

Later, because of a famine in the land of Canaan,
Abraham left the place of his altar and went to Egypt
(12:10). Abraham had many heartaches in Egypt, but he
finally returned to "Beth-el, unto the place where his tent
had been at the beginning, between Beth-el and Hai; unto the
place of the altar, which he had made there at the first: and
there Abram called on the name of the Lord" (13:3,4). Here
again, Abraham lost time while he was out of fellowship with
God, for it was never intended that Abraham leave Canaan
and go to Egypt.

Abraham's grandson Jacob also wasted time at Haran
because he refused to follow God's program. Jacob spent 20
years at Haran with his father-in-law Laban. Even after Jacob
returned to the land, he waited another ten years before he
completely returned to the Lord and obeyed Him.

Later, the nation of Israel lost 38 years because of their
refusal to follow God. It is important for every believer to
realize that time spent out of fellowship with God is wasted
time.

Perhaps you look back on wasted years and think that
you have hardly any time left to offer the Lord. The
important thing, however, is for the disobedient believer to
confess his sins to the Lord and then to faithfully serve Him
with whatever time he has left. No one knows how much
time he has left to serve the Lord, so let us walk in obedience
and honor Him in all that we do today.

Great Leadership

The evidence of divine leadership was first given to the
Israelites in the form of the guiding cloud. The cloud first
appeared after the Israelites were delivered from Egypt. "The
Lord went before them by day in a pillar of a cloud, to lead
them the way; and by night in a pillar of fire, to give them
light; to go by day and night: he took not away the pillar of
the cloud by day, nor the pillar of fire by night, from before
the people" (Ex. 13:21,22).

As the Israelites prepared to leave Mount Sinai, the cloud
was again the evidence of God's presence, although at this

time it was associated with the tabernacle. "On the day that the tabernacle was reared up the cloud covered the tabernacle, namely, the tent of the testimony: and at even there was upon the tabernacle as it were the appearance of fire, until the morning. So it was alway: the cloud covered it by day, and the appearance of fire by night. And when the cloud was taken up from the tabernacle, then after that the children of Israel journeyed: and in the place where the cloud abode, there the children of Israel pitched their tents. At the commandment of the Lord the children of Israel journeyed, and at the commandment of the Lord they pitched: as long as the cloud abode upon the tabernacle they rested in their tents" (Num. 9:15-18).

So conscious were the Israelites of the guiding presence of God that "whether it were two days, or a month, or a year, that the cloud tarried upon the tabernacle, remaining thereon, the children of Israel abode in their tents, and journeyed not: but when it was taken up, they journeyed" (v. 22).

Any doubts as to who planned the strategy and led the Israelites were removed by the appearance of the cloud and the fire. The God of creation was the captain of the host—He called all the signals.

Later, the identity of the captain of the host was emphasized to Joshua. When Joshua was near Jericho, he saw a man with sword drawn and asked him, "Art thou for us, or for our adversaries?" (Josh. 5:13). The man answered, "Nay; but as captain of the host of the Lord am I now come. And Joshua fell on his face to the earth, and did worship, and said unto him, What saith my lord unto his servant? And the captain of the Lord's host said unto Joshua, Loose thy shoe from off thy foot; for the place whereon thou standest is holy. And Joshua did so" (vv. 14,15). It is important that we also know our captain.

God's provision of the cloud and the fire in association with the tabernacle was a clear, visible, undeniable and miraculous way of evidencing His divine presence with the Israelites. The cloud was miraculous in that it never dissipated nor did it move in the way that clouds commonly move. It often stayed in one place for an indefinite period of time (Num. 9:22). This cloud moved only when God wanted it to move, and even then it did not necessarily move in the direction of the wind. The Israelites could not initiate the moving of the cloud; it was God's prerogative.

We do not know exactly what the cloud looked like, but it was evident to the Israelites that God was with them if they remained in the presence of the cloud. At night the cloud took on the appearance of fire so that the camp had light even at night. As a result, the Israelites could move by night or by day.

Leading and Following

The cloud illustrates the principle of leading and following. It was God's responsibility to lead, and it was the people's responsibility to follow. The activity of the cloud was explicitly identified with the voice of God—"At the commandment of the Lord the children of Israel journeyed, and at the commandment of the Lord they pitched: as long as the cloud abode upon the tabernacle they rested in their tents" (Num. 9:18). The command at this time was given through Moses, but trumpets were later used to order the movements of the Israelites.

Israel's responsibility was to follow the signal of God. If the cloud moved, they were to move; if it did not move, they were not to move. Obedience to God is always the key to any spiritual success. If any believer wants to be successful in God's eyes, he must be obedient to God. God may lead the believer in ways he cannot understand, but the only responsibility of the Christian at such times is to follow Him.

Although the leadership of the Israelites was certainly divine, it also had human aspects. The Lord told Moses, "Make thee two trumpets of silver; of a whole piece shalt thou make them: that thou mayest use them for the calling of the assembly, and for the journeying of the camps. And when they shall blow with them, all the assembly shall assemble themselves to thee at the door of the tabernacle of the congregation.... And the sons of Aaron, the priests, shall blow with the trumpets; and they shall be to you for an ordinance for ever throughout your generations" (10:2,3,8).

As clear as the communications and revelations from God may be, He often chooses to use human leadership so that believers will not miss His directions through carelessness. Thus, the trumpets were blown by appointed leaders at certain times. Moses would consult with Aaron and his sons, and then the trumpets would be blown. If the people took their eyes off the cloud and closed their ears to the trumpets, they could not be led by God.

How thankful we should be today to have the unmistakable Word of God to give us leadership! Each believer should have the same attitude that the psalmist had as he prayed: "Search me, O God, and know my heart: try me, and know my thoughts: and see if there be any wicked way in me, and lead me in the way everlasting" (Ps. 139:23,24). Each of us who knows Jesus Christ as personal Saviour should desire to be led by God.

The Bible has much to say about the way believers are led. Before the Lord Jesus Christ ascended into heaven, He told the disciples, "Howbeit when he, the Spirit of truth, is come, he will guide you into all truth: for he shall not speak of himself; but whatsoever he shall hear, that shall he speak: and he will shew you things to come" (John 16:13). So the distinct ministry of the Holy Spirit is to guide believers into truth.

The leading of the Holy Spirit is not reserved for only some special group of believers; it is available to all believers. The Apostle Paul said, "For as many as are led by the Spirit of God, they are the sons of God" (Rom. 8:14). The Apostle Paul also told believers, "Walk in the Spirit, and ye shall not fulfil the lust of the flesh. . . . If we live in the Spirit, let us also walk in the Spirit" (Gal. 5:16,25).

As believers in Christ we need to recognize that God does not save us from condemnation and then just leave us here in this world to make it through our own self-efforts. Some Christians apparently attempt to live that way, but that is not the way God intended for us to live. A person cannot know what is best for himself; he must rely on the wisdom of God. Every believer needs to obey the injunctions of Proverbs 3:5-7: "Trust in the Lord with all thine heart; and lean not unto thine own understanding. In all thy ways acknowledge him, and he shall direct thy paths. Be not wise in thine own eyes: fear the Lord, and depart from evil."

I personally receive much help in finding God's leadership
by meditating on Psalm 25. Psalm 119 is also a great
encouragement—it points to the Word of God as the heavenly
means of leadership.

Israel's First Move

The Bible says, "It came to pass on the twentieth day of
the second month, in the second year, that the cloud was
taken up from off the tabernacle of the testimony. And the
children of Israel took their journeys out of the wilderness of
Sinai; and the cloud rested in the wilderness of Paran" (Num.
10:11,12).

The tabernacle was in the center of the camp, so the
cloud was visible to all. As soon as the cloud lifted, the
Israelites knew they were to move. "They departed from the
mount of the Lord three days' journey: and the ark of the
covenant of the Lord went before them in the three days'
journey, to search out a resting place for them. And the
cloud of the Lord was upon them by day, when they went
out of the camp" (vv. 33,34).

The 11 months at Sinai had brought about many changes
in the life of Israel. The people had arrived at Sinai a fugitive
and unorganized people; they left a well-organized nation,
molded into a commonwealth of 12 tribes. All was
beautifully ordered. At this time God used the special
training Moses had received in Egypt. "Moses was learned in
all the wisdom of the Egyptians, and was mighty in words
and in deeds" (Acts 7:22).

Moses had spent the first 40 years of his life being trained
in the courts of Pharaoh as a possible successor to Pharaoh.
As such, Moses was trained in organization and was the
general of the Egyptian army. He learned all that would be
necessary to lead the greatest nation on earth at that time.
Moses used all the knowledge he had accumulated in leading
the Israelites. It was not, however, the unaided genius of
Moses that God used. God leads through minds competent to
receive and transmit His teaching. In Moses' case, his mental
abilities were used to transmit to Israel an order of

organization that was second to none. What Moses had learned in the world was translated into use for the glory of God.

The Israelites left Sinai as a mighty nation in battle array. They had been furnished with a code of laws, including sanitary regulations, which have been a model for civilized peoples of the world. They had also been provided with a system of sacrifices that continued for centuries. These sacrifices prophetically pointed to the priesthood of the Lord Jesus Christ for believers.

The tabernacle was completed and furnished, providing a special place to meet God. The cloud hovered over the tabernacle as an evidence that God's presence was with the people. When the people saw the cloud lifting and heard the blasting of the trumpets, they moved as they had been instructed. The tribe of Judah went first, and then Issachar, Zebulun and the other tribes followed in order. What a beautiful array it must have been to see three million people moving in such orderliness!

Even though the presence of God was clearly evident to the people, they complained. "And when the people complained, it displeased the Lord: and the Lord heard it; and his anger was kindled; and the fire of the Lord burnt among them, and consumed them that were in the uttermost parts of the camp" (Num. 11:1). God had been dealing with the Israelites on the basis of pure grace, but now He began to deal with them on the basis of the Law. Their murmuring was punishable, so God sent fire to destroy them.

But Moses stood in the gap again: "The people cried unto Moses; and when Moses prayed unto the Lord, the fire was quenched" (v. 2). The psalmist wrote: "Therefore he said that he would destroy them, had not Moses his chosen stood before him in the breach, to turn away his wrath, lest he should destroy them" (Ps. 106:23). Moses was faithful in interceding for his people.

Although Moses had wonderful opportunities for self-advancement, never was his selflessness more clearly evident than when he boldly and persistently prayed to God for Israel. In so doing, Moses averted God's judgments on the often-apostate nation.

The Mixed Multitude

The Scriptures are totally honest when giving information about a person. For instance, many great moments of Moses' life are revealed, but the Scriptures also tell of his weaker moments. One such occasion involved the mixed multitude that came with the Israelites out of Egypt.

The mixed multitude was probably a group of Gentiles who left Egypt with the Israelites. They are first mentioned in Exodus 12:38. After the Israelites had left Mount Sinai, "the mixt multitude that was among them fell a lusting: and the children of Israel also wept again, and said, Who shall give us flesh to eat? We remember the fish, which we did eat in Egypt freely; the cucumbers, and the melons, and the leeks, and the onions, and the garlick: but now our soul is dried away: there is nothing at all, beside this manna, before our eyes" (Num. 11:4-6).

Although the complaining was started by the mixed multitude, the Israelites were also guilty of complaining. This indicates how infectious a complaining attitude can be. Because every person has a sin nature, it does not take long even for believers to become disheartened and to develop an attitude of complaining against the goodness of God. After salvation, Christians too often remember what they enjoyed in the world and occasionally long for the pleasures of sin. When this happens, the believer is guilty of leaving his first love.

The Church of Ephesus was guilty of this, and Christ told it, "Remember therefore from whence thou art fallen, and repent, and do the first works; or else I will come unto thee quickly, and will remove thy candlestick out of his place, except thou repent" (Rev. 2:5). Romans 8:5-8 emphasizes that the believer is to seek the things of the Spirit, not the things of the flesh. Verse 7 reveals that the carnal, or fleshly, mind is "enmity against God." Therefore, those who live to fulfill the desires of the flesh cannot please God.

Christians who have not grown spiritually as they should, through the reading of God's Word and applying it to daily life, find it easy to murmur as the Israelites did. Only a small minority may begin the complaining, but the Christian who is not mature is also susceptible. Just as the bark of one dog can start a whole group of dogs barking, one complaining believer can affect an entire group.

Many pastors have had their hearts broken, and church work has been greatly hampered by a few disgruntled people who influence the entire church. Every church group seems to have a few people who find it easy to complain about anything. Unless the other believers are mature, they will soon follow the pattern of the murmuring, weak believer.

The Israelites may have given no thought to being dissatisfied with the manna that had been miraculously provided for them. But when they heard the complaint of the mixed multitude, they also decided they were tired of eating the same food day after day.

The mixed multitude is a reminder of those who are not believers. The New Testament refers to an unbeliever as a "natural" man, and I Corinthians 2:14 says, "The natural man receiveth not the things of the Spirit of God: for they are foolishness unto him: neither can he know them, because they are spiritually discerned."

Believers who are caught up in a worldly spirit or attitude are referred to as carnal. First Corinthians 3:1,2 says, "And I, brethren, could not speak unto you as unto spiritual, but as unto carnal, even as unto babes in Christ. I have fed you with milk, and not with meat: for hitherto ye were not able to bear it, neither yet now are ye able." These carnal, or fleshly, believers are not able to concentrate on the deep things of God because they are still thinking about fulfilling the desires of the flesh. They find it easy to complain if they are not satisfied, and their complaints can have a deadening effect on others.

God Deals With the Complaints

Notice how God dealt with the murmuring of the mixed multitude. God told Moses, "Say thou unto the people, Sanctify yourselves against to morrow, and ye shall eat flesh: for ye have wept in the ears of the Lord, saying, Who shall give us flesh to eat? For it was well with us in Egypt: therefore the Lord will give you flesh, and ye shall eat" (Num. 11:18). As if this promise were not enough, God added: "Ye shall not eat one day, nor two days, nor five days, neither ten days, nor twenty days; but even a whole month, until it come out at your nostrils, and it be loathsome unto you: because that ye have despised the Lord which is among you, and have wept before him, saying, Why came we forth out of Egypt?" (vv. 19,20).

Notice Moses' response to what God said. At this point Moses revealed that he had moved from being a great intercessor to being a doubter. God promised to supply meat for an entire month, but Moses said, "The people, among whom I am, are six hundred thousand footmen; and thou hast said, I will give them flesh, that they may eat a whole month. Shall the flocks and the herds be slain for them, to suffice them? Or shall all the fish of the sea be gathered together for them, to suffice them?" (vv. 21,22).

God rebuked Moses for his doubt, but He rebuked him gently: "Is the Lord's hand waxed short? Thou shalt see now whether my word shall come to pass unto thee or not" (v. 23). Moses had doubts about God's ability to supply meat for an entire month. Possibly, his doubts were aggravated by his great weariness and by the heavy burden of leading the people. Satan has a way of attacking us when we are down. Remember Amalek? He came when the Israelites were tired and weak; he struck from behind, surprising Israel (see Ex. 17:8-16).

God remained faithful to His promise; He supplied meat for a month just as He said He would. "There went forth a wind from the Lord, and brought quails from the sea, and let them fall by the camp, as it were a day's journey on this side, and as it were a day's journey on the other side, round about the camp, and as it were two cubits high upon the face of the earth" (Num. 11:31). The expression "two cubits high upon the face of the earth" has been variously interpreted. At first glance it seems that the quail were piled that high on the earth. But a legitimate interpretation of the expression is that God caused the quail to fly two cubits, or about three feet, above the ground so the Israelites could catch them.

The people gathered all they could and were beginning to enjoy the feast they had so longed for, but "while the flesh was yet between their teeth, ere [before] it was chewed, the wrath of the Lord was kindled against the people, and the Lord smote the people with a very great plague" (v. 33).

In commenting about the Israelites and this incident, the psalmist said, "They soon forgat his works; they waited not for his counsel: but lusted exceedingly in the wilderness, and tempted God in the desert. And he gave them their request; but sent leanness into their soul" (Ps. 106:13-15).

God may answer believers today in the same way. If we are guilty of complaining and continue to ask God for things just to satisfy our own fleshly desires, He may grant our request, but the result will be spiritual leanness.

Are you out of fellowship with the Lord? Are you seeking to be satisfied with things rather than with the Person of Christ? If so, learn from the example of the Israelites, confess your sin and be restored to fellowship. You will then discover that the Word of God is more precious than you ever thought possible. But when unconfessed sin is in your life, the Word of God becomes tiresome, and one is tempted to complain about the same spiritual diet day after day. But the believer who realizes the awfulness of sin will be so appreciative of God's grace and forgiveness that the Word of God will be a thrill to his heart. As Jeremiah said, "Thy words were found, and I did eat them; and thy word was unto me the joy and rejoicing of mine heart: for I am called by thy name, O Lord God of hosts" (Jer. 15:16).

Chapter 24

Moses Personally Attacked

Crises do not produce heroes, nor do they make cowards. However, when a person is exposed to extraordinary circumstances, strengths and weaknesses come to light that even he did not know he had. As a storm beats against an oak tree, it may reveal the strength of the tree and its ability to stand, or it may reveal hidden decay as the tree collapses under the storm.

Few men can be in a position of influence and power and not be adversely affected. Many can stand under reproof and rebuke and be benefited, but human nature is such that the glamour of position and power becomes a snare.

Someone has said, "We are not what we are because of what we do; we do what we do because of what we are." Another way to put it is that "character determines the deed" or "the deed only reveals the character."

Moses was severely tested in his high position of power. There were three specific attacks, or severe tests, that involved three people: himself, Miriam and Korah.

Discouragement Attacks Moses

Moses himself was involved in the sin of discouragement. Moses was a tried servant, but he was also a tired one, and he became guilty of charging God with unfairness. When the people grumbled because they had only manna to eat, "Moses heard the people weep throughout their families, every man in the door of his tent: and the anger of the Lord was kindled greatly; Moses also was displeased" (Num. 11:10).

In his displeasure Moses said to the Lord, "Wherefore hast thou afflicted thy servant? And wherefore have I not found favour in thy sight, that thou layest the burden of all this people upon me? Have I conceived all this people? Have I begotten them, that thou shouldest say unto me, Carry them in thy bosom, as a nursing father beareth the sucking child, unto the land which thou swarest unto their fathers? Whence should I have flesh to give unto all this people? For they weep unto me, saying, Give us flesh, that we may eat. I am not able to bear all this people alone, because it is too heavy for me. And if thou deal thus with me, kill me, I pray thee, out of hand, if I have found favour in thy sight; and let me not see my wretchedness" (vv. 11-15).

Moses had finally become so discouraged he could not take it any longer, so he complained to God. His complaining was different, however, than the complaining of the people. They had taken out their complaints on him, but he did not respond by attacking them; instead, he went to God and poured out his heart to Him. What a lesson this is for every believer! Each one needs to take his burdens to the Lord in prayer. God understood what Moses was going through. As the psalmist said, God "knoweth our frame; he remembereth that we are dust" (Ps. 103:14).

Caught in a weak moment, Moses lost sight of the sovereignty of God and began to feel sorry for himself. This did not happen very often in Moses' life, but it shows how human Moses was. Self-pity is destructive and reflects itself both in a person's moral life and in his spiritual life. It is common for people, because of their weak sin natures, to fall prey to the attacks of Satan at such a time. Only Jesus Christ, who was the God-Man, was always able to resist the attacks of Satan.

Moses was particularly discouraged because he had just interceded for the people, asking that they be spared from further judgment by God. Now they were murmuring again. God was providing manna miraculously, and yet the people complained about this provision.

This reveals that even 15 months after they had left Egypt, the people still had their hearts fixed on Egypt. Moses was physically exhausted, and then his patience became exhausted. He was vulnerable to Satan's attack.

Elijah had a similar experience. He had been on Mount Carmel and had experienced tremendous victory for the Lord (see I Kings 18). Because of Elijah's strong stand for the Lord, he became responsible for destroying 850 false prophets. After this he ran "before Ahab to the entrance of Jezreel" (v. 46). Then, when Elijah heard that Jezebel planned to do to him what he had done to the false prophets, "he arose, and went for his life, and came to Beer-sheba" (19:3). Elijah left his servant at Beersheba and then "went a day's journey into the wilderness, and came and sat down under a juniper tree: and he requested for himself that he might die; and said, It is enough; now, O Lord, take away my life; for I am not better than my fathers" (v. 4). Elijah was exhausted physically, which made him vulnerable to Satan's attacks.

When Moses was physically exhausted, he was also susceptible to Satan's attack of discouragement. He was so distraught that he wanted to die if the Lord did not change the situation with the people. In his discouragement Moses apparently felt that God had heaped all the burdens on him and that there was no divine help when it was really needed.

God's Reaction to Moses' Discouragement

Because the Lord understood all that Moses was going through, He did not rebuke him. Instead, the Lord told Moses, "Gather unto me seventy men of the elders of Israel, whom thou knowest to be the elders of the people, and officers over them; and bring them unto the tabernacle of the congregation, that they may stand there with thee. And I will come down and talk with thee there" (Num. 11:16,17).

Even though God would be speaking specifically with Moses, the 70 elders would hear what God had to say to him. The Lord told Moses what He planned to do: "I will take of the spirit which is upon thee, and will put it upon them; and they shall bear the burden of the people with thee, that thou bear it not thyself alone" (v. 17).

Moses did as he was instructed. He "went out, and told the people the words of the Lord, and gathered the seventy men of the elders of the people, and set them round about the tabernacle. And the Lord came down in a cloud, and spake unto him, and took of the spirit that was upon him, and gave it unto the seventy elders: and it came to pass, that, when the spirit rested upon them, they prophesied, and did not cease" (vv. 24,25).

God alleviated Moses' aloneness in his responsibility by providing 70 others to share the load. It is commonly thought that the Spirit which was on Moses was divided among the 70 elders. I cannot agree with this position, however, because it is impossible to diminish the Spirit of God. One does not draw off portions of the Holy Spirit as he draws off water from a well. Rather, it seems more accurate to understand verse 25 as teaching that the same Spirit who was on Moses was also given to the 70 elders. Thus, the Spirit who was on Moses was not diminished, but He also rested on the 70 for this special task.

The entire Spirit of God filled, or controlled, each man completely for the task at hand. Just as a flame of fire reaches out to engulf other objects, the Holy Spirit's resting on Moses was extended to the others so that the entire group could be effective for the Lord. There were then 71 lights instead of just one.

Just as one could use the fire from one candle to light 70 others, the Holy Spirit in His full essence was on the 70 elders without being diminished in Moses' life. If God chose to create new stars, He would not have to diminish the light from the sun to give brilliance to the stars. Instead, God would use the same force operable in the sun to give light to the stars.

Concerning the Holy Spirit, it is important to observe the difference between His relationship with believers in the Old Testament and believers in the New Testament. During Old Testament times, the Holy Spirit came on whomever God chose and rested on them or worked through them to accomplish a specific task as God willed and purposed. When the task was accomplished, the Holy Spirit apparently then left that person. This is why David prayed, "Do not take Thy Holy Spirit from me" (Ps. 51:11, NASB).

During New Testament times, however, the Holy Spirit indwelt every believer, as He does today. Romans 8:9 says, "If anyone does not have the Spirit of Christ, he does not belong to Him" (NASB). The fact that every believer's body is inhabited by the Holy Spirit is also seen in I Corinthians 6:19: "Do you not know that your body is a temple of the Holy Spirit who is in you, whom you have from God, and that you are not your own?" (NASB).

Moses' Character Revealed

When God distributed the Spirit that was on Moses to the 70 elders, they began to prophesy (Num. 11:25). This created a situation that revealed the noble character of Moses. When two men were discovered continuing in their prophesying and it was not understood why, a young man ran to tell Moses. Joshua, a special servant to Moses, said, "My lord Moses, forbid them" (v. 28). But notice the beautiful response of Moses: "Enviest thou for my sake? Would God that all the Lord's people were prophets, and that the Lord would put his spirit upon them!" (v. 29).

Moses harbored no jealousy at all. Joshua was jealous for his master, but he did not need to be. However, even this was an indication of Joshua's total loyalty to Moses. He did not want others usurping the authority that belonged only to Moses. Joshua did not want Moses' prestige diminished in any way.

But envy and jealousy found no lodging in Moses' generous nature. He could safely leave such matters in the hands of God, because he had not chosen his own responsibility of leadership—that was God's doing. This is a reminder of something the Lord Jesus said which applies to present-day believers: "Ye have not chosen me, but I have chosen you, and ordained you, that ye should go and bring forth fruit, and that your fruit should remain: that whatsoever ye shall ask of the Father in my name, he may give it you" (John 15:16).

Moses was in touch with God, and a spiritual leader in touch with God does not need to be concerned about his prestige or prerogatives—he can leave those in God's hands.

Psalm 37:5,6 reveals what the believer needs to do: "Commit your way to the Lord, trust also in Him, and He will do it. And He will bring forth your righteousness as the light, and your judgment as the noonday" (NASB). God will take care of the believer and will eventually vindicate him just as surely as the sun shines at noonday.

Moses' reaction revealed a spirit of greatness. He rejoiced when others shared honor with him. When a person's desires are eagerly and intently concentrated on seeing God's will done, the glory of that light extinguishes the fire of self-ambition. A true and faithful servant is willing to be anything—or nothing—if only the divine purpose of God is accomplished.

Miriam and Aaron Attack Moses

Because Moses was used so distinctly by God in leading Israel, it was not unusual for others to be jealous of his leadership position. Numbers 12:1 says, "Miriam and Aaron spake against Moses because of the Ethiopian woman whom he had married: for he had married an Ethiopian woman."

Miriam and Aaron were Moses' older sister and brother. But even they took issue with Moses' leadership, although at first their complaints concerned his wife. Numbers 12 does not specifically say what Miriam and Aaron found objectionable about Moses' wife, but jealousy must have been the main problem.

Moses' wife had just recently joined him at Mount Sinai. Moses had married when he was in the wilderness in the "school" of God. When he returned to Egypt to deliver Israel, however, he went alone. So Moses was without his wife for over a year. Then his father-in-law brought her to him at Mount Sinai.

During the time Moses was without his wife, it is likely that Miriam took care of the housekeeping duties and looked after Moses' welfare. But with the return of Moses' wife, Miriam was put in second place, and she revolted by attacking Moses' leadership.

It is understandable that Miriam was jealous, because she had had a distinctive part in Moses' life. She had watched over him when he was a baby and was hidden among the reeds on the River Nile (see Ex. 2:3,4). Miriam had actively supported Moses when he led the Israelites out of Egypt and had even led the women in a song of praise after their escape (see 15:20,21).

But then Miriam and Aaron complained about Moses' wife, perhaps because they were excluded from that inner family circle. Miriam and Aaron may have gossiped together about Moses' wife. Perhaps Miriam was the instigator of the gossip, but Aaron joined her in it—the Bible indicates that both were involved in this complaining against Moses. Both Miriam and Aaron were older than Moses, and perhaps it was difficult for them to bow to the leadership of their younger brother.

This jealousy took its usual hypocritical turn. Miriam and Aaron did not talk to Moses about his wife; instead, they complained about his authority. How easy it is to disguise jealousy beneath a cloak of zeal for the law of God or to think of oneself as pure while rebuking somebody else's faults. Real jealousy originates from power hunger, and it usually breaks out in faultfinding, just as it did in this case.

Miriam and Aaron said, "Hath the Lord indeed spoken only by Moses? Hath he not spoken also by us?" (Num. 12:2). But even though they did not realize the seriousness of the charge, the Bible says, "And the Lord heard it" (v. 2).

If only believers would always remember that the Lord is listening in on their conversations, which means He hears all of their accusations. If they would keep this in mind, many gossiping tongues would be silenced. God is listening to every word you say to someone about another person.

The psalmist said, "The Lord knoweth the thoughts of man, that they are vanity" (Ps. 94:11). There are no thoughts a person has that the Lord does not know. The psalmist also said, "Search me, O God, and know my heart: try me, and know my thoughts: and see if there be any wicked way in me, and lead me in the way everlasting" (139:23,24).

Someone has said, "When we think we are judging another, God is often judging our own state." It is a trait of the flesh when aroused to jealousy to cut others down to fit one's own pattern.

Because we all have a sin nature, we tend to think that we can exalt ourselves by disparaging others. This is especially true in the political world. One person running for office endeavors to make himself look the most qualified for the position by putting down the other candidates. Perhaps

Miriam and Aaron thought the only way to add to their prestige was to take away from Moses' prestige.

Moses' Meekness

At this point the Bible says, "(Now the man Moses was very meek, above all the men which were upon the face of the earth)" (Num. 12:3). This was God's estimate of Moses. When Miriam and Aaron made their charges, Moses did not answer a word—he reflected the character of God.

Believers today have the Holy Spirit living within them, and they manifest the fruit of the Spirit as they submit to Him (see Gal. 5:22,23).

The Apostle Peter told believers, "For even hereunto were ye called: because Christ also suffered for us, leaving us an example, that ye should follow his steps: who did no sin, neither was guile found in his mouth: who, when he was reviled, reviled not again; when he suffered, he threatened not; but committed himself to him that judgeth righteously" (I Pet. 2:21-23).

Our ability to respond in this way is made possible by the indwelling Christ. That Christ indwells believers is evident from Colossians 1:27: "Christ in you, the hope of glory." Because Christ was in him, the Apostle Paul went on to say in verse 29, "For this purpose also I labor, striving according to His power, which mightily works within me" (NASB).

The Bible's reference to Moses' being "very meek" (Num. 12:3) does not mean that he was weak. Meekness is not weakness. The weak return blow for blow and blurt out their wrath because they are unable to control their passion. Meekness, on the other hand, does not defend itself. Only a strong person can remain quiet when he is provoked and even turn the provocation into an intense love for the person accusing him. No wonder Jesus said, "Blessed are the meek: for they shall inherit the earth" (Matt. 5:5).

Because of Moses' meekness, he did not get angry with Miriam and Aaron, which caused God to have great praise for him. Meekness is really the result of true humility. Humility refers to one's attitude, especially a person's attitude toward God. Meekness is the outward manifestation to others of the inner relationship and attitude toward God.

A meek person is under control; in particular, he is under the control of God, for only God can give a person the mastery of himself when he is provoked.

When the Bible refers to being "filled with the Spirit" (Eph. 5:18), it refers to a person's being under the control of the Holy Spirit. The Holy Spirit forms the life and attitudes of Christ in the believer. When the believer is under the control of the Holy Spirit, he will react toward his enemies the same way Christ reacted toward His.

Meekness indicates that there is no sense of self-assertion. The meek person is not vindictive nor is he quick to defend himself. Moses relied on the Lord to vindicate him when he was charged by Miriam and Aaron. Thus, in Moses we see a combination of great moral and spiritual strength as well as genuine humility. All of these are marks of a man of God. The person who walks in right relationship with God does not need to vindicate himself. The believer is assured in Psalm 37:6 that God "will bring forth your righteousness as the light, and your judgment as the noonday" (NASB).

Question for Believers

Each believer needs to answer a searching question: Are my eyes fixed on the single purpose of glorifying God? If so, the fires of self-ambition will be extinguished. When a believer desires to glorify God above all else, he will be willing to do anything and to be anything so that the purpose of God can be accomplished.

The Apostle Paul gave believers admonitions about living for the glory of God. Paul said, "Let no one seek his own good, but that of his neighbor. . . . Whether, then, you eat or drink or whatever you do, do all to the glory of God" (I Cor. 10:24,31, NASB). Concerning himself, Paul said, "Just as I also please all men in all things, not seeking my own profit, but the profit of the many, that they may be saved" (v. 33, NASB).

It is good for a believer to ask himself if he is as concerned about seeing God's working through others as he is about God's working through himself. The sin nature causes a person to want to be on center stage. We are all like this, so we must come to grips with this tendency. We become competitive in the Christian life and find it difficult to pray for Christians who are not part of our church or our work.

But in the Body of Christ there should be no competing with each other. We are members of the same body (I Cor. 12:12,13), and when one member suffers, we should all suffer with him. When one member is honored, we should all rejoice (v. 26).

We need to spend time in the Word and be alone with God until we are more concerned about His honor than our own. We do not have to worry about competition from other believers; our concern is only to glorify the Lord in all that we do. When a Christian is more concerned about God's honor than about his own, God will take care of his worries about competition from fellow believers. Granted, it is much easier to say this than to really live it, but we must come to grips with this problem if we are going to have victory in our Christian lives. We must be aware of the indwelling Christ and rely on Him to give us victory in these areas.

Since Jesus Christ lives within the believer, the characteristics of Christ will be expressed through the believer when self is out of the way. And what are the characteristics of Christ? Notice what kind of an attitude the Lord Jesus Christ had: "Have this attitude in yourselves which was also in Christ Jesus, who, although He existed in the form of God, did not regard equality with God a thing to be grasped, but emptied Himself, taking the form of a bondservant, and being made in the likeness of men. And being found in appearance as a man, He humbled Himself by becoming obedient to the point of death, even death on a cross" (Phil. 2:5-8, NASB).

A meek and quiet spirit are very valuable in the sight of God, but how does the believer obtain such a spirit? First, claim the meekness of Christ. There was no guile, or deceit, in Jesus Christ, and He did not retaliate against His enemies (see I Pet. 2:21-23). Ask Christ to produce this kind of meekness in you. The Lord Jesus said, "Take my yoke upon you, and learn of me; for I am meek and lowly in heart: and ye shall find rest unto your souls" (Matt. 11:29). In any moment of provocation, turn at once to the Lord Jesus Christ, and claim His meekness.

Second, cultivate the habit of silence. The psalmist said, "What time I am afraid, I will trust in thee" (Ps. 56:3). Isaiah 30:15 tells the believer, "In quietness and in confidence shall be your strength." James 1:19 admonishes, "Let every man be swift to hear, slow to speak, slow to wrath."

Third, consider the harm done to the aggressors. One cannot say unkind and bitter words about others without hurting himself more than others.

Fourth, let God vindicate your cause. Moses trusted God to vindicate him, so he did not try to defend himself. God heard the unjust accusations, and a righteous God would not leave such injustice without correction. Commit yourself to the Lord, and He who judges righteously will vindicate you (see Ps. 37:5,6). The believer can safely leave his case with the Lord, knowing that God will bring to pass what is right and necessary.

God's Response to Miriam and Aaron

Even though Moses did not respond to the charges of Miriam and Aaron, "the Lord spake suddenly unto Moses, and unto Aaron, and unto Miriam, Come out ye three unto the tabernacle of the congregation" (Num. 12:4). Thus we see that the Lord took immediate action when accusations were made against the leader He had chosen. The Lord had heard the accusations made by Miriam and Aaron, and He spoke audibly to them and commanded that they come to the tabernacle.

At the tabernacle, "the Lord came down in the pillar of the cloud, and stood in the door of the tabernacle, and called Aaron and Miriam: and they both came forth. And he said, Hear now my words: If there be a prophet among you, I the Lord will make myself known unto him in a vision, and will speak unto him in a dream. My servant Moses is not so, who is faithful in all mine house. With him will I speak mouth to mouth, even apparently, and not in dark speeches; and the similitude of the Lord shall he behold: wherefore then were ye not afraid to speak against my servant Moses?" (vv. 5-8).

At least three specific elements in this passage need special attention. First, God made it clear to Miriam and Aaron that He revealed Himself to prophets by visions and dreams (v. 6). Although this was God's normal way of revealing Himself to mankind, He made it clear to Miriam and Aaron that this was not the way He revealed Himself to Moses.

Second, God chose to reveal Himself to Moses in a most intimate way—"mouth to mouth, even apparently, and not in dark speeches; and the similitude of the Lord shall he behold" (v. 8).

Third, the Lord asked Miriam and Aaron, "Wherefore then were ye not afraid to speak against my servant Moses?" (v. 8).

Miriam and Aaron were guilty before God because of their accusations of Moses. The Bible says, "The anger of the Lord was kindled against them; and he departed" (v. 9).

Notice the consequences of the accusations made by Miriam and Aaron: "Miriam became leprous, white as snow" (v. 10). When Aaron saw what had happened to Miriam, he said to Moses, "I beseech thee, lay not the sin upon us, wherein we have done foolishly, and wherein we have sinned" (v. 11). This admission by Aaron was a confession of his sin. Even though I John 1:9 had not yet been written, the truth it states was as applicable in Aaron's time as in ours: "If we confess our sins, he is faithful and just to forgive us our sins, and to cleanse us from all unrighteousness."

Because Aaron confessed his sin by admitting it, he was forgiven by God, and judgment did not fall on him. However, Miriam experienced judgment, indicating she was unwilling at that time to admit her sin.

Aaron pleaded for his sister in the condition that had been brought on her. Aaron said to Moses, "Let her not be as one dead, of whom the flesh is half consumed when he cometh out of his mother's womb" (Num. 12:12). Miriam's flesh was decomposing as a result of the leprosy, and Aaron was desperately pleading that his older sister not be like a stillborn child that comes into the world with decomposed flesh.

Moses Intercedes for Miriam

In response to Aaron's plea, Moses "cried unto the Lord, saying, Heal her now, O God, I beseech thee" (Num. 12:13).

Moses revealed his godlike character by pleading for Miriam instead of rebuking her in anger. He interceded for his older sister and appealed to God on the basis of His name *El*, which is related to *Elohim*, the name used in reference to His creative work. Moses appealed for an act that only the God of creation could accomplish—making living flesh from dead flesh.

Moses' godlike character is seen in that he appealed for Miriam's healing, even though he was the one being directly attacked by her accusations.

The way a believer responds to others depends on his own relationship to the Lord. The New Testament tells believers, "Woe unto you, when all men shall speak well of you! For so did their fathers to the false prophets. But I say unto you which hear, Love your enemies, do good to them which hate you, bless them that curse you, and pray for them which despitefully use you" (Luke 6:26-28).

Notice God's response to Moses' intercessory prayer for Miriam: "The Lord said unto Moses, If her father had but spit in her face, should she not be ashamed seven days? Let her be shut out from the camp seven days, and after that let her be received in again" (Num. 12:14).

Miriam was kept outside the camp for seven days while the Israelites waited before they moved on (v. 15). The Lord responded in grace to the intercessory prayer of Moses but only after justice was done. Speaking out against the servant that God had chosen to lead the Israelites was a great sin, and God revealed to the people how serious He considered it to be.

The awfulness and hideousness of Miriam's sin was exposed. She was not restored to the camp until she had paid for the sin of haughtiness and envy by being shut outside the camp in humiliation for seven days. She did not atone for her sin—no person can do that—but she did experience the consequences of her sin. She also experienced the timeless truth that a person reaps whatever he sows (Gal. 6:7).

All Israel knew about her sin and its punishment because they were delayed in their journey for seven days. Think of it—three million people had to wait for one person! She may have committed her sin privately, but she was exposed to public shame. It is good to remember that no sin is really private. What any individual does has an effect on others.

It is also important to remember that any consequences the believer suffers for his sin cannot be compared to what Christ suffered for the sin of the world. The Bible says, "Wherefore Jesus also, that he might sanctify the people with his own blood, suffered without the gate" (Heb. 13:12). Because of what the Lord Jesus Christ did for us, let all of us who know Him as Saviour do what the following verse exhorts: "Let us go forth therefore unto him without the camp, bearing his reproach" (v. 13).

Korah Attacks Moses

Moses had undergone the attack of Satan through personal discouragement and the attack by Miriam concerning his authority. Now he was about to undergo the most subtle of all attacks. Note how the attacks became progressively more severe. As we grow in our knowledge of God, He often tests us more severely to develop a stronger character. But we should always remember I Corinthians 10:13: "No temptation has overtaken you but such as is common to man; and God is faithful, who will not allow you to be tempted beyond what you are able, but with the temptation will provide the way of escape also, that you may be able to endure it" (NASB).

The rebellion of Korah occurred several years after Miriam and Aaron allowed their jealousy to erupt into accusations against Moses. Korah's rebellion is described in Numbers 16. Following him in his rebellion were 250 princes described as "men of renown" (v. 2). Of course, they were not renowned before God but before men. These princes were highly respected leaders among the Israelites.

Korah and these princes "gathered themselves together against Moses and against Aaron, and said unto them, Ye take too much upon you, seeing all the congregation are holy, every one of them, and the Lord is among them: wherefore then lift ye up yourselves above the congregation of the Lord?" (v. 3). This accusation and attack on Moses was similar to the previous attack by Miriam and Aaron but seemed much more severe. Both cases involved jealousy of the leadership of another, although at this time Aaron was accused along with Moses of lording it over the people.

Korah and his followers indicated that the leadership of Moses and Aaron was no longer needed. Korah and his followers pointed out, "All the congregation are holy, every one of them, and the Lord is among them" (v. 3). Korah and his men were pointing out that any one of the Israelites was just as qualified as Moses and Aaron to lead the people. In this charge they specifically ignored God's prerogative of choice, for He had distinctly chosen Moses and Aaron to lead the people.

Korah and his followers also implied that they were qualified to do the priestly tasks when they asked Moses and Aaron, "Wherefore then lift ye up yourselves above the congregation of the Lord?" (v. 3). This question really leveled an accusation at God, because He had distinctly put Moses and Aaron into the positions they held. Moses had been reluctant to accept God's call, but finally God persuaded him to obey. It must have hurt Moses deeply to have Korah and his followers charge him with placing himself above the others.

Any suggestion that every person was qualified to be a priest was seriously out of line. God guarded the priesthood closely—anyone who intruded into the priestly office was put to death. This indicates how calloused Korah and his followers had become. They were even thinking of taking upon themselves the priestly activities.

Korah and the 250 princes also charged Moses with not bringing them into the land as he had promised. They asked Moses, "Is it a small thing that thou hast brought us up out of a land that floweth with milk and honey, to kill us in the wilderness, except thou make thyself altogether a prince over us? Moreover thou hast not brought us into a land that floweth with milk and honey, or given us inheritance of fields and vineyards: wilt thou put out the eyes of these men?" (vv. 13,14).

What an accusation! It was not Moses' responsibility to bring the Israelites into the land; it was God's responsibility. The people were the ones causing the delay.

Moses' Response to Korah

Notice how Moses responded to the various charges. First, "he fell upon his face" (Num. 16:4). This is a reference to the way Moses prostrated himself before God. Then he responded by telling Korah and his followers: "Even to morrow the Lord will shew who are his, and who is holy; and will cause him to come near unto him" (v. 5).

Later, Moses spoke to the other Israelites concerning Korah and his followers: "Hereby ye shall know that the Lord hath sent me to do all these works; for I have not done them of mine own mind. If these men die the common death of all men, or if they be visited after the visitation of all men, then the Lord hath not sent me. But if the Lord make a new thing, and the earth open her mouth, and swallow them up, with all that appertain unto them, and they go down quick into the pit; then ye shall understand that these men have provoked the Lord" (vv. 28-30).

Those were strong words, but Korah and his followers had committed a gross sin. They failed to realize that their position among the Israelites was appointed by God and that they were to be content in that position, just as Moses had been appointed by God and was to be content in his position. This truth is especially seen during the Church Age, because God has placed believers in the Body to perform specific functions. First Corinthians 12 discusses at length how believers need each other and how they must work together properly if they are to honor the Lord.

Moses made the real issue clear when he told Korah and his followers, "For which cause both thou and all thy company are gathered together against the Lord: and what is Aaron, that ye murmur against him?" (Num. 16:11). Always remember that an accusation against God's chosen one is a direct accusation against God Himself.

Moses declared that a unique judgment would fall on Korah and his men. If that judgment did not fall, then Moses was willing to admit that he was not God's leader. But when Moses finished speaking, "the earth opened her mouth, and swallowed them up, and their houses, and all the men that appertained unto Korah, and all their goods. They, and all that appertained to them, went down alive into the pit, and the earth closed upon them: and they perished from among the congregation" (vv. 32,33).

But notice the result of this judgment of God. The next day the Israelites "murmured against Moses and against Aaron, saying, Ye have killed the people of the Lord" (v. 41). Instead of teaching the Israelites a lesson, the judgment on Korah and his followers had only caused the Israelites to question God and to defend those who rebelled against Him. This was the lowest kind of ingratitude. The intercession of Moses and Aaron had saved the congregation from God's judgment, but these same people turned against their leaders after the death of the rebels.

The Lord told Moses, "Get you up from among this congregregation, that I may consume them as in a moment" (v. 45). Before Moses and Aaron could intercede and make atonement for the people, a plague struck which killed 14,700 (see vv. 46-49). Moses and Aaron had been accused by the Israelites of being murderers. But they were really the saviors of the people, for had they not interceded, all would have been destroyed.

All of this resulted because of the rebellion of Korah and those who followed him. The awfulness of their sin can be measured by the penalty God inflicted on them.

Consider the ways that Moses' character manifested itself under such pressure. First, Moses let God vindicate him as the chosen leader, along with Aaron. Moses did not defend himself before those who challenged his position.

Second, even though the people opposed him, Moses interceded to save these same people from the wrath of God, and a great multitude owed their lives to him.

Third, although Moses interceded for the people, he did not shirk his God-given responsibility as a leader. He stood firm in his position; he did not run away and give up. He stood still and let God do the fighting.

Fourth, although he was personally challenged, Moses handled these incidents in such a way that the people were struck with awe and fear toward God. Moses magnified God rather than himself.

Chapter 25

Kadesh-Barnea: Place of Decision

After the time of Miriam's purification from the leprosy God brought upon her, "the people removed from Hazeroth, and pitched in the wilderness of Paran" (Num. 12:16). The wilderness of Paran was south of the land of Palestine. As the Israelites journeyed toward the Promised Land, it was necessary for them to go through the wilderness of Paran. At the northern edge of this wilderness was a place known both as "Kadesh" and "Kadesh-barnea." Kadesh-barnea was just south of the Promised Land and figured prominently in Israel's history. From this place the spies were sent into the land of Canaan and then returned "unto the wilderness of Paran, to Kadesh; and brought back word unto them" (13:26).

The Israelites and the Believer

In Israel's history Kadesh-barnea became much more than a stopping place; it became a place of decision. A study of the history of Israel reveals many parallels that can be drawn to the individual believer in the present age. This is especially true of Israel's travels from Egypt to Canaan. Israel came out of Egyptian captivity, passed through the wilderness and eventually entered the land. This parallels an individual as he passes through his spiritual training period. Believers often reveal carnality during this important phase of life.

The natural state of an individual is mentioned in I Corinthians 2:14: "The natural man receiveth not the things of the Spirit of God: for they are foolishness unto him: neither can he know them, because they are spiritually

271

discerned." The "natural man" is the person who has not trusted in Jesus Christ as his personal Saviour. This parallels the Israelites in Egypt before they were saved by the blood of the lamb.

The Bible refers to carnal believers in I Corinthians 3:1: "And I, brethren, could not speak unto you as unto spiritual, but as unto carnal, even as unto babes in Christ." These were believers because they were "in Christ." However, they were immature believers who were being trained in the spiritual walk and for spiritual warfare. It is a characteristic of immature Christians to long for the things of the world, just as the Israelites in the wilderness longed for the things in Egypt.

The spiritual believer is referred to in I Corinthians 2:15: "He that is spiritual judgeth all things, yet he himself is judged of no man." This compares to the Israelites when they finally entered the land and claimed their rightful possessions.

Thus we see that three stages often occur in a believer's life, although not every believer goes through a lengthy time in the carnal stage. It is important, however, for the individual believer to study Israel's history and to learn valuable lessons. Concerning the Old Testament experiences of Israel, I Corinthians 10:6 says, "Now these things happened as examples for us, that we should not crave evil things, as they also craved" (NASB). Verse 11 says, "Now these things happened to them as an example, and they were written for our instruction, upon whom the ends of the ages have come" (NASB).

The Book of Hebrews emphasizes these same truths: "But with whom was he grieved forty years? Was it not with them that had sinned, whose carcases fell in the wilderness? And to whom sware he that they should not enter into his rest, but to them that believed not? So we see that they could not enter in because of unbelief. Let us therefore fear, lest, a promise being left us of entering into his rest, any of you should seem to come short of it" (3:17—4:1). Hebrews 4:9 says, "There remaineth therefore a rest to the people of God." Verse 10 adds, "For he that is entered into his rest, he also hath ceased from his own works, as God did from his."

Hebrews 4 refers to the need of the believer to rest in Jesus Christ even though he is walking on earth. The believer is to quit trying to accomplish things in his own strength and to accept by faith what Jesus Christ has for him and wants to do in and through him. The scriptural injunction to the believer concerning Israel is: "Let us labour [be diligent] therefore to enter into that rest, lest any man fall after the same example of unbelief" (v. 11).

Kadesh-barnea became a place with special meaning for the Israelites because the course of their history was changed there. That is why it is proper to speak of Kadesh-barnea as a place of decision.

The way the name "Kadesh-barnea" is used concerning Israel is comparable to the way the word "waterloo" is commonly used today. Inasmuch as Napoleon was defeated at Waterloo, it is now common to refer to a person's defeat as his waterloo. Because of what happened to Israel at Kadesh-barnea, it is also valid to refer to an individual believer's being at his Kadesh-barnea; that is, at the place of decision.

The believer must decide whether to remain at Kadesh-barnea in the desert and the place of defeat or to rest in Jesus Christ and go on to maturity, just as Israel eventually entered the land. The choice is up to the individual believer; no one can make it for him. Each person who knows Christ as Saviour must decide whether he will remain in the place of spiritual infancy and defeat or go on to the place of victory and spiritual maturity.

The Israelites had been delivered from Egypt by the blood of the lamb and had been separated from Egypt by the Red Sea. This set up the potential for their entrance into Canaan. What God had done for the people was so well known that even other nations feared the Israelites (see Josh. 2:9-11).

God had provided for Israel in the desert by giving a cloud to protect and to guide, manna for food and water for drink. He also protected them from enemies such as Amalek. The people were given the Law and were organized into a great commonwealth.

By the time the Israelites arrived at Kadesh-barnea, about two years had elapsed since they had crossed the Red Sea.

Those two years had been spent in training so they would learn to walk by faith and to be ready to do spiritual warfare in Canaan. So as they stood at Kadesh-barnea, they were faced with a great test—they had to decide whether or not they would take God at His word and walk and conquer by faith. They had to decide whether or not they would go on to spiritual victory.

Canaan and the Believer

It is important to note that Canaan does not represent heaven, as some songs indicate. Canaan was a place of warfare and provides a parallel to the spiritual warfare engaged in by the believer. The believer's spiritual warfare is detailed in Ephesians 6:10-18. This is really the abundant life that Christ spoke of in John 10:10: "I am come that they might have life, and that they might have it more abundantly."

Rather than thinking of Canaan as an illustration of heaven, it is more accurate to think of it as representing life "in the heavenlies" while the believer is here on earth. The Book of Ephesians—commonly considered the New Testament counterpart to the Old Testament Book of Joshua—says much about the believer's life in the heavenlies. The Apostle Paul was used of God to write Ephesians, and he said, "Blessed be the God and Father of our Lord Jesus Christ, who hath blessed us with all spiritual blessings in heavenly places in Christ" (1:3). Paul also said that God "hath raised us up together, and made us sit together in heavenly places in Christ Jesus" (2:6). The phrase "in heavenly places" in both of these verses is a reference to the heavenlies.

The believer who lives on the basis of his position in the heavenly realm is characterized by an abundant life. Second Peter 1:3 reveals that God has made everything available that is necessary for the believer to live this abundant life: "[He] hath given unto us all things that pertain unto life and godliness."

So Canaan really stands for the victorious Christian experience that is possible for the believer here and now. Kadesh-barnea represents the place of decision the believer comes to as he progresses spiritually in this life.

The Desert and the Believer

A present-day believer who has a wildernesslike Christian life is similar to the Israelites in the desert. They wandered here and there without a special sense of direction. It is easy for a Christian today to be caught up in the routine and not have any sense of direction about what he should be doing. Even local churches can have programs only for the sake of programs without really having a purpose in mind that produces something beneficial in the believer's life.

A Christian in the midst of a wilderness experience is not a fruitful Christian, just as Israel led a fruitless life in the desert. The Israelites were characterized by unbelief which expressed itself in their lives through doubt, frustration and complaining. They did not have the confidence in God to realize that He was using adverse circumstances to accomplish something for their good. Romans 8:28 specifically states this truth: "We know that all things work together for good to them that love God, to them who are the called according to his purpose."

In the wilderness Israel's main virtue was a negative one—they were not doing what the Egyptians were doing (although they secretly longed to do those things). There was nothing positive or spiritually aggressive about the life of Israel while in the desert.

Many Christians today are like the Israelites of old—they are characterized by a negative position rather than a positive one. They do not drink, dance, smoke, swear, cheat or lie. But after listing what they do not do, it is sometimes very difficult to see any positive elements in their lives. One often looks in vain for aggressive spiritual warriors. Believers are told, "Finally, my brethren, be strong in the Lord, and in the power of his might" (Eph. 6:10).

The reality of the spiritual warfare of the believer is seen in Ephesians 6:12: "For we wrestle not against flesh and blood, but against principalities, against powers, against the rulers of the darkness of this world, against spiritual wickedness in high places." Instructions for this spiritual warfare include directions to put on the whole armor of God so that the believer will be able to stand victoriously (vv. 13-17). In addition, the believer is to be "praying always with all prayer and supplication in the Spirit, and watching thereunto with all perseverance and supplication for all saints" (v. 18).

Each believer needs to ask himself if he is still wandering around in the desert or if he is really engaged in spiritual warfare with the Lord. We must wage spiritual war against the evil forces that keep souls bound and blinded. We who know Christ as Saviour need to demonstrate positive lives through prayer, the teaching of the Word, personal testimony and the help we give in whatever way we can.

The nation of Israel was useless to God as long as it lived in the wilderness. God did not forsake them, but they were useless in the sense that they were not accomplishing anything for Him. So, too, Christians today who live on the wilderness plane of life accomplish little, if anything, for God. The exhortation to such believers is: "Therefore leaving the elementary teaching about the Christ, let us press on to maturity, not laying again a foundation of repentance from dead works and of faith toward God" (Heb. 6:1, NASB).

At Kadesh-barnea Israel was at a crucial point in its national life. Two years had passed since the people had been redeemed from Egypt, and the land they had long dreamed of was before them. Kadesh-barnea was essentially the gateway to the land of Canaan.

The land of Canaan had been an important focus of their thinking for many years. God had promised Abraham seed, or descendants, and a land more than 400 years earlier (see Gen. 12:1-3). The promises of seed and land always go together, but the descendants of Abraham had been separated from the land for many years.

Egypt had been used by God for a special purpose in the life of Israel. In Egypt the Israelites were put by themselves because the Egyptians would not intermarry with them. But finally, Pharaoh's power over the Israelites had been broken, and Israel was on its way to the Promised Land.

At Kadesh-barnea the nation faced an hour of crisis. The people were at a place of great decision. This was the greatest moment for that generation of Israelites.

To go forward would mean immediate possession with no Jordan River to cross, no more years of desert wandering and no death in the wilderness because of disobedience. What would their decision be? Would they enter the land? Israel stood at the moment of destiny with untold potential. A mistake here would cast the die and mark the course for future generations and would cause them to think of the past and what might have been. And as John Greenleaf Whittier said, "For of all sad words of tongue or pen, the saddest are these: 'It might have been!' "

A New Testament Passage

Before examining what happened to the Israelites at Kadesh-barnea, consider a New Testament passage that has been frequently misunderstood by many believers. It relates to the subject of deciding about going on to maturity, and that is why it is important to consider this passage in connection with the decision that faced Israel.

The passage is in the Book of Hebrews. This book emphasizes the need for the believer to go on to maturity. Early in the book the writer asks, "How shall we escape, if we neglect so great salvation?" (2:3). The reference is not to unbelievers but to believers. The entire Book of Hebrews was addressed to Hebrew Christians. The author was concerned that believers go on to a salvation characterized by maturity and not stop with a salvation that only delivers from condemnation.

As the author developed his theme, he referred to Melchizedek and then made statements that are highly significant for every believer who desires to go on to maturity. Writing by inspiration of God, he said, "Of whom we have many things to say, and hard to be uttered, seeing ye are dull of hearing. For when for the time ye ought to be teachers, ye have need that one teach you again which be the first principles of the oracles of God; and are become such as have need of milk, and not of strong meat. For every one that useth milk is unskilful in the word of righteousness: for he is a babe. But strong meat belongeth to them that are of full age, even those who by reason of use have their senses exercised to discern both good and evil. Therefore leaving the principles of the doctrine of Christ, let us go on unto perfection; not laying again the foundation of repentance from dead works, and of faith toward God" (5:11—6:1).

Then follow the difficult verses that so many stumble over: "For it is impossible for those who were once enlightened, and have tasted of the heavenly gift, and were made partakers of the Holy Ghost, and have tasted the good word of God, and the powers of the world to come, if they shall fall away, to renew them again unto repentance; seeing they crucify to themselves the Son of God afresh, and put him to an open shame" (vv. 4-6).

The writer of Hebrews made it clear in 5:11-14 that, at a time when the Christians to whom he was writing should be teaching others, they themselves needed to be taught. In effect he was saying, "You need to be taught again the ABCs of God's revelation to mankind." They were unable to take solid spiritual food, and the indication is that anyone who is unable to take solid food is immature.

Having said that, the writer of Hebrews said, "Therefore leaving the principles of the doctrine of Christ, let us go on unto perfection; not laying again the foundation of repentance from dead works, and of faith toward God" (6:1). In other words, it was not necessary to again lay foundational truths since they had already been laid. The believer is not to continue to dwell on the gospel and its foundational truths. Having trusted Jesus Christ as personal Saviour, he is then to go on to maturity. A believer who remains at the gospel stage is immature. Having once received spiritual life, he needs the food of God's Word in order to go on to maturity.

But what about those controversial verses that say a person cannot be renewed to repentance if he falls away? I personally believe the author is talking about believers, for he refers to them as having been "once enlightened" and having "tasted of the heavenly gift" (v. 4). He also says they "were made partakers of the Holy Ghost" (v. 4). Also, they had "tasted the good word of God, and the powers of the world to come" (v. 5).

The writer was saying that, for those who have experienced salvation, it is impossible for them to be renewed to repentance as they were when they first trusted Christ for salvation. For them to even think of such would be to recrucify the Son of God in their minds and expose Him to

KADESH-BARNEA: PLACE OF DECISION

shame and contempt by their conduct. A person cannot be born again over and over again.

Even though this is a complex passage, let us consider what it does not teach. Some are under the impression that it teaches the possibility that a believer can lose his salvation; that is, he can "fall away" from his salvation. Although many believe this, none is able to say precisely how much sin it takes to cause a falling away from salvation. Is it one sin or two or three or more? Or does it have to do with how gross the sin is? But then, is not one sin just as bad as another in the eyes of God?

Those who believe this passage teaches that a believer can lose his salvation usually do not emphasize what the rest of the passage says—that once he falls away, it is impossible to renew him again. This would mean that the person who lost his salvation could never again be saved. Who, then, is really saved? Have not all believers at one time or another fallen into sin?

But I believe the entire Book of Hebrews was written to Christians to tell them how to go on to a mature Christian life. What the author was writing about in Hebrews 6 was not the matter of losing one's salvation but of going on to maturity. The words "fall away" in verse 6 refer to those who refuse to go on with God into a life of maturity. So when a believer realizes his need of going on to maturity and deliberately opposes doing so, he cannot be renewed to repentance; that is, he then forfeits his opportunity to go on to maturity.

By refusing to go into the land, Israel was refusing to go on to spiritual maturity. This was a deliberate act of unbelief and a rejection of God's continuing purpose for them. This refusal denied God's ability to complete what He had promised, even though the nation had seen Him perform many miracles in its behalf. So Hebrews 6 refers to going on to spiritual maturity, a maturity found only in the risen and ascended Christ. The people to whom this passage was written were already believers, and Jesus Himself said concerning believers, "I give unto them eternal life; and they shall never perish, neither shall any man pluck them out of my hand. My Father, which gave them me, is greater than all;

and no man is able to pluck them out of my Father's hand"
(John 10:28,29).

What a shame, however, that, although some know Jesus
Christ as personal Saviour, their lives are characterized by a
refusal to really take God at His word in daily living. These
do not go on to spiritual maturity. The Old Testament
includes many lessons for these people to learn, and that is
why we focus attention on the Israelites as they stood at
Kadesh-barnea, ready to enter the land of Canaan. Would
they believe God and keep moving forward, or would they be
characterized by unbelief and refuse to go any farther? The
latter would be a deliberate act of unbelief and a refusal to
accept their better knowledge.

Israel Asks for Spies

Rather than going into the land immediately, the
Israelites called for spies to be sent in first. The Bible says,
"The Lord spake unto Moses, saying, Send thou men, that
they may search the land of Canaan, which I give unto the
children of Israel: of every tribe of their fathers shall ye send
a man, every one a ruler among them" (Num. 13:1,2).

If these are the only two verses one reads on this subject,
he might think that the Lord wanted the spies to be sent into
Canaan, and this would absolve the Israelites from
responsibility. Comparison with another passage of scripture
indicates otherwise, however. Several years later, when Moses
was rehearsing for the Israelites what had taken place at
Kadesh-barnea, he gave additional information concerning
this incident. Actually, his review took place 38 years later,
and the Israelites were only then getting ready to enter the
land. But before they entered Canaan, Moses reminded them
of what had taken place back at Kadesh-barnea.

"And when we departed from Horeb, we went through
all that great and terrible wilderness, which ye saw by the
way of the mountain of the Amorites, as the Lord our God
commanded us; and we came to Kadesh-barnea. And I said
unto you, Ye are come unto the mountain of the Amorites,
which the Lord our God doth give unto us. Behold, the Lord
thy God hath set the land before thee: go up and possess it,
as the Lord God of thy fathers hath said unto thee; fear not,

neither be discouraged. And ye came near unto me every one of you, and said, We will send men before us, and they shall search us out the land, and bring us word again by what way we must go up, and into what cities we shall come. And the saying pleased me well: and I took twelve men of you, one of a tribe" (Deut. 1:19-23).

Notice in particular that Moses said the Israelites asked for these spies to be sent in and that he agreed with them. It is apparent that God had not wanted the Israelites to send spies into the land; He wanted them to take Him at His word and go in by faith. But because the people wanted the spies to see what the land was like, God granted permission for this to be done.

This reveals a distinction between God's direct will and His permissive will. This distinction is frequently found in the Scriptures. God permits some things simply because of the hardness of peoples' hearts. Because of Israel's unbelief, God was longsuffering with them along the way. That is why God permitted them to send spies into the land, even though He did not want them to do so. This reveals that the people were characterized by unbelief. Even though God had enabled them to overcome the greatest nation in the world at that time (Egypt), they could not trust Him to overcome the much smaller nations in the land of Canaan.

In addition to being characterized by unbelief, the Israelites were also characterized by self-will. Concerning the Israelites, the psalmist said, "They quickly forgot His works; they did not wait for His counsel, but craved intensely in the wilderness, and tempted God in the desert. So He gave them their request, but sent a wasting disease among them" (Ps. 106:13-15, NASB). The King James Version translates this last verse: "He gave them their request; but sent leanness into their soul" (v. 15). This reveals that God sometimes permits what is not in His direct will. It also reveals that the individual loses out spiritually.

What a paradox! The Israelites were to walk by faith, but they wanted to send spies into the land. What does faith want with spies? Apparently they were more concerned about walking by sight than by faith.

Many believers today find it extremely difficult to take God at His word. Instead of walking by faith, they want proofs about the future beyond what God has said and the power He has demonstrated. They are just like the Israelites who wanted to send spies into the land so they would know what it was like and how strong it was. Then they would choose whether or not to go in. Every believer should remember II Corinthians 5:7: "(For we walk by faith, not by sight.)"

God's Promises

God knew the difficulties that Israel would face, and He knew how to surmount them. Had He not proven this during the two years since the Israelites left Egypt? Even while they were in Egypt, God had made a promise and then kept it: "I will bring you out from under the burdens of the Egyptians, and I will rid you out of their bondage, and I will redeem you with a stretched out arm, and with great judgments: and I will take you to me for a people, and I will be to you a God: and ye shall know that I am the Lord your God, which bringeth you out from under the burdens of the Egyptians. And I will bring you in unto the land, concerning the which I did swear to give it to Abraham, to Isaac, and to Jacob; and I will give it you for an heritage: I am the Lord" (Ex. 6:6-8).

God had promised to deliver them out of the land (v. 6). Had He not done so? He had promised to take them to Himself (v. 7). Had He not done so? He had promised to bring them into the land (v. 8). What would keep Him from fulfilling this promise also?

What an application exists here for present-day believers! Remember, the land of Canaan, as it parallels the Christian's life, refers to involvement in spiritual warfare. As such, it is a parallel of the abundant life that God wants every believer to have (see John 10:10). Just as God had accomplished things for Israel in the past and was also able to do so in the future, God is able to bring the present-day believer into a victorious life.

Philippians 1:6 says to the believer, "Being confident of this very thing, that he which hath begun a good work in you will perform it until the day of Jesus Christ." God had begun a good work in Israel, and He was able to give them all they needed in the future. Why did they need spies? And God has provided salvation for all who believe, so once an individual comes into right relationship with Him, he is to walk in reliance on God, not on the basis of sight.

If you know Jesus Christ as your Saviour, God has begun a good work in you, and He is able to perfect it. But, of course, He needs your cooperation of faith. God will not override your will to bring you to the place of spiritual maturity. But any believer who does not go on to spiritual maturity cannot blame a lack of God's provisions for this. Second Peter 1:3 clearly reveals that God has made available all we need for "life and godliness."

Romans 8:31,32 also reveals the marvelous way God works in behalf of a believer: "What shall we then say to these things? If God be for us, who can be against us? He that spared not his own Son, but delivered him up for us all, how shall he not with him also freely give us all things?" No wonder verse 37 says, "In all these things we are more than conquerors through him that loved us." Because of all that God has done for us and has made possible for us, let us go on to maturity by trusting Him all the way.

God is faithful to His Word. There is no need to doubt the wonderful promises He has made. Numbers 23:19 says, "God is not a man, that he should lie; neither the son of man, that he should repent: hath he said, and shall he not do it? Or hath he spoken, and shall he not make it good?" This is the kind of wonderful God we have!

Our God is the same God that Israel had. Instead of trusting Him and believing His word, they demanded that spies be sent into the land first. Such a demand was equivalent to saying that they could not believe God or trust His power to enable them to overcome any obstacle they would find. They thought it was necessary first to know for sure what God was talking about. They evidenced a tremendous lack of faith.

Instead of taking God at His word, they thought they had to confirm it by man's approval. And this same thing often happens today. The Lord burdens an individual to do a particular thing, but he sometimes refuses to begin without first getting man's approval.

True faith interprets circumstances through a realization of who God is. As one truly knows God, he will realize that circumstances amount to nothing. Weak faith (which is actually unbelief) must be bolstered by human investigation and visible proof. This is why there is such an emphasis today on experience—believers are unwilling to take God at His word. True faith looks from God to the circumstances, which erases all questions. On the other hand, weak faith shuts out God and sees only the difficulty. It creates a multitude of unanswered questions.

Israel seemed to be wary of entire dependence on God; they wished to think for themselves and act on their own reasoning. But as II Corinthians 3:5 says, "Not that we are fit (qualified and sufficient in ability) of ourselves to form personal judgments or to claim or count anything as coming from us; but our power and ability and sufficiency are from God" (Amplified).

In reality, the spies which Israel sent into the land of Canaan investigated in order to verify divine truthfulness. They set themselves up as judges of God. But true faith takes God at His word.

Two years of training with God was sufficient to prove Him, but the people stubbornly resisted the clear word of God and disbelieved. Notice God's reaction to the Israelites' unbelief: "But with whom was he grieved forty years? Was it not with them that had sinned, whose carcases fell in the wilderness? And to whom sware he that they should not enter into his rest, but to them that believed not? So we see that they could not enter in because of unbelief" (Heb. 3:17-19).

True faith rests in the Person of Christ. Hebrews 11:6 says, "But without faith it is impossible to please him: for he that cometh to God must believe that he is, and that he is a rewarder of them that diligently seek him."

The Report of the Spies

Moses chose an individual from each of the 12 tribes and sent the men to spy out the land of Canaan. They spied out the land for 40 days and then returned to give their report. "They went and came to Moses, and to Aaron, and to all the congregation of the children of Israel, unto the wilderness of Paran, to Kadesh; and brought back word unto them, and unto all the congregation, and shewed them the fruit of the land. And they told him, and said, We came unto the land whither thou sentest us, and surely it floweth with milk and honey; and this is the fruit of it. Nevertheless the people be strong that dwell in the land, and the cities are walled, and very great: and moreover we saw the children of Anak there. The Amalekites dwell in the land of the south: and the Hittites, and the Jebusites, and the Amorites, dwell in the mountains: and the Canaanites dwell by the sea, and by the coast of Jordan" (Num. 13:26-29).

The spies first verified God's word concerning the worth of the land. They described it as a place flowing with milk and honey and even displayed samples of the fruit they brought back. How interesting that they had verified what God had said and what they previously had been unable to believe. They had seen the productivity of the land, so they were no longer taking it by faith but by sight.

Ten of the 12 spies gave a glowing report of the productivity of the land but added a "nevertheless" when they referred to the people living there (v. 28). This indicates that they were looking at circumstances, because a person looking from God to circumstances never says "nevertheless." But as these spies gave their report, they indicated their lack of faith in God. They had seen the giants in the land, and because the spies were afraid of them, they thought God would not be able to overcome them. They were interpreting everything in the light of their own experience rather than interpreting everything on the basis of who God is.

How common this fallacy is among believers today; they base almost everything on experience instead of on the Word of God. The conclusion of the ten spies was: "We be not able to go up against the people; for they are stronger than we" (v. 31). But notice that their report is referred to as "an evil report" (v. 32). The spies, of course, did not think it was an evil report; they considered it to be a wise, carefully thought out report. They said, "The land, through which we have gone to search it, is a land that eateth up the inhabitants thereof; and all the people that we saw in it are men of a great stature. And there we saw the giants, the sons of Anak, which come of the giants: and we were in our own sight as grasshoppers, and so we were in their sight" (vv. 32,33).

Notice that in their report the spies said, "All the people that we saw in it are men of a great stature" (v. 32). That was not really true. Although they might have seen many of great stature, not all of them were giants. But this only shows that the spies' hearts were filled with fear, which greatly influenced their interpretation of everything.

The spies were so overwhelmed by the people of the land that they said, "We were in our own sight as grasshoppers, and so we were in their sight" (v. 33). The obstacles looked overwhelming because the spies were interpreting everything from a human viewpoint.

The Report of Caleb and Joshua

But not all of the spies were guilty of unbelief. Two of them, Caleb and Joshua, did not agree with the report of the others. "Caleb stilled the people before Moses, and said, Let us go up at once, and possess it; for we are well able to overcome it" (Num. 13:30).

What a different report! Joshua and Caleb had seen the same difficulties as the other spies, but the key difference was their faith. Faith brings God into the picture; unbelief shuts Him out. The way that God's power is kept from operating by unbelief is clearly seen in the report of the ten spies. They surely had been at the Red Sea when God opened it, allowed Israel to pass through and then closed it to destroy the armies of the greatest nation in the world. But because of the unbelief of these spies, they had such a small God that they appeared to be grasshoppers in the eyes of others.

How big is your God? It is easy to sing "How great Thou art," but it is quite another thing to believe this when faced with difficult circumstances. An observer might think that some of us should sing, "How small Thou art." This was especially true of the spies who fixed their attention on the circumstances rather than on God.

Notice what the spies were trusting in—the military might of the nation. When they saw the inhabitants of the land and then considered their own military might, the spies decided they were unable to take the land. Because they saw things only from a human viewpoint, their eyes were fixed on the walled cities and the giants. Unbelief never looks beyond the circumstances.

Faith, on the other hand, although it never minimizes the difficulties after seeing them, looks into the face of God and relies on Him. But because faith looks first at God, it sees the difficulties to be extremely small by comparison.

So, in contrast to the negative report of the ten spies, Joshua and Caleb gave a positive report. When the Israelites heard the reports, they believed the negative report and were so discouraged they wanted to appoint a captain and return to Egypt (14:4). Moses and Aaron were horrified by such a thought, and they fell on their faces before the Israelites (v. 5). Joshua and Caleb tore their clothes as they heard such unbelief expressed, and they told the people, "The land, which we passed through to search it, is an exceeding good land. If the Lord delight in us, then he will bring us into this land, and give it us; a land which floweth with milk and honey. Only rebel not ye against the Lord, neither fear ye the people of the land; for they are bread for us: their defence is departed from them, and the Lord is with us: fear them not" (vv. 7-9).

The unbelieving spies considered the inhabitants of the land to be giants, but as Joshua and Caleb looked at them, they considered them to be "bread for us" (v. 9). In other words, Joshua and Caleb's faith was so great that they thought the Israelites would eat up the inhabitants of the land just as a person eats bread. But notice that they placed one condition on such a victory: "if the Lord delight in us" (v. 8). Their confidence was in the Lord, not in military might.

Joshua and Caleb made it clear as to why military might was not the real consideration: "Their defence is departed from them, and the Lord is with us: fear them not" (v. 9). Joshua 2 indicates why the people were defenseless. Rahab shared with two spies (sent into the land at a later time) that the people had been living in fear of the Israelites ever since they had heard about their crossing the Red Sea and their victory over other armies (see vv. 10,11).

Numbers 13 and 14 makes it evident that ten of the spies
interpreted God in light of circumstances, whereas the other
two spies (Joshua and Caleb) interpreted circumstances in
light of God. Because of the faith Joshua and Caleb had in
God, they said, "Let us go up at once," and, "We are well
able to overcome it" (13:30). Do you wonder how you will
be able to overcome the obstacles in your life? If you know
Jesus Christ as your Saviour, I John 4:4 applies directly to
you: "Greater is he that is in you, than he that is in the
world." This is why the Apostle Paul said, "Christ in you, the
hope of glory" (Col. 1:27). Certainly the walls of circumstances will be high, but God is even higher. Certainly the
giants are strong, but God is stronger—He is almighty.

Faith is not indifferent nor is it reckless; rather, it looks
the difficulty straight in the face because it has seen God and
draws strength from Him. Therefore believers are told, "Be
strong in the Lord, and in the power of his might" (Eph.
6:10). To faith there is never a wall too high, never a city too
great and never a giant too strong.

Reaction of the Israelites

Notice what happened when Joshua and Caleb took a
strong stand for the Lord: "All the congregation bade stone
them with stones" (Num. 14:10). Think of it—the people
wanted to kill the only two spies who had any confidence in
God! This is often how fickle even believers become. They
react to those who really take God at His word and want to
move ahead.

If God had not promised to bring the people into the
land, He might have destroyed them completely right there.
And if it were not for the grace of God, He might immediately destroy some people today who disregard the complete
salvation they have. For instance, those who are unconcerned
about having an abundant life show total disregard for the
words of Christ: "I am come that they might have life, and
that they might have it more abundantly" (John 10:10).

And some refuse to take God at His word concerning the
security that each believer has in Christ. The Lord Jesus
Christ said, "My sheep hear my voice, and I know them, and
they follow me: and I give unto them eternal life; and they

shall never perish, neither shall any man pluck them out of my hand. My Father, which gave them me, is greater than all; and no man is able to pluck them out of my Father's hand" (vv. 27-29). Those who claim they can take themselves out of the hand of God are actually implying that they are greater than God. Concerning salvation, the Bible promises, "He which hath begun a good work in you will perform it until the day of Jesus Christ" (Phil. 1:6).

Do not misunderstand. Just because a believer is secure in Christ does not mean he should willfully sin. The Apostle Paul dealt with this very subject in the Book of Romans. He said, "That as sin hath reigned unto death, even so might grace reign through righteousness unto eternal life by Jesus Christ our Lord. What shall we say then? Shall we continue in sin, that grace may abound? God forbid. How shall we that are dead to sin, live any longer therein?" (5:21—6:2).

Paul told believers, "For, brethren, ye have been called unto liberty; only use not liberty for an occasion to the flesh, but by love serve one another" (Gal. 5:13). Believers are told in I Peter 2:16, "As free, and not using your liberty for a cloke of maliciousness, but as the servants of God."

The person who has experienced the regenerating work of the Holy Spirit in his life will not want to sin even though he will often sin. The Holy Spirit lives within the believer (I Cor. 6:19), and He convicts the person of sin when it is committed. Those who do not confess their sin at first sometimes have to go through severe chastening (see Heb. 12:8-11) before they come to their spiritual senses and confess their sin to God. And believers are promised: "If we confess our sins, he is faithful and just to forgive us our sins, and to cleanse us from all unrighteousness" (I John 1:9).

It is hard to believe that the Israelites wanted to stone Joshua and Caleb for telling them the truth about God. But Joshua and Caleb were experiencing a principle stated in II Timothy 3:12: "All who desire to live godly in Christ Jesus will be persecuted" (NASB). If we live according to man-made rules, we will be applauded for our accomplishments. But when we renounce all dependence on our own ability, testify to God's grace and depend only on Him, we will suffer persecution.

Chapter 26

Kadesh-Barnea: Result of Decision

The report of the ten spies influenced the course of the entire nation of Israel. When the spies gave the glowing report about the land and added their "nevertheless" (Num. 13:28), the people became as filled with fear as the spies. "All the congregation lifted up their voice, and cried; and the people wept that night" (14:1). This is a good example of the fact that the opinion of relatively few (actually ten) can have a significant influence on a multitude (about three million people). The New Testament refers to the way an individual affects others: "For none of us liveth to himself, and no man dieth to himself" (Rom. 14:7). What a solemn responsibility each person has before God and man! It is exceedingly important that we be true and full of faith in what we say and do in our relationships with others and with God.

Reaction to the Positive Report

As so often is the case today, the negative report of the spies carried more weight with the Israelites than the positive report. Caleb quieted the people to give them his message: "Let us go up at once, and possess it; for we are well able to overcome it" (Num. 13:30). But although the people were quiet while Caleb spoke, they soon broke into loud crying because they believed the report of the ten spies rather than that of Caleb and Joshua. Mob psychology took over, even as it did when Christ entered Jerusalem in what is commonly referred to as His Triumphal Entry (see Matt. 21:1-11). Although many acclaimed Him as Messiah at that time, the

290

official leadership of Judaism rejected Him, and a few days later the cry was "Crucify him, crucify him" (Luke 23:21).

After the ten spies had given their evil report, "all the congregation lifted up their voice, and cried; and the people wept that night" (Num. 14:1). They were frightened and discouraged by the report of these ten spies, and true faith seemed to find no place in them. They gave up all hope of ever entering the land of Canaan.

The Israelites "murmured against Moses and against Aaron: and the whole congregation said unto them, Would God that we had died in the land of Egypt! Or would God we had died in this wilderness!" (v. 2). What utter despair they were in! These who had witnessed such great miracles of God had no confidence in Him for the future and even wished they were dead.

They asked, "Wherefore hath the Lord brought us unto this land, to fall by the sword, that our wives and our children should be a prey? Were it not better for us to return into Egypt?" (v. 3). They even blamed God for the progress they had made up to that time. Had it not been for God, they would not have made it that far, but they did not remember this. Note especially that they were concerned about their wives and children. They were concerned about their little ones, but we will see later that these were the ones included in God's promise for the future and that God preserved.

The Israelites were so discouraged that they said, "Let us make a captain, and let us return into Egypt" (v. 4). God would never have allowed them to do that. In His great mercy and grace He had broken Egypt's power over them, and under no circumstances would He have allowed them to return to Egypt.

Their sin was not merely despair and despondency but outright unbelief that accused God of wrongdoing. This is evident from what Moses said later when he was reviewing Israel's history. Moses reminded the people, "Notwithstanding ye would not go up, but rebelled against the commandment of the Lord your God: and ye murmured in your tents, and said, Because the Lord hated us, he hath brought us forth out of the land of Egypt, to deliver us into the hand of the Amorites, to destroy us" (Deut. 1:26,27).

God had lovingly and mightily led them out of Egypt, but the people accused Him of hating them. How low can people sink in unbelief?

The men who led the people to this state of mind and decision were not to influence Israel anymore. Their judgment was quickly sealed by the Lord. Numbers 14:36,37 says, "And the men, which Moses sent to search the land, who returned, and made all the congregation to murmur against him, by bringing up a slander upon the land, even those men that did bring up the evil report upon the land, died by the plague before the Lord." This is a sobering reminder that "it is a fearful thing to fall into the hands of the living God" (Heb. 10:31).

Not only did the Israelites not believe God, but they also accused Him of thinking evil and wanting to do evil. How sad it is when a person comes to this low state. This is sometimes the case with those who lose loved ones—they become so embittered that they even accuse God of not loving them.

A Final Appeal

After the ten spies gave their evil report, which was believed by the people, God's men—Moses, Aaron, Joshua and Caleb—knew that the people had passed the place of no return in their willful unbelief. In their rebellion the people had sealed their own doom by voting for retreat, even though they knew God's ability. Moses and Aaron "fell on their faces before all the assembly" (Num. 14:5), and Joshua and Caleb "rent their clothes" (v. 6). Joshua and Caleb told the people, "The land, which we passed through to search it, is an exceeding good land. If the Lord delight in us, then he will bring us into this land, and give it us; a land which floweth with milk and honey. Only rebel not ye against the Lord, neither fear ye the people of the land; for they are bread for us: their defence is departed from them, and the Lord is with us: fear them not" (vv. 7-9).

This was the final appeal that Joshua and Caleb made to the rebellious Israelites with the hope of reversing their decision not to enter the land. Joshua and Caleb did not yet fully realize how God viewed this terrible sin of unbelief.

The confidence of Joshua and Caleb was in the Lord, and

they knew that He was able to bring the Israelites into the land successfully. But when they finished speaking, "all the congregation bade stone them with stones" (v. 10). The people wanted to kill these men of God for telling them the truth.

This reveals that the people had passed the point of no return. They had deliberately sinned—by an act of the will they had turned against God. Even though they had seen many miracles performed for them by God, they rejected Him against better knowledge. They refused to go on with Him. This is where Hebrews 6 relates to this part of the history of Israel. The Israelites had been enlightened, had tasted of the heavenly gift, had been made partakers of the Holy Spirit, had tasted of the good word of God and of the powers of the world to come (Heb. 6:4,5). But after knowing and experiencing all this, if they refused to go on with the Lord, it would be impossible to renew them to repentance—they would never again be given the opportunity to make this decision.

I do not believe that either Numbers 14 or Hebrews 6 refers to salvation; rather, these chapters refer to a child of God going on with the Lord in a deeper relationship of maturity. The death spoken of later is not spiritual death but physical.

God's government is just. Israel shut God out in unbelief; therefore, when the people later attempted to go up against the Canaanites, they went alone because God refused to go with them. So it became a battle of giants against grasshoppers instead of giants against God. Since they abandoned God in unbelief, He abandoned them in their presumption.

God Speaks

As soon as the congregation wanted to stone those who told them the truth, "the glory of the Lord appeared in the tabernacle of the congregation before all the children of Israel" (Num. 14:10). How awesome this must have been! God had something to say to those who refused to take Him at His word, and His appearance was evident to all.

God told Moses, "How long will this people provoke me? And how long will it be ere they believe me, for all the signs which I have shewed among them? I will smite them with the pestilence, and disinherit them, and will make of thee a greater nation and mightier than they" (vv. 11,12). This was God's first announcement of the judgment that was to come on the Israelites because of their unbelief. The judgment for their unbelief was physical death and disinheritance, not loss of salvation. Their salvation was based on the blood shed back in Egypt, for it was there that they acted by faith and applied the blood according to God's instructions. But because of their unbelief they were to be judged by God.

The judgment on the Israelites was not a complete destruction of the nation. Notice that God again offered to make of Moses a great nation, just as He had earlier (see Ex. 32:10). In spite of such a significant offer, notice that Moses interceded for the people.

Moses told the Lord, "Then the Egyptians shall hear it, (for thou broughtest up this people in thy might from among them;) and they will tell it to the inhabitants of this land: for they have heard that thou Lord art among this people, that thou Lord art seen face to face, and that thy cloud standeth over them, and that thou goest before them, by daytime in a pillar of a cloud, and in a pillar of fire by night. Now if thou shalt kill all this people as one man, then the nations which have heard the fame of thee will speak, saying, Because the Lord was not able to bring this people into the land which he sware unto them, therefore he hath slain them in the wilderness. And now, I beseech thee, let the power of my Lord be great, according as thou hast spoken" (Num. 14:13-17).

Even though there would be extremely hard times ahead, Moses again made it clear that he chose to suffer affliction with the Israelites rather than to enjoy the pleasures of sin for a season (Heb. 11:25). Moses did not want to go into the land without the other Israelites.

Moses' intercession had two basic appeals. First, Moses did not want God to let the heathen nations have any basis for denying God's omnipotence. Moses reminded God that all nations knew He dwelt in the midst of the nation of Israel (v. 14). Moses pleaded that if God killed the people, it would indicate to other nations that He did not have the ability to bring Israel into the land of Canaan (v. 16).

Second, Moses pleaded on the basis of the greatness of God. Moses said, "Let the power of my Lord be great, according as thou hast spoken, saying, The Lord is longsuffering, and of great mercy, forgiving iniquity and transgression, and by no means clearing the guilty, visiting the iniquity of the fathers upon the children unto the third and fourth generation. Pardon, I beseech thee, the iniquity of this people according unto the greatness of thy mercy, and as thou hast forgiven this people, from Egypt even until now" (vv. 17-19).

This is another of the great intercessions of Moses—a man whom God had offered to make the head of a new nation. Moses was concerned about what others would say about God as well as how the character of God would be maligned. Moses wanted the greatness of God's mercy and grace to be evident to all through the pardoning of the Israelites.

The Lord answered Moses, "I have pardoned according to thy word: but as truly as I live, all the earth shall be filled with the glory of the Lord. Because all those men which have seen my glory, and my miracles, which I did in Egypt and in the wilderness, and have tempted me now these ten times, and have not hearkened to my voice; surely they shall not see the land which I sware unto their fathers, neither shall any of them that provoked me see it" (vv. 20-23). This pronouncement of God surely reminds us of Hebrews 6:4-6.

Judgment Announced

God pardoned the people, but justice had to be meted out. Because the people had refused to believe Him, they would not be able to enter the land of Canaan. They had tested the Lord in the wilderness ten different times, and this incident brought an end to God's longsuffering for that generation. Those ten incidents of testing had occurred during the two years after they left Egypt.

The older generation of Israelites would not see the land, but there were two exceptions—Caleb and Joshua. God said, "But my servant Caleb, because he had another spirit with him, and hath followed me fully, him will I bring into the land whereinto he went; and his seed shall possess it" (Num. 14:24). Later, Joshua was mentioned, when God told Moses to tell the people, "Doubtless ye shall not come into the land, concerning which I sware to make you dwell therein, save Caleb the son of Jephunneh, and Joshua the son of Nun" (v. 30).

The first announcement of judgment came when God made it clear that He would punish the people because of their disbelief (see vv. 11,12). The second announcement came when God told the older generation that none of them except Joshua and Caleb would see the land (see vv. 22-24,30). Then the third announcement of judgment was heard throughout all Israel.

The Lord said to Moses and Aaron, "How long shall I bear with this evil congregation, which murmur against me? I have heard the murmurings of the children of Israel, which they murmur against me. Say unto them, As truly as I live, saith the Lord, as ye have spoken in mine ears, so will I do to you: your carcases shall fall in this wilderness; and all that were numbered of you, according to your whole number, from twenty years old and upward, which have murmured against me" (vv. 27-29).

In addition to sparing Joshua and Caleb from this judgment, God also spared the younger generation. God said, "But your little ones, which ye said should be a prey, them will I bring in, and they shall know the land which ye have despised" (v. 31).

All over 20 who had seen God's great wonders but had refused to enter the land were to be destroyed in the wilderness. The only exceptions were Caleb and Joshua, who brought back a good report. Those under 20 were also to be spared and brought into the land. This younger generation was not responsible for the decision their parents made in refusing to enter the land.

What a shame that those who were 20 years old and older had to spend the next 38 years in aimless wandering in the desert, simply waiting to die. There was no inheritance for them. They did not lose their salvation, but they lost their inheritance. Because of their unbelief and failure to take God at His word, they led lives of fruitless misery.

God did not forsake them; He was with them even in

their desert experiences. He continued to provide the manna, the water and the cloud, but the hope of entering Canaan was lost forever to this generation. They were doomed to abide by their fateful decision in refusing to enter the land.

Even Joshua and Caleb, who dared to believe God, had to return to the wilderness with the others. Joshua and Caleb had to suffer along with them for 38 more years. This is an example of the way decisions affect other people. But the faith of Joshua and Caleb was characterized by great patience. Because they believed God, they were able to endure even the experiences of the desert without losing hope.

After God pronounced that none would enter the land except Joshua and Caleb and the younger generation, the Bible records God's judgment on the ten spies. They were judged by physical death right there and then. "The men, which Moses sent to search the land, who returned, and made all the congregation to murmur against him, by bringing up a slander upon the land, even those men that did bring up the evil report upon the land, died by the plague before the Lord" (Num. 14:36,37). Surely this judgment caused the others to realize that the Lord was not to be trifled with. This surely underscored in their minds that God expects to be taken at His word and not mocked by unbelief.

After Moses communicated to the people the messages of God, "the people mourned greatly. And they rose up early in the morning, and gat them up into the top of the mountain, saying, Lo, we be here, and will go up unto the place which the Lord hath promised: for we have sinned" (vv. 39,40).

Although they confessed their sin—at least with their lips if not with their heart—this did not keep them from reaping the results of their deliberate turning against God's leadership. They had sinned against better knowledge, and they were to suffer the consequences of it.

Israel's Sin of Presumption

Notice that, after they learned that the Lord would not let them go into the land, they made a rash decision to "go up unto the place which the Lord hath promised" (v. 40). Earlier, God had wanted them to do this, and they had refused; when God said they would not enter the land, they presumed to go anyway. This was simply adding one sin to another. Their sin of unbelief led them to the sin of presumption, as well as the sin of self-confidence.

Moses told them, "Wherefore now do ye transgress the commandment of the Lord? But it shall not prosper. Go not up, for the Lord is not among you; that ye be not smitten before your enemies" (vv. 41,42). Moses explained that the Amalekites and Canaanites would have to be faced and that the Israelites would fall by the sword because they had turned away from the Lord (v. 43). God was not going with them; He could not be mocked.

In spite of Moses' words of caution, however, "they presumed to go up unto the hill top: nevertheless the ark of the covenant of the Lord, and Moses, departed not out of the camp. Then the Amalekites came down, and the Canaanites which dwelt in that hill, and smote them, and discomfited them, even unto Hormah" (vv. 44,45). So we see what happens when people presume upon God's grace.

They had sinned by refusing to enter the land as God said they should; then they had sinned by presuming to go when He said they could not. The result was inevitable—they were driven back because God's blessing was not on them. Neither Moses nor the ark moved from the camp nor did God and the cloud accompany them. The people were acting entirely apart from the direction of God. Earlier, God had told them, "To morrow turn you, and get you into the wilderness by the way of the Red sea" (v. 25). They were then driven back into the wilderness toward the Red Sea from which they had come.

The first two years of their wilderness experience were a necessary discipline for the people, even though it was probably a longer time than was actually needed for them to cover the distance. But they learned slowly, and we see that after two years they still had not learned to actually take God at His word. As a result of their unbelief and refusal to enter the land, they spent 38 more years in the desert, wandering here and there.

Even though they were God's chosen people, they had been disapproved for their failure to believe God at this crucial time. Salvation was not the issue at stake; rather, going on to maturity with the Lord was involved. But because they refused to believe the word of the Lord, they were severely judged. God refused to go with them against the Canaanites, and He let them be driven back. However, because of the grace and mercy of the Lord, He returned with them to the wilderness for 38 more years. Every day of this time God provided manna and water as well as the shelter of the cloud by day and the light of the pillar of fire by night. The Apostle Paul later spoke of God's longsuffering when he said, "For a period of about forty years He put up with them in the wilderness" (Acts 13:18, NASB).

The people deserved to be in the wilderness alone, without God's sustaining grace, but in His longsuffering He was with them during the entire time. God had made an unconditional promise to Abraham, and not even the unbelief of the people could thwart His presence or His provision for the nation. Although the Israelites had been faithless, God remained faithful to His word. This is a reminder of the New Testament truth: "If we believe not, yet he abideth faithful: he cannot deny himself" (II Tim. 2:13).

The mercy of the Lord to Israel is also indicated by the fact that, even though the older generation had refused to enter the land, God still spoke to the nation about eventually entering it. Numbers 15 begins with the words "And the Lord spake unto Moses, saying, Speak unto the children of Israel, and say unto them, When ye be come into the land of your habitations, which I give unto you" (vv. 1,2).

Thus we see that God did not allow the younger generation to forget about eventually going into the land. God then passed on to the Israelites through Moses the instructions they would need concerning offerings when they entered the land. How ironic that, although the older generation feared to enter the land because of their young ones, only the young ones were able to enter. There is a solemn lesson here for believers today. Although we are to be concerned about our children and grandchildren, we must guard against thinking that even the Lord cannot take care of them and that the younger generation is hopeless. God is still on the throne, and He never forsakes His own. God is not dead; He is able to fulfill His will and purposes.

New Testament Applications

The New Testament refers to these Old Testament incidents in reminding believers not to be guilty of the same faults. Believers are told not to "grumble, as some of them did, and were destroyed by the destroyer. Now these things happened to them as an example, and they were written for our instruction, upon whom the ends of the ages have come" (I Cor. 10:10,11, NASB).

The Book of Hebrews also draws on these Old Testament incidents as warnings to believers. Christians are told: "And with whom was He angry for forty years? Was it not with those who sinned, whose bodies fell in the wilderness? And to whom did He swear that they should not enter His rest, but to those who were disobedient? And so we see that they were not able to enter because of unbelief" (3:17-19, NASB).

Hebrews 4 continues: "Therefore, let us fear lest, while a promise remains of entering His rest, any one of you should seem to have come short of it" (v. 1, NASB). The passage goes on to tell of the lack of faith in God that the Israelites had. Verse 9 contains the application to believers today: "There remaineth therefore a rest to the people of God. For he that is entered into his rest, he also hath ceased from his own works, as God did from his. Let us labour [be diligent] therefore to enter into that rest, lest any man fall after the same example of unbelief" (vv. 9-11).

The "rest" mentioned in this passage is a reference to Christian maturity. It is a rest that results from taking God at His word and applying it to daily life. It is not the rest of heaven or the rest of death but the rest of a position of maturity in Christ Jesus. As indicated in Hebrews 4, this relationship is entered by faith. It is a relationship in which a Christian trusts, or relies on, the Lord Jesus Christ for all of his needs. The mature believer has rest from fear, rest from worry, rest from frustrations and rest from all of the horrible, diabolical side effects that result from fear, worry and frustration.

Many Christians are living far beneath the privileges they have in Christ. As a result their lives are full of worry, fear and guilt, and many even lack the assurance of their salvation. Just as the Israelites were afraid of obstacles when they refused to enter the land, the believer who refuses to enter into a mature relationship with the Lord fears many things in his life. But by active faith, it is possible for a believer to enter into this mature relationship in which he has complete confidence (rest) in Christ.

This active faith is mentioned in Philippians 2:12,13: "Work out your own salvation with fear and trembling. For it is God which worketh in you both to will and to do of his good pleasure." Notice carefully that these verses do not say to work "for" your salvation but to work "out" your salvation. This portion of God's Word is addressed to those who already know Jesus Christ as Saviour—salvation is already in them, but they need to work it out, or express it.

Notice that, according to verse 13, God does two things in the life of a believer. God works in the believer "both to will and to do of his good pleasure." God not only does the work in and through the believer, but He even gives him the desire, or will, to want to magnify Christ in all that he does.

God does not override the personality of the believer in what He does. The Christian must cooperate with God in order for the work of God to be produced in and through his life. Just as an automobile's power steering and power brakes do not work by themselves but must first be activated, so the believer must activate the power of God in his life through faith. The confidence (faith) that a believer has in God activates God to work in and through him. This faith, or trust, relationship is the abundant life spoken of by Christ Himself, recorded in John 10:10. This abundant life is available by faith, for as the believer cooperates with God, he will discover the work of God being accomplished in his life.

It is a shame that many Christians are satisfied with only salvation, or deliverance from condemnation, but ignore and reject the need to go on to a mature relationship with the Lord. Remember Kadesh-barnea. Because the Israelites refused to go on at the place of decision, the result was 38 years of fruitless wandering in the desert. Those years were void of significant accomplishment; the nation was simply marking time until the older generation died off.

A Transition Period

The 38 years of wandering in the wilderness served as a transition period in the history of the Israelites, and it was significant in three ways. First, they neither advanced nor retreated geographically—they simply wandered aimlessly in the wilderness. When the judgment was over 38 years later, they returned to Kadesh-barnea, from which the younger generation moved on toward the land. What happened to Israel then is true of a lot of believers today. They are wandering aimlessly in the Christian life, having no sense of direction and not accomplishing anything significant for the Lord.

Many churches are this way; they go through a routine week after week but do little that is really worthwhile for the Lord. Weak believers and weak churches are only marking time; they are not really moving in a definite direction toward any particular goal.

Second, the population of the nation of Israel was significantly affected during their years of wandering in the wilderness. A generation of over 600,000 warriors died and was buried in the wilderness. Moses referred to this later, saying that the Lord spoke to him "when all the men of war were consumed and dead from among the people" (Deut. 2:16). Actually, all of the older generation, except Joshua and Caleb, died off before the nation was allowed to enter the land. The graves in the wilderness were a daily reminder of God's judgment.

Although there were many deaths in the wilderness, there were also many births as the younger generation grew to adulthood and had children. Thus, the total population was somewhat stabilized, even though so many were dying off.

Third, spiritually, a new hope was born for Israel. The original covenant that God made with Abraham was reaffirmed. Preparations were made at the end of the 38 years to enter the land. Although so many had died off, key leaders were still left to minister to the people—Moses, Aaron, Joshua and Caleb. The earlier promises of the covenant were reaffirmed to Moses when God said, "Behold, I have set the land before you: go in and possess the land which the Lord sware unto your fathers, Abraham, Isaac, and

Jacob, to give unto them and to their seed after them" (Deut. 1:8).

After the years of wandering in the wilderness, God commanded Moses to rise up and begin to march toward the land with the younger generation. But what a sad time it was in Israel's history when so many people lost their lives in the wilderness because of their refusal to take God at His word and to enter the land.

An Example for Believers

As we have stated, Israel's experience serves as a warning to all of us today who know Jesus Christ as personal Saviour. In a sense, every believer comes to a Kadesh-barnea in his life. This is the place of special decision; it is a fork in the road in his Christian life, and he must decide which direction he will go. If he goes on to spiritual maturity, there is eternal potential for his well-being, but if he refuses to go on to spiritual maturity, there will be aimless wandering, just as the Israelites experienced.

Each unsaved individual must make a decision when he is faced with the sin issue and with salvation, which is in Jesus Christ. Each person must decide whether he will reject what Christ has accomplished for him on the cross and continue going his own way or whether he will admit his sinfulness and trust Jesus Christ as his personal Saviour. Those who realize their need and place their faith in Christ as Saviour receive forgiveness of sins and eternal life. What decision have you made in this regard? Are you still trusting yourself and what you can do, or are you trusting Jesus Christ and what He has done for you?

If you have received Christ as your Saviour, your concern should be to glorify Him in every aspect of life and to have an ever-deepening relationship with Him. Each believer comes to a place of decision, or a Kadesh-barnea, concerning the maturing process in his life. He must decide whether he will go on with the Lord and trust Him completely for every aspect of life or whether he will be content with just being delivered from condemnation.

This place of decision for the believer has a road that leads to victory and usefulness, but it also has a road that leads to despair, disapproval and uselessness. To choose the wrong road is to decide in favor of fear, worry and frustration. Someone has said, "Decisions are the hinges on which the doors of destiny turn." This is not only true of individual believers; it is also true of local churches. Individuals and churches can become stagnant unless they make decisions that lead them on in the way of victory and usefulness.

Just as God had to set aside one entire generation of Israelites before He could bring the nation into the land, there are no doubt instances when God has had to set aside an entire generation in a local church while He waited for another generation to grow to maturity and go on to victory. As Proverbs 29:18 says, "Where there is no vision, the people perish."

The message for the believer today is found in Hebrews 6:1: "Let us go on unto perfection." As has been mentioned, the word translated "perfection" actually means "maturity." When a believer comes to a fork in the road in his spiritual life, it is important that he make the decision that leads him on to maturity. Believers are not to stagnate or go back spiritually as Israel did, wandering aimlessly in the wilderness and wanting to go back to Egypt.

No matter how discouraged we may be with the way our Christian life has been in the past, we cannot go back and start over. Therefore, the only thing to do is to go on from where we are at this point. The Apostle Paul emphasized that Jesus Christ is the foundation in the believer's life (I Cor. 3:11). The need is to continue building on that foundation, not to try laying another foundation (see v. 12).

A believer who is in the wilderness of self is useless to God. The individual may go through the motions of the Christian life, but he does not really magnify God in his life. So also, a local church that is constantly divided over petty issues evidences that it is still in the wilderness of self and is not accomplishing anything significant for God.

A believer's progress from the time of salvation to spiritual maturity parallels the experience of Israel during the journey from Egypt to Canaan. The nation was delivered from Egypt by blood, just as an individual is delivered from condemnation by the shed blood of Christ. Deliverance from

Egypt is comparable to the individual's being delivered from sin and damnation.

Great Salvation

The individual who trusts Christ as Saviour possesses a great salvation. This salvation is far more than just deliverance from condemnation. Hebrews 2:3 asks, "How shall we escape, if we neglect so great salvation?" The salvation referred to is a salvation that leads to spiritual maturity. It is wonderful that sin has been atoned for, but in addition to that, Satan's power has been broken as far as the believer is concerned (see v. 14). At the time of salvation God provides all that the individual needs for eternal life and godliness (II Pet. 1:3,4). All of this is available to those who become the sons of God by receiving Jesus Christ as personal Saviour (John 1:12).

By believing in Christ, a person comes into possession of salvation, and then the person's need is to work out—by continuous faith—that salvation in and through his life (see Phil. 2:12,13). Nothing is lacking in what God has provided for us, for we "are complete in him" (Col. 2:10).

God also gives the believer a wonderful position in Christ in the heavenlies. Ephesians 2:6 says God "hath raised us up together, and made us sit together in heavenly places in Christ Jesus." This position in Christ reveals that the believer is positionally in the place of the victor because Christ is victorious over all. The Lord Jesus Christ has given us all the weapons necessary for the spiritual warfare we face. The Bible says, "For though we walk in the flesh, we do not war after the flesh: (for the weapons of our warfare are not carnal, but mighty through God to the pulling down of strong holds;) casting down imaginations, and every high thing that exalteth itself against the knowledge of God, and bringing into captivity every thought to the obedience of Christ" (II Cor. 10:3-5).

God has given the believer all he needs for spiritual victory. But the believer must choose whether or not he will go on to the place of spiritual victory and maturity, which involves a continuous application of faith in the indwelling Christ (see Gal. 2:20). This is why Hebrews 6:1 encourages believers to go on, and verse 3 says, "And this will we do, if God permit." Have you wondered what is meant by the words "if God permit"? I believe this refers to the type of experience Israel had at Kadesh-barnea. God wanted them to go on into the land, but they refused because of their unbelief. When God announced the judgment that would come on them, they changed their minds and wanted to go into the land, but God would not permit it. They had experienced so many spiritual blessings and had witnessed the magnificent powers of God, but even with such knowledge they had refused to go on to victory when God gave them the opportunity.

So remember Israel's situation as you consider decisions you must make in your spiritual life. Although they had been away from Egypt for two years and had seen the display of God's power, they sinned against better knowledge. They looked at themselves, and they looked at the giants, but they refused to look at God. As a result, God had to set them on the shelf, and the nation spent the next 38 years in fruitless activity because the people refused to believe God. May our lives always be characterized by active belief, which results in victorious (mature) Christian living.

Chapter 27

Moses Sins Under Pressure

Because of the unbelief which the Israelites displayed at Kadesh-barnea, the next 38 years were spent in aimless wandering while the older generation died. All, that is, except Joshua and Caleb.

Numbers 20 reveals that Miriam died at Kadesh-barnea, but the leadership of the nation was still in the hands of Moses and Aaron. Throughout Moses' life he had been characterized by faithfulness and selflessness, but a situation developed that caused his life to end in a minor key. He was presented with a situation, and under the pressure of it he did not glorify the Lord. As a result he was not able to enter the Promised Land. At first it might seem that this was a severe penalty for what one might consider a small matter. However, a careful analysis of this incident shows that it was not such a small matter after all.

No Water

After the years of wandering in the wilderness, the Israelites returned to Kadesh-barnea, where Miriam died (Num. 20:1). There was no water for the people to drink, so they sided against Moses and Aaron and said, "Would God that we had died when our brethren died before the Lord! And why have ye brought up the congregation of the Lord into this wilderness, that we and our cattle should die there? And wherefore have ye made us to come up out of Egypt, to bring us in unto this evil place? It is no place of seed, or of figs, or of vines, or of pomegranates; neither is there any water to drink" (vv. 3-5).

Notice what the complaint of the people really was. They had seen the solemn judgment God had meted out on their parents and grandparents over a period of 38 years. Perhaps some of the older generation were still living at this time, but most of them had died in the wilderness and had been buried by the younger ones. The younger generation knew very well why God had judged Israel—because of unbelief.

The same Israelites who grumbled because of the lack of water had seen the fatherliness of God toward them through Moses, their aged leader. God had provided all they needed—even out in the desert during the 38 years of aimless wandering. But although they had experienced the provisions of their miracle-working God, they vehemently took issue with Moses and ultimately with God as they faced a lack of water. They charged Moses with having brought them to "this evil place" (v. 5). They were not in the land of Canaan yet, but apparently they referred to it in their grumbling and even called God's Promised Land an "evil place."

It had been 40 years since the Israelites had left the land of Egypt, and they had experienced God's constant supply during all those 40 years. But their children insulted God by questioning His goodness and wisdom. What a wonder that God did not strike them dead right there!

Notice how Moses and Aaron responded—they "went from the presence of the assembly unto the door of the tabernacle of the congregation, and they fell upon their faces: and the glory of the Lord appeared unto them" (v. 6). What a great God Moses and Aaron had! He was a God of judgment because He was a righteous God, but He was also a God of compassion, and He revealed Himself to them.

God told Moses what to do: "Take the rod, and gather thou the assembly together, thou, and Aaron thy brother, and speak ye unto the rock before their eyes; and it shall give forth his water, and thou shalt bring forth to them water out of the rock: so thou shalt give the congregation and their beasts drink" (v. 8).

Observe the threefold instructions: (1) "Take the rod"; (2) "gather thou the assembly together"; (3) "speak ye unto the rock before their eyes."

Two Rods and Two Rocks

The rod that Moses took was a distinctive rod. Numbers 20:9 says, "And Moses took the rod from before the Lord, as he commanded him." The indication is that this was a different rod than the one commonly used by Moses.

Nearly 40 years had passed since Moses had used his rod to deliver the Israelites from Egypt. He also used his own rod when he struck the rock in Horeb to bring forth water, as recorded in Exodus 17. At that time God told Moses, "Go on before the people, and take with thee of the elders of Israel; and thy rod, wherewith thou smotest the river, take in thine hand, and go. Behold, I will stand before thee there upon the rock in Horeb; and thou shalt smite the rock, and there shall come water out of it, that the people may drink" (vv. 5,6). Moses did as the Lord instructed, and the people had water.

The rock mentioned in Exodus 17 foreshadowed Christ on the cross because there He was smitten. However, the rock of Numbers 20 foreshadowed the ascended Christ, who now intercedes as a high priest for believers. The significant difference in the rocks of Exodus 17 and Numbers 20 is also indicated in that a different word for "rock" is used in these two passages. Although both rocks speak of Christ, God was endeavoring to communicate two different things to us concerning the Person of Christ.

In Exodus 17 the rock was smitten, just as Christ was "smitten of God" (Isa. 53:4) and was "bruised for our iniquities" (v. 5). The rock of Numbers 20 foreshadowed Christ in the heavens, as referred to in Hebrews 9:24: "For Christ is not entered into the holy places made with hands, which are the figures of the true; but into heaven itself, now to appear in the presence of God for us." Hebrews 7:25 tells what Christ is doing in heaven for us: "Wherefore he is able also to save them to the uttermost that come unto God by him, seeing he ever liveth to make intercession for them." Because Christ ever lives, He has an "unchangeable priesthood" (v. 24). So the rock of Numbers 20 refers to this priestly work of Christ after His resurrection, ascension and exaltation at the right hand of the Father.

Not only was there a difference between the two rocks, but there was also a difference between the two rods. As mentioned previously, God told Moses to "take the rod" (Num. 20:8), and "Moses took the rod from before the Lord" (v. 9). During the other incident where water was needed (Ex. 17), God told Moses, "Take . . . thy rod, wherewith thou smotest the river, take in thine hand, and go. Behold, I will stand before thee there upon the rock in Horeb; and thou shalt smite the rock, and there shall come water out of it, that the people may drink" (vv. 5,6). That rod was clearly identified as the one which Moses used at the Red Sea. However, the rod of Numbers 20 is the one Moses took "from before the Lord" (v. 9).

The background concerning this rod that Moses took from before the Lord is given in Numbers 17. After Korah and his followers questioned the authority of Moses and Aaron over the Israelites, God told Moses to take a rod from each of the 12 tribes and to write their names on them. He was also to write the name of Aaron on the rod of Levi. Moses was instructed to lay the rods in the tabernacle, and God said, "It shall come to pass, that the man's rod, whom I shall choose, shall blossom: and I will make to cease from me the murmurings of the children of Israel, whereby they murmur against you" (v. 5). On the next day "the rod of Aaron for the house of Levi was budded, and brought forth buds, and bloomed blossoms, and yielded almonds" (v. 8).

Then note what the Lord instructed Moses: "Bring Aaron's rod again before the testimony, to be kept for a token against the rebels; and thou shalt quite take away their murmurings from me, that they die not" (v. 10). So the rod was placed in the ark of the covenant as a testimony to Israel of God's choice of Moses and Aaron as the leaders of the nation.

Hebrews 9:4 says that the ark of the covenant contained "the golden pot that had manna, and Aaron's rod that budded, and the tables of the covenant." Aaron's rod was a priestly rod, in contrast to the rod of Moses, which was a rod of judgment.

Foreshadowings of Christ

In this second incident where water was needed, Moses was not to use the rod of judgment but the priestly rod to bring forth water. Another distinction between the two incidents is that in Exodus 17 Moses went alone with the rod of judgment, whereas in Numbers 20 he was instructed to go with Aaron and to speak to the rock (v. 8). Aaron was the high priest, so this adds significance to the occasion and further emphasizes the priestly aspect of the rock as it foreshadowed the intercessory work of the Lord Jesus Christ.

At the incident of Exodus 17, which took place right after the Israelites had come out of Egypt, the emphasis was judgment; at the incident of Numbers 20, which took place just prior to their entering the land, the emphasis was on priestly work. Israel had been redeemed from Egypt by blood, just as redemption is provided for all through the shed blood of Jesus Christ. So judgment was the key element associated with the rock in Exodus 17.

Just prior to entering the land, however, the great need of Israel was to rely on God for everything. Thus, the rock of Numbers 20 represented Christ, the High Priest, at the right hand of the Father, who only needs to be spoken to. There was to be no striking of the rock, inasmuch as it prefigured Christ, who had already been smitten. Since His death was sufficient to pay the penalty for all sin, there was no need for Him to be smitten again. That the rock of Numbers 20 foreshadowed the Lord Jesus Christ is evident from I Corinthians 10:4: "They drank of that spiritual Rock that followed them: and that Rock was Christ."

The Scriptures make it clear that Christ died for sin once and for all. Romans 6:9,10 says, "Knowing that Christ being raised from the dead dieth no more; death hath no more dominion over him. For in that he died, he died unto sin once: but in that he liveth, he liveth unto God."

Concerning Christ, the Book of Hebrews says, "Nor yet that he should offer himself often, as the high priest entereth into the holy place every year with blood of others; for then must he often have suffered since the foundation of the world: but now once in the end of the world [ages] hath he appeared to put away sin by the sacrifice of himself. . . . So Christ was once offered to bear the sins of many; and unto them that look for him shall he appear the second time without sin unto salvation" (9:25,26,28). The Book of

Hebrews also states, "We are sanctified through the offering of the body of Jesus Christ once for all. . . . For by one offering he hath perfected for ever them that are sanctified" (10:10,14). Death came to Christ only once; now He ever lives to make intercession (7:25).

In the incident of Numbers 20 the rock foreshadowed the exalted Christ, and that is why it needed only to be spoken to. It is so important that this distinction between the smitten Christ and the exalted Christ as He is foreshadowed in the two rocks be maintained.

Since the Lord Jesus Christ has been judged on the cross by having all of the sins of the world placed on Him, those of us who have received Him as Saviour need now to speak to Him for our needs. And just as His death was effective for all sin, His intercessory work is effective for all of our needs.

Hebrews 10:19-23 reveals the boldness believers can have in approaching the throne of grace. This significant passage says, "Having therefore, brethren, boldness to enter into the holiest by the blood of Jesus, by a new and living way, which he hath consecrated for us, through the veil, that is to say, his flesh; and having an high priest over the house of God; let us draw near with a true heart in full assurance of faith, having our hearts sprinkled from an evil conscience, and our bodies washed with pure water. Let us hold fast the profession of our faith without wavering; (for he is faithful that promised)."

The injunction to hold fast to the profession of our faith is similar to the earlier exhortation in Hebrews: "Let us go on unto perfection [maturity]" (6:1). To go back (v. 6) would be to crucify Christ again.

Just as Christ was smitten only once, the Holy Spirit is given to believers only once. Thereafter they simply come to Him and drink to the full. This is the analogy used by Christ Himself when He said, "If any man thirst, let him come unto me, and drink. He that believeth on me, as the scripture hath said, out of his belly shall flow rivers of living water. (But this spake he of the Spirit, which they that believe on him should receive: for the Holy Ghost was not yet given; because that Jesus was not yet glorified.)" (John 7:37-39).

Moses Strikes the Rock

In spite of the fact that God had told him to take the rod and speak to the rock, Moses momentarily lost his self-control and lashed out at the Israelites. He said, "Hear now, ye rebels; must we fetch you water out of this rock?" (Num. 20:10).

In his anger, instead of speaking to the rock as God had instructed, "Moses lifted up his hand, and with his rod he smote the rock twice" (v. 11). In a way this was the most crucial moment in the life of Moses, and it holds some serious lessons for us today. In one brief, impulsive act, this great man of God forfeited his opportunity to lead the people of Israel into the Promised Land. He had led them for nearly 40 years—from Egypt to the edge of Canaan—but God refused to let him go into the land because of his disobedience at this point.

After Moses struck the rock twice, the Lord told him and Aaron, "Because ye believed me not, to sanctify me in the eyes of the children of Israel, therefore ye shall not bring this congregation into the land which I have given them" (v. 12).

We might excuse Moses for hitting the rock instead of speaking to it, but his actions were significant because of what the rock foreshadowed. Even though we might overlook something and think it was only a slight sin, let us not forget that God looks at matters differently than we do. Isaiah 55:8,9 says, "For my thoughts are not your thoughts, neither are your ways my ways, saith the Lord. For as the heavens are higher than the earth, so are my ways higher than your ways, and my thoughts than your thoughts."

We cannot tell God what to do nor can we counsel Him; He has all wisdom and is absolutely righteous in all His acts. The Apostle Paul realized this, and he exclaimed, "How fathomless the depths of God's resources, wisdom, and knowledge! How unsearchable His decisions, and how mysterious His methods! For who has ever understood the thoughts of the Lord, or has ever been His adviser? Or who has ever advanced God anything to have Him pay him back? For from Him everything comes, through Him everything lives, and for Him everything exists. Glory to Him forever!" (Rom. 11:33-36, Williams).

Some Christians today think that we should not emphasize the sins of a person like Moses. It is true that the sins of a person should not be overemphasized in contrast to his acts that glorify the Lord; however, it is what a person does with his sin that makes him great in the eyes of God. All are sinners, but not all are willing to face that fact and cry out to God for forgiveness. As I John 1:9 indicates, those who confess their sins are forgiven by God, but it takes great strength of character to admit sin and confess it to the Lord. Great is the person who comes clean before God concerning his sin.

In the Bible God does not present a false concept of those He used mightily. Whether it was David or Moses or someone else, God reveals the sin they were guilty of but also reveals how they claimed forgiveness and became great men with Him. In spite of the fact that David committed terrible sins, he was known as a man after the heart of God (I Sam. 13:14). He came clean before the Lord concerning his sin, and Psalm 51 records his confession.

Consequences of Moses' Sin

Even though God forgives sin, there are often consequences that must be suffered in this life. Such was the case with Moses. He was the greatest prophet who ever lived other than Christ (see Deut. 34:10), but because of this sin he was not able to enter the land of Canaan. God forgave him of the sin, but there were still consequences to be suffered.

Moses and Aaron suffered the consequences because they misrepresented Christ in this second incident of bringing water from the rock. Since this second rock foreshadowed Christ in His high-priestly work as one who only needs to be spoken to, they did not exalt Him when they struck the rock—and especially when they struck it twice. Thus, Moses and Aaron had to reap the consequences of their disobedience. The reason the consequences were so severe was that much more was involved than is seen on the surface of this passage of scripture.

Because of Moses' and Aaron's unbelief God was not sanctified in the eyes of the people; it was as if they were putting Christ to an open shame the second time. Numbers

20 indicates that God brings chastisement on those who, by their actions, imply that Christ can be put to open shame again.

The sobering lesson from this incident concerning Moses and Aaron is that God deals more severely with leaders, especially when their public action brings dishonor to His glory. God told them, "Because ye believed me not, to sanctify me in the eyes of the children of Israel, therefore ye shall not bring this congregation into the land which I have given them" (v. 12). The New Testament refers to leaders' having greater responsibility when it says, "Let not many of you become teachers, my brethren, knowing that as such we shall incur a stricter judgment" (James 3:1, NASB).

But whether you are a leader or not, it is important that you come clean before God concerning sin if you know Jesus Christ as your Saviour. The Apostle John told believers, "My little children, these things write I unto you, that ye sin not. And if any man sin, we have an advocate with the Father, Jesus Christ the righteous [one]" (I John 2:1). Jesus Christ pleads the case of those who have trusted Him as personal Saviour. And because His shed blood on the cross was effective in paying for all sin, His intercession is effective for all who call on Him. "Let us therefore come boldly unto the throne of grace, that we may obtain mercy, and find grace to help in time of need" (Heb. 4:16).

So although Moses had to suffer as a result of his sin, forgiveness was available because of God's mercy. And out of His grace God also provided for the people of Israel. Even though Moses had struck the rock twice instead of speaking to it, God manifested His grace to the people in that He supplied the water they needed: "The water came out abundantly, and the congregation drank, and their beasts also" (Num. 20:11).

What a wonderful God we have! His grace produces results even when He is poorly represented. The people did not suffer because of their leader's sin. Man's unbelief does not nullify the power of God. As II Timothy 2:13 says, "If we believe not, yet he abideth faithful: he cannot deny himself."

Even though Moses was told at this time that he would not be able to enter the land because of his act of unbelief, he later asked the Lord for permission to enter the land. When Moses later reviewed the history of the nation for the Israelites, he told them, "And I besought the Lord at that time, saying, O Lord God, thou hast begun to shew thy servant thy greatness, and thy mighty hand: for what God is there in heaven or in earth, that can do according to thy works, and according to thy might? I pray thee, let me go over, and see the good land that is beyond Jordan, that goodly mountain, and Lebanon. But the Lord was wroth with me for your sakes, and would not hear me: and the Lord said unto me, Let it suffice thee; speak no more unto me of this matter" (Deut. 3:23-26).

So although Moses' sin was forgiven, he had to suffer its consequences by not being allowed to enter the Promised Land. Sin leaves its effect. Galatians 6:7 says, "Whatsoever a man soweth, that shall he also reap." Moses did not lose his salvation because of his sin, but he lost much in the way of reward during his earthly life because he did not accomplish the goal that for years he had his eyes fixed on.

Chapter 28

Great in His Farewell

The last year of Moses' life was as full of work as any other prior to it. The conquest of the land east of Canaan took place during that year. The two Canaanite chiefs, Sihon and Og, were conquered, and the land on the east of the Jordan was designated for two and a half tribes of Israel.

Then followed a series of farewell addresses, which contained Moses' last charges to the people. The Book of Deuteronomy records these addresses, which were full of emotion and stirring appeals. Moses spoke much about the past, revealed his gratitude to God as well as his fear of God, and spoke of the results of self-interest and the danger of sin as the people prepared to enter the land. The farewell messages of Moses revealed how greatly he loved his people, for he poured out his heart to them and was so concerned for their future.

A New Leader

In the last year of Moses' life Joshua was appointed to succeed him as Israel's leader. In Moses' concern for the people, he asked God, "Let the Lord, the God of the spirits of all flesh, set a man over the congregation, which may go out before them, and which may go in before them, and which may lead them out, and which may bring them in; that the congregation of the Lord be not as sheep which have no shepherd" (Num. 27:16,17).

Notice that Moses was concerned that the Israelites not be "as sheep which have no shepherd." The Lord Jesus Christ used a similar analogy in John 10 when He revealed Himself as "the good shepherd" (v. 14).

Note the five qualifications that Moses stipulated for the future leader. Numbers 27:17 lists them. He was to be a man who: (1) "may go out before them"—one who would lead them; (2) one who "may go in before them"—one who could intercede in behalf of the people; (3) one who "may lead them out"—one who would be an able leader in warfare; (4) one who "may bring them in"—one who would lead them into the land; (5) one who would give proper leadership so that "the congregation of the Lord be not as sheep which have no shepherd." These are significant qualifications which Moses realized would be needed by the one who would successfully lead that great people.

This passage also reveals the principle that those in places of responsibility should be careful to establish proper leadership under them. This is a principle we have sought to carry out at Back to the Bible. I remember clearly that we sought for God's man to head up the Missions Department about 25 years ago. We waited for over two years for God's man, but it was well worth the wait. G. Christian Weiss has served the Lord and Back to the Bible ably since he was sent to us by God. When we needed another assistant, we waited on God for His choice. That choice was Ord Morrow, who joined us in 1959. We know that we must wait on God so that the leadership is distinctly His choice, not just ours.

After Moses made known his request for a leader, the Lord said to him, "Take thee Joshua the son of Nun, a man in whom is the spirit, and lay thine hand upon him; and set him before Eleazar the priest, and before all the congregation; and give him a charge in their sight. And thou shalt put some of thine honour upon him, that all the congregation of the children of Israel may be obedient. And he shall stand before Eleazar the priest, who shall ask counsel for him after the judgment of Urim before the Lord: at his word shall they go out, and at his word they shall come in, both he, and all the children of Israel with him, even all the congregation" (vv. 18-21).

Joshua was the individual who was to succeed Moses, the greatest prophet who ever lived other than Christ (see Deut.

34:10). Joshua was one of the spies who had brought back a good report of the land and had encouraged the people to believe God and take the land (see Num. 14:6-9). As he was chosen as Moses' successor, he was specifically described as being "a man in whom is the spirit" (27:18). Although he possessed the Spirit, Joshua was not to receive his directions directly from the Lord as did Moses. Moses knew the Lord "face to face" (Deut. 34:10), but Joshua was to receive his instructions through Eleazar the priest (Num. 27:21). Moses was not only a prophet, but in a sense he was also a priest, since he received revelation directly from God. Joshua, however, received God's message from the high priest, who in turn received revelation from God. Somehow God communicated with the priest through the Urim and Thummim, and then the priest communicated God's will to Joshua.

After God instructed him concerning Joshua, "Moses did as the Lord commanded him" (v. 22). Moses' life was characterized by obedience. He laid his hands on Joshua and bestowed honor on him. God had said, "Thou shalt put some of thine honour upon him, that all the congregation of the children of Israel may be obedient" (v. 20).

Moses' Birthday Message

Especially significant in the last year of Moses' life was the celebration of his 120th birthday. Moses said to the Israelites, "I am an hundred and twenty years old this day; I can no more go out and come in: also the Lord hath said unto me, Thou shalt not go over this Jordan. The Lord thy God, he will go over before thee, and he will destroy these nations from before thee, and thou shalt possess them: and Joshua, he shall go over before thee, as the Lord hath said" (Deut. 31:2,3).

In his birthday message, Moses gave solemn charges to the Israelites and to Joshua. He charged Israel with the responsibility to go into the land and take it from the nations inhabiting it. Moses told the Israelites, "The Lord shall give them up before your face, that ye may do unto them according unto all the commandments which I have commanded you. Be strong and of a good courage, fear not, nor be afraid of them: for the Lord thy God, he it is that doth go with thee; he will not fail thee, nor forsake thee" (vv. 5,6).

Moses then gave a solemn charge to Joshua: "Be strong and of a good courage: for thou must go with this people unto the land which the Lord hath sworn unto their fathers to give them; and thou shalt cause them to inherit it. And the Lord, he it is that doth go before thee; he will be with thee, he will not fail thee, neither forsake thee: fear not, neither be dismayed" (vv. 7,8).

After Moses had made his solemn charges to Israel and to Joshua, God said to Moses, "Behold, thy days approach that thou must die: call Joshua, and present yourselves in the tabernacle of the congregation, that I may give him a charge" (v. 14). The Lord Himself then appeared "in a pillar of a cloud" (v. 15) and said to Moses, "Behold, thou shalt sleep with thy fathers; and this people will rise up, and go a whoring after the gods of the strangers of the land, whither they go to be among them, and will forsake me, and break my covenant which I have made with them. Then my anger shall be kindled against them in that day, and I will forsake them, and I will hide my face from them, and they shall be devoured, and many evils and troubles shall befall them; so that they will say in that day, Are not these evils come upon us, because our God is not among us?" (vv. 16,17).

So God warned what would happen after the people entered the land; there would be apostasy with its resulting judgment. But to Joshua there was the charge "Be strong and of a good courage: for thou shalt bring the children of Israel into the land which I sware unto them: and I will be with thee" (v. 23).

Moses then delivered a final charge to the Levites. After he had finished writing the Law in a book, he told the Levites, "Take this book of the law, and put it in the side of the ark of the covenant of the Lord your God, that it may be there for a witness against thee. For I know thy rebellion, and thy stiff neck: behold, while I am yet alive with you this day, ye have been rebellious against the Lord; and how much more after my death?" (vv. 26,27).

Moses' Song and Benediction

Moses then called all the leaders together and delivered to them what is commonly known as "The Song of Moses." This song, recorded in Deuteronomy 32, is one of the most sublime compositions on record. It has been called the "Magna Charta of Prophecy."

Moses' song can only be compared to one other song—the song of the Lamb. The song of Moses and the song of the Lamb are both mentioned in Revelation 15:3: "And they sing the song of Moses the servant of God, and the song of the Lamb, saying, Great and marvellous are thy works, Lord God Almighty; just and true are thy ways, thou King of saints."

After Moses had delivered his song to the Israelites, he pronounced a great benediction on them. This benediction is recorded in Deuteronomy 33, which begins with the words "And this is the blessing, wherewith Moses the man of God blessed the children of Israel before his death" (v. 1).

The chapter concludes with these significant words: "There is none like unto the God of Jeshurun, who rideth upon the heaven in thy help, and in his excellency on the sky. The eternal God is thy refuge, and underneath are the everlasting arms: and he shall thrust out the enemy from before thee; and shall say, Destroy them. Israel then shall dwell in safety alone: the fountain of Jacob shall be upon a land of corn and wine; also his heavens shall drop down dew. Happy art thou, O Israel: who is like unto thee, O people saved by the Lord, the shield of thy help, and who is the sword of thy excellency! And thine enemies shall be found liars unto thee; and thou shalt tread upon their high places" (vv. 26-29).

How characteristic it was of Moses to extol the love and care of Almighty God!

Chapter 29

Great in His Death

Moses was not only great in his works, his meekness and his farewell, but he was also great in his death.

We have looked at the inner life of this noble man, and we have seen that all he accomplished was because his heart was fixed on the Lord. His soul's secret abiding place was in God. To Moses, God was his home, his help and his stay. Moses recognized that he was nothing in himself and that everything he accomplished was because of God's indwelling presence. Because Moses relied completely on God, he was greatly used by God in a way no other individual, apart from the Lord Jesus Christ, has been used.

What was accomplished in Moses' life was due to the indwelling Holy Spirit, who fulfilled the work of God in Moses' life. During Old Testament times, the Holy Spirit did not indwell every believer as He does today. The Holy Spirit came upon chosen believers to empower them for service, enabling them to accomplish God's specific work. Since the Day of Pentecost, however, the Holy Spirit has indwelt every believer. The Apostle Paul emphasized this truth when he referred to each believer's body as a temple of the Holy Spirit (I Cor. 6:19). The ministry of the Spirit in Old and New Testament times and today is to work out through the believer that which God has worked in him. This is especially indicated in Philippians 2:12,13, where believers are told: "Work out your own salvation with fear and trembling. For it is God which worketh in you both to will and to do of his good pleasure."

As Moses drew to the close of his life, he was great in his death just as he had been great in his life. At this point a backward look gives perspective to a forward look. He was forbidden to enter the land because he struck the rock instead of speaking to it. This sin was so serious because of what the rock foreshadowed—Christ's intercessory ministry.

Moses' Last Request

Although Moses' life had been lived as a great symphony, it ended in a minor key. In his last request of God, he asked for something that was denied. This is especially significant when one realizes all that Moses had been granted by God as he had interceded in the past. God was on the verge of destroying the Israelites more than once, but Moses had stood in the gap and had successfully interceded for them. The psalmist said, "Therefore he said that he would destroy them, had not Moses his chosen stood before him in the breach, to turn away his wrath, lest he should destroy them" (Ps. 106:23).

The last request of Moses, which was rejected by God, is recorded in Deuteronomy 3:23-27. Moses told the Israelites, "I besought the Lord at that time, saying, O Lord God, thou hast begun to shew thy servant thy greatness, and thy mighty hand: for what God is there in heaven or in earth, that can do according to thy works, and according to thy might? I pray thee, let me go over, and see the good land that is beyond Jordan, that goodly mountain, and Lebanon. But the Lord was wroth with me for your sakes, and would not hear me: and the Lord said unto me, Let it suffice thee; speak no more unto me of this matter. Get thee up into the top of Pisgah, and lift up thine eyes westward, and northward, and southward, and eastward, and behold it with thine eyes: for thou shalt not go over this Jordan."

This denial of Moses' request was especially significant in light of Moses' great intercessions at Mount Sinai and at Kadesh-barnea, as well as for Miriam and Korah.

Moses was greatly disappointed about not being able to enter into the land. He said to the Israelites, "The Lord was wroth with me for your sakes, and would not hear me: and the Lord said unto me, Let it suffice thee; speak no more unto me of this matter" (v. 26).

Moses' sin was forgiven because he had confessed it to God, and he had been restored to full fellowship with God. However, the judicial consequences of his sin remained. This is the principle by which God works even today. Galatians 6:7,8 says, "Be not deceived; God is not mocked: for whatsoever a man soweth, that shall he also reap. For he that soweth to his flesh shall of the flesh reap corruption; but he that soweth to the Spirit shall of the Spirit reap life everlasting." So there are judicial consequences even though the person confesses his sin and is restored to fellowship with God. When sin is confessed, however, the person suffers no eternal consequences because of it.

God told Moses not to ask again for permission to enter the land. Although the Bible tells us to "pray without ceasing" (I Thess. 5:17) and to "ask," "seek" and "knock" (Matt. 7:7), God makes it clear at times that we are not to ask again.

This was true in the Apostle Paul's life. He had a "thorn in the flesh" (II Cor. 12:7) and asked the Lord three times to remove it from him. God's response, however, was "My grace is sufficient for thee: for my strength is made perfect in weakness" (v. 9). God made it clear to Paul that the thorn was to keep him from becoming too exalted because of the revelation he had received from God.

Moses Confesses

Although Moses' last request was not answered, his great character was seen in that he confessed his sin before all of the Israelites. He "besought the Lord at that time" (Deut. 3:23), but his request was denied. The Lord told him to go to the top of Pisgah, where he would see the Promised Land, but he would not be able to enter it (v. 27).

When God denied his request, Moses did not continue to beg God to let him enter the land. Just as Moses had accepted God's word many other times in his life, he accepted this denial, even though it was not what he preferred to hear.

Because of Moses' nature, it is safe to assume that he did not make only a general confession about his sin of striking the rock instead of speaking to it. While no verse says it in so many words, Moses was the type who faced sin specifically.

We need to follow Moses' example—we need to face sin squarely and not minimize or explain it away. There are those who say, "Lord, if I have sinned, please forgive." It is true that sometimes we do not know where or how we might have sinned, but at those times we should be like the psalmist and pray, "Search me, O God, and know my heart: try me, and know my thoughts: and see if there be any wicked way in me, and lead me in the way everlasting" (Ps. 139:23,24).

When God puts His finger on the sin we have committed, it is then our responsibility to agree with God concerning it—this is actually what "confess" means. When we agree with God that it is sin, then we can claim the promise of God that He forgives when we confess (I John 1:9).

We are often slow to humble ourselves as Moses did and readily admit a great sin. A private sin needs to be confessed only to God because only He and the individual know about it. A public sin, however, needs to be confessed publicly, in addition to being confessed to God. The confession should be as extensive as the sin, no less and no more.

Some do not believe that even public sin should be confessed publicly because, they say, it lowers one in the eyes of the people. But just the opposite is true. When the people know an individual has sinned, he will never have a good testimony before them again until he admits his sin.

Moses' admission of his sin elevated him in the estimation of the people because he had come clean with them as he had with God concerning his sin. When God put His finger on the sin in Moses' life, Moses readily admitted it to God and to the people.

Moses' meekness at this point in his life is seen in that he showed no trace of jealousy or envy when his successor was announced. The Lord told Moses, "But charge Joshua, and encourage him, and strengthen him: for he shall go over before this people, and he shall cause them to inherit the land which thou shalt see" (Deut. 3:28).

Moses did something that is extremely difficult to do. With beautiful self-emptiness he stepped down from his elevated position, threw his mantle over the shoulders of his successor and encouraged him to discharge with holy fidelity the duties of that high office from which he had to resign.

Moses publicly stepped down from his position and put

his full approval on Joshua as God had asked him to do.
"Moses called unto Joshua, and said unto him in the sight of
all Israel, Be strong and of a good courage: for thou must go
with this people unto the land which the Lord hath sworn
unto their fathers to give them; and thou shalt cause them to
inherit it. And the Lord, he it is that doth go before thee; he
will be with thee, he will not fail thee, neither forsake thee:
fear not, neither be dismayed" (31:7,8).

Even in Moses' dying moments, he humbled himself
under the mighty hand of God. He accepted the discipline
imposed on him by God, and he did not murmur at the
refusal of his request. Because of this humble attitude, Moses
was later exalted by God. Moses was great in his life, but he
was just as great in his dying moments.

Moses Views the Land

Although God's discipline kept Moses out of Canaan,
God's grace conducted him to Pisgah's top, where, in the
Lord's company, he was permitted to view the land.
Actually, three names are used in reference to the place from
which Moses viewed the Promised Land—Pisgah, Nebo and
Abarim. This may seem confusing, but the different names
refer to different parts of the same general location. Mount
Nebo was the head, or summit, of Mount Pisgah, which was a
portion of the mountain range called Abarim.

"The Lord spake unto Moses that selfsame day, saying,
Get thee up into this mountain Abarim, unto mount Nebo,
which is in the land of Moab, that is over against Jericho; and
behold the land of Canaan, which I give unto the children of
Israel for a possession" (Deut. 32:48,49). The day referred to
by the words "selfsame day" (v. 48) was the day of Moses'
120th birthday (see 31:2). What an unusual birthday
celebration! Although Moses was not allowed to enter the
Promised Land, he was allowed to see it as no other man ever
saw it.

Deuteronomy 34:1-3 records the breathtaking view of
the land that Moses had. It was possibly the greatest
emotional experience in his lifetime. These verses say, "And
Moses went up from the plains of Moab unto the mountain
of Nebo, to the top of Pisgah, that is over against Jericho.

And the Lord shewed him all the land of Gilead, unto Dan, and all Naphtali, and the land of Ephraim, and Manasseh, and all the land of Judah, unto the utmost sea, and the south, and the plain of the valley of Jericho, the city of palm trees, unto Zoar."

God must have given Moses a special ability to see and caused the sky to be clear that day so Moses could view the land. After showing Moses the land, God said to him, "This is the land which I sware unto Abraham, unto Isaac, and unto Jacob, saying, I will give it unto thy seed: I have caused thee to see it with thine eyes, but thou shalt not go over thither" (v. 4).

The entire passage of Deuteronomy 32:48—34:4 gives a complete description of those events preceding Moses' death. Here we see the typically selfless heart of Moses. There was not a word of self-pity or mourning; there was not even an expression of his great excitement about having God show him all the lands of Israel's inheritance.

Even at the mature age of 120—after faithfully leading his people through agonizing years of tribulation—he was still in prime physical condition: "His eye was not dim, nor his natural force abated" (34:7). And, as was typical of Moses, he obeyed his Master to the end. A phrase that characterized the life of Moses was "Moses did as the Lord commanded him" (Num. 27:22).

Moses' Triumph in Death

God's last command to Moses was that he was to go to the mountaintop and die there, after having viewed the land. God told Moses, "Get thee up into this mountain Abarim, unto mount Nebo, which is in the land of Moab, that is over against Jericho; and behold the land of Canaan, which I give unto the children of Israel for a possession: and die in the mount whither thou goest up, and be gathered unto thy people; as Aaron thy brother died in mount Hor, and was gathered unto his people" (Deut. 32:49,50).

Moses was to go alone. This was his last step of obedience, and even this demonstrates the aloneness of Moses.

Aloneness is the price that often has to be paid for great leadership. But aloneness must not be confused with loneliness. The Christian leader realizes that, even though he must stand alone at times, God stands with him, so there is no loneliness. God's most effective work in the heart of an individual is often accomplished when that person is alone.

Alone Moses worked, suffered, met God and legislated for his people. But never was this aloneness as apparent as when he was unattended—even by Joshua, his ever-faithful servant—as he walked up Mount Nebo to die. Alone he climbed the craggy steep. Alone he gazed on the landscape before him. And alone he lay down to die. At the moment of death he was absolutely alone—no one in Israel stood by him.

Yet God was with Moses. In a sense, God was Moses' undertaker, and the angels were his pallbearers. God was also the custodian of the grave, for no one knew where Moses was buried.

No tombstone was placed on Moses' grave—no monument to indicate the remains of this great man of God. The epitaph of Moses was not on a tombstone but was recorded in God's eternal Word, written there by the Holy Spirit Himself. No finer epitaph of Moses could be recorded than what is stated in Deuteronomy 34:10-12: "And there arose not a prophet since in Israel like unto Moses, whom the Lord knew face to face, in all the signs and the wonders, which the Lord sent him to do in the land of Egypt to Pharaoh, and to all his servants, and to all his land, and in all that mighty hand, and in all the great terror which Moses shewed in the sight of all Israel." This is God's epitaph for this great man.

Hebrews 11:27 could also be an epitaph of Moses' life: "He endured, as seeing him who is invisible." What a eulogy! One reads of what many accomplished in the temporal and visible realm, but this man was ruled by the invisible. What a man of faith!

The Book of Jude reveals that there was a battle for the body of Moses after his death. Verse 9 says, "Yet Michael the archangel, when contending with the devil he disputed about the body of Moses, durst not bring against him a railing accusation, but said, The Lord rebuke thee." There is nothing to indicate why the Devil wanted the body of Moses—perhaps he wanted his body in a place where people could come and worship him, because the Devil loves to foster dead religions. The Devil was defeated in this endeavor, however, because God would not let the Devil create a mecca to which pilgrims could travel to worship a dead person.

But God superintended over Moses' death, and He "buried him in a valley in the land of Moab, over against Beth-peor: but no man knoweth of his sepulchre unto this day" (Deut. 34:6). God cared for His servant during his lifetime; He also cared for him in his death.

Friend, is the God of Moses your God also? Do you realize how much God cares for you? God does not change; He loves His own even in death. Perhaps you say, "But Moses was a man of special character and total obedience." So he was, but this characteristic is possible for any believer today. The Christian who has obedience to God as his rule of life experiences the joy of knowing the same God that Moses knew.

God had a special relationship with Moses, for He knew him "face to face" (v. 10). So precious was this relationship that God would not even permit the angels to bury Moses. What an example this is of the faithfulness of God to His own! Just as God had been faithful to Moses in his life, so He was faithful to him in his death.

What a great God we have! He is not only faithful to us during our lifetime with the various special needs we have, but He is also faithful to us even in death. Remember that Moses' God is our God; He is a never-changing God.

Notice especially that Moses did not die from some disease in his old age. The Bible says, "Moses was an hundred and twenty years old when he died: his eye was not dim, nor his natural force abated" (v. 7). Moses did not die as a withered, feeble old man but in the fullness of strength. Time had only made him venerable but not weak.

Lessons From Moses' Death

It is greatly interesting to trace Moses' life from the brink of a river, where he lay as a helpless baby, to the top of Pisgah, where he stood in the company of his God and gazed with undimmed vision on the inheritance of Israel. Think of it—120 years between those two events. They were years of serving and believing God for his own needs and for the needs of his people. No other life is so described in the Bible as Moses'.

None of us is called of God to a position in service as Moses had. But every believer is called of God to give the kind of service Moses did—each one is to be faithful. The Bible says, "Moreover it is required in stewards, that a man be found faithful" (I Cor. 4:2). Because as believers in Jesus Christ we are the stewards of God, it is exceedingly important that we be faithful in our service. God says, "Be thou faithful unto death, and I will give thee a crown of life" (Rev. 2:10).

Several important lessons can be gleaned from Moses' death. First, in death we, too, stand alone. We may not be absolutely alone as Moses was—there may be friends and loved ones around us—but in a real sense we are alone with God no matter who else is there. This is why each person needs to be sure of his individual relationship with God.

Second, we meet God on our own record, not on someone else's. As Moses faced God in death, his mother's or his father's relationship with God was not important. Only his own relationship with God mattered. So it is with each one of us; each one is responsible for his own personal relationship with the Lord.

Third, all that surrounded Moses' death was "according to the word of the Lord" (Deut. 34:5). Our lives and deaths are also ordered by God. Concerning man, Job 14:5 says, "Seeing his days are determined, the number of his months are with thee, thou hast appointed his bounds that he cannot pass." No one knows the time of his death, when he will be required to give account to God, but this time has been determined by the Lord.

Fourth, the death of a saint is precious in God's eyes. God exercised loving care over Moses at death, and every believer's death somehow brings glory to the Lord. The psalmist said, "Precious in the sight of the Lord is the death of his saints" (Ps. 116:15). John 21:19 also indicates that a believer's death glorifies the Lord. Jesus had explained how Peter would die, and verse 19 records: "This spake he, signifying by what death he should glorify God."

Fifth, the Lord takes no pleasure in the death of the wicked. Moses had been dearly beloved by God, and he would be in the presence of God immediately after his death. But this is not true of an unbeliever; thus, Ezekiel 33:11 says, "As I live, saith the Lord God, I have no pleasure in the death of the wicked."

Sixth, the Lord knows where all the bodies of the dead are. Just as the Lord knew where Moses' body was even though no one else did, God also knows the location of the remains of every dead person. Although the remains of a body of a believer may have turned to dust long ago, that believer's body will be resurrected from the grave when the Lord Jesus Christ returns. The Bible says, "For the Lord himself shall descend from heaven with a shout, with the voice of the archangel, and with the trump of God: and the dead in Christ shall rise first" (I Thess. 4:16).

The Lord not only knows where the remains of believers are, but He also knows where the remains of unbelievers are. The unsaved dead of all ages will someday be resurrected to stand before the Great White Throne Judgment: "And I saw a great white throne, and him that sat on it, from whose face the earth and the heaven fled away; and there was found no place for them. And I saw the dead, small and great, stand before God; and the books were opened: and another book was opened, which is the book of life: and the dead were judged out of those things which were written in the books, according to their works. And the sea gave up the dead which were in it; and death and hell delivered up the dead which were in them: and they were judged every man according to their works. And death and hell were cast into the lake of fire. This is the second death. And whosoever was not found written in the book of life was cast into the lake of fire" (Rev. 20:11-15).

But remember, God receives no pleasure from the death of the wicked (Ezek. 33:11). What God desires is that each person believe in Jesus Christ as his personal Saviour. John 1:12 assures us, "As many as received him, to them gave he power to become the sons of God, even to them that believe on his name." John 5:24 says, "He that heareth my word, and believeth on him that sent me, hath everlasting life, and shall not come into condemnation; but is passed from death unto life." First John 5:12 promises, "He that hath the Son hath life; and he that hath not the Son of God hath not life." If you do not know Jesus Christ as your Saviour, may you realize your sinful condition and place your trust in Him as your Saviour from condemnation before it is eternally too late.

The Mount of Triumph

It was not the end of the story when Moses saw the Promised Land and died before the Lord and was buried by God. There is a glorious sequel—the overwhelming disappointment of not being able to enter the land had a joyous destiny.

Nebo and Pisgah were not the last mountains on which Moses was destined to stand. About 1500 years after Moses was on Nebo and Pisgah, he appeared on another mountain with Elijah and the Lord Jesus Christ—the Mount of Transfiguration.

The Gospel of Luke records that Jesus "took Peter and John and James, and went up into a mountain to pray. And as he prayed, the fashion of his countenance was altered, and his raiment was white and glistering. And, behold, there talked with him two men, which were Moses and Elias [Elijah]: who appeared in glory, and spake of his decease [departure] which he should accomplish at Jerusalem" (9:28-31).

The desire of Moses' heart had at last been granted! He had yearned to enter the land, but God had not permitted him to do so earlier. However, he appeared in the land not only with Elijah but also with the Lord Jesus Christ Himself. God had given Moses a foretaste of the glory that was to follow by allowing him to view the land from the top of Pisgah. Then he actually entered the Promised Land in the company of the Lord of Glory.

On the Mount of Transfiguration notice that Moses and Elijah "spake of his decease which he should accomplish at Jerusalem" (v. 31). The Transfiguration occurred just prior to the Lord's going to the cross to shed His blood for the sin of the world, and Moses and Elijah were encouraging the Lord concerning what He had to face.

The fact that Moses was not able to enter the land during his lifetime but was able to do so later is a lesson to us that final reward does not always come here and now. The believer's greatest rewards are future. In a sense, this can be spoken of as a "delayed reward." Great men of faith never have to have the reward at the present—they look to a reward that is beyond. This is evident from Hebrews 11, which says of great men of faith, "All these, having gained approval through their faith, did not receive what was promised, because God had provided something better for us, so that apart from us they should not be made perfect" (vv. 39,40, NASB).

The glorious thing to remember is that God has a plan whereby we share in future rewards. Therefore, it is imperative that we keep our eyes on the future and on the glories that will come later. What a joy it will be to someday sit with Abraham, Isaac and Jacob, as well as Moses and Elijah, to rejoice in the God of our salvation!

God's rewards for Moses' faithful service did not come during his lifetime, but they resulted from a decision he made at the age of 40. "By faith Moses, when he was come to years, refused to be called the son of Pharaoh's daughter; choosing rather to suffer affliction with the people of God, than to enjoy the pleasures of sin for a season; esteeming the reproach of Christ greater riches than the treasures in Egypt: for he had respect unto the recompence of the reward" (Heb. 11:24-26). On the Mount of Transfiguration Moses was beginning to see the full and rich rewards for the decision he had made over 1500 years earlier.

This same principle is also true for the believer today. His rewards are primarily future. In fact, the last chapter of the Bible records these words of the Lord Jesus Christ: "Behold, I come quickly; and my reward is with me, to give every man according as his work shall be" (Rev. 22:12).

Stages of Moses' Rewards

Moses' rewards came in different stages. First, he was given an unparalleled view of the Promised Land from the

vantage point of Mount Nebo. Second, he stood with Elijah
and the Lord on the Mount of Transfiguration. Third, he still
has a special reward awaiting him in connection with the
Second Coming of the Lord Jesus Christ. This third aspect is
a debatable one, but it is my personal conviction that Moses
will be one of the two witnesses spoken of in Revelation 11.

During the Tribulation the Antichrist will kill everyone
who refuses to worship him. But in the middle of the
seven-year Tribulation, God will bring in two witnesses, of
whom it is said: "I will give power unto my two witnesses,
and they shall prophesy a thousand two hundred and
threescore days, clothed in sackcloth" (v. 3). The two
witnesses prophesy for three and a half years, which is a
reminder to us that God is never without a witness, even
during the darkest times of spiritual declension.

Concerning the two witnesses, God said, "If any man will
hurt them, fire proceedeth out of their mouth, and devoureth
their enemies: and if any man will hurt them, he must in this
manner be killed. These have power to shut heaven, that it
rain not in the days of their prophecy: and have power over
waters to turn them to blood, and to smite the earth with all
plagues, as often as they will" (vv. 5,6).

If one of these witnesses is Moses, then the indication is
that God will give him a final opportunity to be vindicated
before men. While on earth, Moses never vindicated himself;
he suffered along with God's people without complaint. But
if he is one of the two witnesses, it is clear that God will
vindicate him before all mankind.

Although the Bible does not specifically say who the two
witnesses are, it is interesting to observe that they will
perform miracles similar to those performed by Moses and
Elijah. Elijah prevented rain during his ministry (see I Kings
17:1; James 5:17,18), and Moses brought plagues on Pharaoh
and the Egyptians (see Ex. 7—12).

If the two witnesses are Moses and Elijah, this is another
reward of God for their faithfulness. But notice what will
happen to the two witnesses: "When they shall have finished
their testimony, the beast that ascendeth out of the
bottomless pit shall make war against them, and shall
overcome them, and kill them. And their dead bodies shall lie
in the street of the great city, which spiritually is called

Sodom and Egypt, where also our Lord was crucified. And they of the people and kindreds and tongues and nations shall see their dead bodies three days and a half, and shall not suffer their dead bodies to be put in graves. And they that dwell upon the earth shall rejoice over them, and make merry, and shall send gifts one to another; because these two prophets tormented them that dwelt on the earth" (Rev. 11:7-10).

But even though God permits the two witnesses to be killed, notice their ultimate triumph: "After three days and an half the spirit of life from God entered into them, and they stood upon their feet; and great fear fell upon them which saw them. And they heard a great voice from heaven saying unto them, Come up hither. And they ascended up to heaven in a cloud; and their enemies beheld them" (vv. 11,12).

As I read this passage and think of Moses, again I ask the question, Could this not be God's final vindication of Moses in the presence of the whole world? Moses died alone, unseen by men, but if one of the two witnesses is Moses, he will be allowed to die in the sight of all men and to be taken to heaven in the sight of all men.

No one knows where Moses' grave was, but during the Tribulation the two witnesses will be seen ascending into heaven. Inasmuch as the Scriptures do not specifically state who the two witnesses are, we must not be dogmatic. But if they are Moses and Elijah—and I personally believe they will be—it would certainly be a fitting reward for these Old Testament prophets.

Conclusion

In bringing to a close the study of the life of Moses, let us remember the progress in Moses' life. He died to self when he went to Pharaoh to deliver the Israelites from Egypt. He died by himself on Mount Nebo after God had permitted him to view the Promised Land. He encouraged Christ concerning His death when he appeared with Elijah on the Mount of Transfiguration. And—if he is one of the two witnesses—he will be vindicated by God before all mankind.

Moses was great in his birth, great in his decisions, great

in his faithfulness and great in his death. Because he lived by faith, his life still speaks to us, even though he is dead.

Among the many lessons we learn from Moses, none could be greater than realizing the need to be in right relationship to God. Do you realize that "all have sinned, and come short of the glory of God"? (Rom. 3:23). Although none of us can escape condemnation by our own efforts (see Eph. 2:8,9), Jesus Christ shed His blood on the cross and thereby became the satisfaction for our sins. "He is the propitiation [satisfaction] for our sins: and not for our's only, but also for the sins of the whole world" (I John 2:2).

But no one is automatically delivered from condemnation just because Jesus Christ died on the cross. It is necessary to receive Him as Saviour by placing one's faith in Him. "As many as received him, to them gave he power to become the sons of God, even to them that believe on his name" (John 1:12). When any person trusts Jesus Christ as his personal Saviour, he is delivered from condemnation and passes from death to life (John 5:24). If you have not placed your trust in Jesus Christ as your Saviour, do so while there is yet time.

Back to the Bible is a nonprofit ministry dedicated to Bible teaching, evangelism and edification of Christians worldwide.

If we may assist you in knowing more about Christ and the Christian life, please write to us without obligation:

Back to the Bible
P.O. Box 82808
Lincoln, NE 68501